GEORGE VILLIERS
SECOND DUKE OF BUCKINGHAM
1628-1687

The Duke of Buckingham.

GEORGE VILLIERS
SECOND DUKE OF BUCKINGHAM
1628-1687

A STUDY IN THE HISTORY OF THE RESTORATION

BY WINIFRED, LADY BURGHCLERE

KENNIKAT PRESS
Port Washington, N. Y./London

GEORGE VILLIERS

First published in 1903
Reissued in 1971 by Kennikat Press
Library of Congress Catalog Card No: 74-118511
ISBN 0-8046-1259-5

Manufactured by Taylor Publishing Company   Dallas, Texas

PREFACE

IN attempting to compile—mainly from original sources hitherto unedited—the biography of one of the most interesting figures of the Stuart epoch, I had, at first, hoped to avoid the presumption of writing English History. But the Duke of Buckingham's name is so closely interwoven with the chronicles of the time, that I soon found this to be impossible. In order, therefore, to make the narrative intelligible, I have, where it was necessary, indicated the course of current events; and whenever it has been possible I have preferred in doing so to use the language of contemporaries.

I have not sought to produce an Apology. There are incidents in the life of George Villiers which the veriest sophistry cannot condone. Yet surely the student of human nature may claim some attention for that eccentric genius whom the satirist describes as "not one but all mankind's epitome." It is always difficult to judge one generation by the ethical standard of another; and in the case of the second Duke of Buckingham it must be remembered that he grew up in an era of transition and reaction—transition from the theological order of thought to the scientific and philosophical; reaction from the reign of the Saints to that of the natural Adam.

These are not conditions favourable to moral equilibrium. Few Englishmen have, however, been so lavishly endowed with gifts of mind and charms of person; and his passionate and constant advocacy of religious freedom speaks as well for his heart as for his brain. But the curse of Reuben was upon him, and, like the first-born of the Patriarch, it was written of George Villiers that, unstable as water, he should not excel.

It is now my privilege to acknowledge the generous furtherance and counsel I have received in the preparation of this monograph.

I desire, first, to offer my humble thanks to His Majesty for permission to reproduce the beautiful Vandyck of the Villiers family, the presence of which at Windsor testifies to the fatherly affection of Charles I. for his orphan wards.

To Lord Denbigh, Sir George Wombwell, Mr Astor, Mr Wykeham Martin of Leeds Castle, Mr Martin Colnaghi and Mr J. Eliot Hodgkin, I owe the interesting portraits and the facsimile letter which adorn this volume.

It is difficult adequately to express my gratitude to the librarians and curators whose invaluable assistance has been ungrudgingly bestowed on me. My thanks are particularly due to Sir Henry Maxwell Lyte, Deputy-Keeper of the Records; to

Mr Horace Headlam of the Record Office; to Mr Sydney Colvin and Mr Beckley of the British Museum; and to Mr Falconer Madan of the Bodleian. Mr Law of the Signet Library, and Dr Clarke of the Advocates' Library, in Edinburgh, have often befriended me; and Dr Montague James, of the Fitzwilliam Museum at Cambridge, interested himself in the researches of a complete stranger. The help I have received is not confined to this country alone. In my researches in the *Archives des Affaires Étrangères*, at the Quai D'Orsay in Paris, I was treated with characteristic French courtesy by the Directeur des Archives, Monsieur Girard de Rialle.

Mr C. H. Firth, the distinguished historian of the Protectorate, was good enough to indicate various MSS. sources of information I should otherwise have neglected to consult. Mr Julian Corbett placed his extensive acquaintance of the period at my disposal; and the Duke of Rutland, whose family connection with Katharine, Duchess of Buckingham, gave him special knowledge of the subject, most kindly read and annotated my first two chapters.

Last, but not least, I owe no small debt of gratitude to Mr Perceval Landon for friendly aid and helpful suggestions unsparingly given to my work during the progress of its publication.

W. B.

Titsey Place,
22nd August 1903.

CONTENTS

CHAP.		PAGE
I.	EARLY YEARS	1
II.	THE CIVIL WAR	18
III.	EXILE	54
IV.	BUCKINGHAM'S MARRIAGE	79
V.	THE RESTORATION	104
VI.	BUCKINGHAM AT COURT	133
VII.	BUCKINGHAM'S OUTLAWRY	163
VIII.	THE TRIUMPH OF BUCKINGHAM	183
IX.	INTRIGUES WITH FRANCE	211
X.	BUCKINGHAM'S VAGARIES	238
XI.	THE FALL OF BUCKINGHAM	262
XII.	BUCKINGHAM IN ADVERSITY	297
XIII.	BUCKINGHAM IN THE TOWER	320
XIV.	BUCKINGHAM AND THE POPISH PLOT	341
XV.	THE END	377

LIST OF ILLUSTRATIONS

THE DUKE OF BUCKINGHAM AS A YOUNG MAN . *Frontispiece*
    From the picture in the possession of Sir George Wombwell, Bart., at Newburgh Priory.

THE DUKE OF BUCKINGHAM AND HIS BROTHER   *To face p.* 18
    From the picture by Vandyck in the possession of H.M. the King at Windsor.

LORD AND LADY FAIRFAX . . . . .   „   80
    From the picture by William Dobson, in the National Portrait Gallery.

FACSIMILE OF A LETTER FROM THE DUKE OF BUCKINGHAM, IN THE POSSESSION OF J. ELIOT HODGKIN, ESQ. . . . .   „   88

GENERAL FAIRFAX . . . . . .   „   130
    From the minature by John Hoskins, in the possession of Mr C. P. Wykeham Martin at Leeds Castle.

LADY SHREWSBURY . . . . . .   „   152
    From the picture by Sir Peter Lely, in the possession of Mr W. Waldorf Astor at Cliveden.

THE DUCHESS OF BUCKINGHAM . . . .   „   198
    From the picture in the possession of Mr C. R. Wykeham Martin at Leeds Castle.

LADY SHREWSBURY AS "MINERVA" . . .   „   290
    From the picture by Sir Peter Lely, in the possession of Mr Martin Colnaghi.

THE DUKE OF BUCKINGHAM . . . .   „   340
    From the picture by Sir Peter Lely, in the National Portrait Gallery.

THE DUCHESS OF RICHMOND . . . .   „   378
    From the picture by Vandyck, in the possession of the Earl of Denbigh at Newnham Paddox.

THE SECOND DUKE OF BUCKINGHAM

CHAPTER I

EARLY YEARS

ON January the 30th, 1627-8, the bells of the Abbey and St Martin's-in-the-fields rang merrily for the birth of a son to the all-powerful Duke of Buckingham.

The child was doubly welcome at Wallingford House, where the young parents had never ceased mourning the loss of their first boy, the baby Earl of Coventry, who had indeed only lived long enough to be an occasion for the quaint muse of his kinsman, Sir John Beaumont.

> "Thou cam'st into the world a little spy,
> Where all things that could please the ear and eye
> Were set before thee; but thou found'st them toys,
> And flew'st with scornful smiles t' eternal joys."[1]

The "little spy," was not the only one to "stay with patience in that nursery of the ground." Hitherto—for the death of his godchild and namesake, the infant Jacobina Villiers, had been as bitter a grief to King James as to her parents—the only heir to the vast possessions which had been lavished

---

[1] "Upon the Earl of Coventry's Departure from us to the Angels," by Sir J. Beaumont. Nichol's "Leicestershire," vol. i. p. 657.

on the beloved "Steenie" was a girl, five years old, Lady Mary, or "Mall"—"the fairest Lady Mary in England,"[1] according to Secretary Conway.

The future Duke[2] was christened by Dr Laud, then Bishop of Bath and Wells, on February the 14th, at Wallingford House, "the King and the Earl of Suffolk being godfathers, and the Queen godmother, by her deputy, the Duchess of Richmond. His Majesty came thither in a long soldier's coat all covered with gold lace and his hair all gawfred and frizzled, which he never used before."[3]

In 1628, *The* Duke, as it was the fashion to call George Villiers, First Duke of Buckingham, stood at the very zenith of his power. Never had Englishman in as short a time attained so dizzy an eminence. Small wonder that after a career of uninterrupted success—to which the favour of the King contributed hardly more than his graciousness of manner and personal beauty—he refused to believe that fortune could even deny him the love of Anne of Austria. The great Cardinal himself appeared an antagonist scarcely more formidable than his critics of the House of Commons, whom the King's warrant had lately relegated to the Tower. From their first meeting, all the energies of the Duke's being were centred in the conquest of the French Queen. Such vestiges of common-sense and prudence as he had hitherto retained were swept away by the mad passion that possessed him; and

---

[1] Goodman's "Court of James I.," vol. ii. p. 290. Conway to Buckingham.

[2] Wood's "Athenae Oxon.," vol. iv. p. 207.

[3] "Court and Times of Charles I.," vol. i. p. 324, 22nd Feb. 1627-8. Rev. J. Meade to Sir M. Stuteville.

indeed something of the visionary infatuation of his mood appears to have communicated itself to the child born at the time. But openly avowed as was George Villiers' devotion for the Queen, it did not impair his affection for his wife, or alienate her heart from him. From this standpoint the romantic story of our hero's father and mother is worthy of a passing notice, for it ranks as almost unique among the accustomed betrothals of the time. In the Jacobean age as a rule, the Court of Wards and the authority of guardians left little scope for Love's young dream.

Lady Katherine Manners, the only daughter of Francis, Sixth Earl of Rutland, a notable heiress in her generation, seemed predestined to an alliance in which her individual fancy would probably carry less weight than any other consideration. When the King's favourite proclaimed himself her suitor, the Earl of Rutland could not indeed refuse his consent to the marriage on which his daughter had passionately set her heart. But it is doubtful whether the match can have commended itself to him. Goadby, the dower-house of Lady Villiers, where Buckingham himself had spent his boyhood, was at no great distance from Belvoir, and the Earl at least can have been under no illusions as to that lady's origin or character. Nor can the exorbitant settlements demanded by Buckingham have inspired him with much belief in the disinterested nature of the young man's affections. Moreover, apart from the personal prejudices which the old noble might well entertain against the new-made peer, the difference of religion appeared to present unsurmountable obstacles. Like her dead mother, Frances Knyvett,

Lady Katherine was a devout Roman Catholic, and much as she loved George Villiers, openly stated that she would not and could not change her faith.

Undoubtedly the fates were not propitious to the union, and the Puritans declared it would never have taken place if the Earl of Buckingham had not cut the Gordian knot "by enticing the maiden to his lodgings." "There," says Arthur Wilson, "he keeps her some time, and then returns her to her father. The stout old Earl sent him this threatening message: That he had too much of a gentleman to suffer such an indignity, and if he did not marry his daughter and repair her honour, no greatness should protect him from his justice. Buckingham, that perhaps made it his design to get the father's good-will this way (being the greatest match of the kingdom), had no reason to mislike the union, therefore he quickly salved up the wound before it got to a quarrel."[1] It is only fair to say that party prejudice may have misrepresented the matter, and a different complexion is put upon it in the explanation given by George Villiers' mother, the Countess of Buckingham.

According to this version the Earl himself had allowed his daughter to spend the day with Lady Buckingham, on the condition that "she should not go out of her sight." Towards evening, however, the Countess was taken ill,[2] and rather than let the girl return under another escort, she kept Katherine as her bed-fellow for the remainder of the night. The next day they went back together to the

[1] "History of King James I.," by A. Wilson.
[2] Letter of Sir Ed. Zouche to Lord Zouche, quoted in "Life and Times of George Villiers, Duke of Buckingham," by Mrs Thomson, vol. i. p. 246.

paternal mansion, only to find that the Countess of Rutland refused to receive her stepchild, and consequently Lady Katherine was reduced to seek Lady Buckingham's protection.

As for Buckingham, in an indignant letter to the outraged father, he bitterly protested that Lady Katherine "never received any blemish in her honour but what came by your own tongue."

Whatever the rights of the story were, the outcome of the scandal was to render the marriage imperative.[1] And as the bridegroom dared not affront public opinion by taking a Papist wife, the nuptial ceremony was preceded by Lady Katherine's recantation in St Martin's parish church, a conversion charitably attributed to the eloquence of the Dean of Westminster, Dr Williams.

The Duchess of Buckingham evidently realised the ideal of submissive wifehood. Her portraits show her comely and amiable; and, in her charming letters, "poor fond Kate," as the King calls her, reveals herself the most warm-hearted and faithful of women. We see her rather bemoaning the absence of her brilliant lord than reproaching him for the repeated infidelities that might easily have estranged a more exacting nature. On his side, George Villiers seems to have been sincerely attached to her, and, strange as it may appear, their intercourse in private, as well as in public, remained affectionate to the last.

In later years it was through his mother that the second Duke loved to trace his descent from the Plantagenets; but, for good or ill, it was from the

[1] Harl. MSS. 1581, p. 134. Duke of Buckingham to Earl of Rutland.

male stock that he drew his strongest characteristics. The first George Villiers, compounded as he was of "a most flowing courtesy and affability [1] to all men who made any address to him," surely transmitted to his child an ample portion of his singular charm. In both alike, wit too often outran prudence.

The pompous Spaniards were aghast at Steenie's deportment in the Royal presence, "his practising of dance-steps and humming of ends of sonnets." And a generation later we find that nervous courtier, Sir John Reresby, quaking with dismay at the caustic comments it pleased our Duke to make on his sovereign. In the infatuated search for the Philosopher's Stone, the son consumed many more thousands in the crucible than the father lavished on the gems and medals of antique Greece, or the masterpieces of Titian's Italy, which crowded his London palace. In one particular, it is true, they were strikingly dissimilar. The imperious spirit of the first George Villiers ever refused to stoop to plot or intrigue. Not all the tortuous precepts of the Royal Machiavelli could implant in him the elementary notions of "kingcraft." On the other hand, the Buckingham of the Cabal moves and has his being in an atmosphere of conspiracy. In this respect he was no unworthy grandson of the old Countess of Buckingham, who, from the menial offices of an obscure manor-house wormed herself into the closest intimacy with James I., and, as the King's crony, became the ultimate dispenser of the Royal loaves and fishes. But, if they differed in their methods, father and son were alike in their aims: and the Nemesis which waits

[1] Clarendon, "History of the Great Rebellion," vol. i. p. 56.

for all careers, unredeemed by an ideal, spared neither the one or the other.

The cradle of the little Earl of Coventry was rocked to the noise of wars and rumours of wars. The year preceding his birth witnessed the defeat of his father before La Rochelle, a disaster of which Holles wrote: "Since England was England it received not so dishonourable a blow."[1] Steenie, indeed, carried himself gallantly enough in this bad business, yet, as his wife bitterly remarks, his walking the trenches "had not made him any whit the more popular man."[2] On his return the King's marked favour only intensified the national rage against the unsuccessful Lord High Admiral; and indeed the echoes of universal execration must have penetrated even to the nursery of Wallingford House.

In 1628, the Petition of Right, succeeded by the Remonstrance, designated the Duke of Buckingham, in Coke's words, as "the cause of all our miseries; the grievance of grievances." Charles prorogued Parliament, and the Duke having raised fresh supplies, mainly by mortgages on his own property, again started for Southampton to retrieve his misfortunes. But the words of the great Parliamentarian had fallen upon a fruitful soil, and before Buckingham could embark, Felton purchased his " poore tenpenny knife."

Not his family only, but the Duchess also—whose condition at this time made it additionally hard to part from her idolised husband—accompanied

---

[1] Gardiner, "Hist. of England," vol. vi. p. 202. Holles to Wentworth.
[2] Gardiner, vol. vi. p. 189.

him on this last expedition. The poor woman was oppressed by forebodings. Every lane and alley of the capital rang with scurrilous ballads. The air was thick with hatred. On the morning of the 23rd of August, the Duchess begged him to take some precautions. Steenie, however, like Henri de Guise before him, was disdainful of such foes. As Le Balafré had met all prophecy of danger from Henri III. with the curt rejoinder, "il n'oserait," so Buckingham assured his friends: "there are no Roman spirits left."

The tragedy has often been described. The shrieks of her sister-in-law, Lady Anglesea, were the first intimation that the unfortunate Duchess received of the terrible event. Clad only in her night-gown, she rushed to the hall, to find her beloved husband dead. The corpse was surrounded by a terror-stricken and bewildered crowd, and the disorder was such that the murderer Felton might have escaped had he so chosen.

An express was immediately despatched to the King, who lodged some four miles distant. Charles was at prayers. The terrible news was whispered in his ear, but his punctilious piety forbade his giving vent to his feelings till the service was concluded. Then he went to his room, flung himself on his bed, and turned his face to the wall.

That same day the King sought out the broken-hearted widow, and assured her "he would be a father to her children, and a husband to herself."

In the midst of her overwhelming grief, the Duchess must have realised that she stood in urgent need of help. During the last year her husband had pledged lands and jewels with prodigal magnificence to assist the master for whose policy he doubtless held himself accountable. When his executors attempted to draw up a statement of his estate, they found he had received no acknowledgment for £50,000 lent to the Crown.

Happily the works of art, which Rubens and Balthasar Gerbier had collected for York House, now proved a mine of gold. A few of these matchless gems were sold to the King, the Earl of Northumberland, and the Abbé Montague, and the immediate necessities of the Duchess were thus relieved.[1]

Under the existing system of the Court of Wards the natural loss of a father was increased tenfold. No prerogative of the Crown was more harmful than the traffickings in the guardianship of minors; and Charles was too well aware of the objections attending this commerce to depute to anyone but himself the care of his "martyr's" children.

A few months after Buckingham's death the Duchess gave birth to a son, to whom the King and Francis, Earl of Rutland, stood sponsors. "They complimented who should give the name. The king named him Francis, and the grandfather gave him his benediction, seven thousand pounds a year."[2] The advent of this boy, early noted for his marvellous beauty, deposed little Mall Villiers from the immediate succession to the Dukedom of Buckingham, though she was still considered the great match of the kingdom. When in the cradle,

---

[1] Brian Fairfax's "Life of G. Villiers, Second Duke of Buckingham." Preface to *Rehearsal*, Arber Ed.
[2] *Idem.*

rumour had bestowed her on Prince Charles Louis, the eldest son of the King and Queen of Bohemia.

Eventually, in 1626, though only four years old, her father betrothed her to Charles, Lord Herbert, heir to the Earl of Montgomery. "My Lord of Pembroke," writes a contemporary, "because he has no heirs of his own body, is now presently to assure my Lord of Montgomery £4000 a year in land, and when the marriage between his son and the Duke's daughter comes to be accomplished, to make it up to £10,000 a year. The Duke to give his daughter £10,000 at the perfecting of the marriage, and £10,000 within a year after."[1]

Such arrangements were common at that time. In the natural course of events, Mall would have remained, till the perfecting of the marriage, with her mother and brothers at York House. But this was not to be; for Lord Francis was only a few months old when the Duchess of Buckingham took a step which proved fatal to the happiness of all her children. She suddenly declared herself a Catholic, and a few weeks later discharged most of the Duke's Protestant servants. Katherine's decision, unfortunate as it was, need not have excited such general surprise. It had perhaps been less the ghostly counsels of Dean Williams than the worldly wisdom of her own family, which had induced her to adopt the religion of her lover. In the dark days of widowhood her mind not unnaturally reverted to her early faith.

[1] "Court and Times of Charles I.," vol. i. p. 123. Mr Pory to Rev. J. Meade, July 1626.

Her constant friend and companion, the Countess of Buckingham, herself a convert to Romanism, and one of the most fervent proselytisers in the fashionable society of the day, did not fail to take advantage of her daughter-in-law's mood. Nor did the old lady rely solely on her own polemical talents. In Lady Buckingham's house, called "The Porche," we are told there lived "three Jesuit priests, to wit, Fisher, Walpole, and Floyd, besides the two others that daily dine there but lodge at the White Lion in King Street."[1] The erudition of Dr Williams himself would have been severely taxed in argument with five Jesuits. But neither to him, nor to Laud, her husband's confessor, does Katherine appear to have submitted her searchings of heart. Nor could her halting belief in the reformed tenets have received much support from George Villiers' beloved sister, Susan, Lady Denbigh. The little seminary of "The Porche" had likewise undermined the latter's peace of mind, and it required all the ingenuity and eloquence of the celebrated Dr Cozens, her spiritual adviser,[2] to retain this good lady within the fold of Canterbury.

The Duchess's recantation had been publicly pronounced in St Martin's-in-the-Fields, but we are not told where her reconciliation to the Church of Rome took place. Though seldom enforced, the penal laws were at this date so severe, that when Lady Falkland made her first confession to a Roman Catholic priest, she did so in a stable,

---

[1] "Records of the Society of Jesus, for the Province of England," by H. G. Foley, vol. i. p. 509.
[2] "The Falklands," by the author of "A Life of a Prig," p. 16.

to avoid involving any householder in her disgrace. Even at this interval of time it is not difficult for us to make allowance for our forefathers' attitude towards the unhappy Papists; for we should remember that in the early years of Charles I. many a tor and down must still have borne the traces of the beacon-fires, which had roused Elizabeth's burghers against the Armada of the King of Spain. The scars of nature are more prompt to heal than are the sullen memories of men to fade. Many a sober-minded Englishman was convinced that no Romanist was capable of genuine loyalty to that Commonwealth whose greatness was mainly due to its Protestant masterbuilders.

The Duchess of Buckingham was, of course, a privileged person, but, on this occasion, Charles's displeasure was serious and not lightly appeased. The Duke of Buckingham and Lord Francis were, therefore, at an early age, transferred from their mother's care to the Court, where they were educated with the young Princes, under the personal supervision of the King, whilst Mall was straightway entrusted to the guardianship of the Pembroke family. Thus, by her unfortunate, though conscientious, resolution, the Duchess practically made orphans of her children.

The Earl of Rutland's death, in 1632, was a further misfortune for the Villiers family. Not only was the Duchess henceforward a lonelier woman, but the loss of so good and wise an influence was no small calamity to his grandson. Lord Rutland had endeared himself to his contemporaries by his unaffected virtues. The poor adored him for his unostentatious charity, and Brian Fairfax records a quaint and kindly habit of the stout old Earl. "Every quarter-day, he sent his steward with bags of money to several prisons, to relieve prisoners and pay their debts."

His death was unexpected. He was overtaken by sickness in the public inn of Bishop's Stortford, and the end was not long delayed. His daughter was hastily summoned, and, holding her hand, he blessed with his dying breath both "his sweetheart" and her children. "It grieves me," he said, "I should see none of them before I die, but I leave them my blessinge."[1] He urged the desirability of the proposed match between my Lord Chamberlain's son and Mall, and he impressed on Katherine, with evident anxiety, that "hee gave his best heroners to his Majestie," and that the "King's Query was to chewse either his best huntinge horse for the hare or his best buck-hunter;" he recalled with satisfaction that his "tombe was allready made," and since he was content that his funeral "should be such as all his ancestors had, which will be no great charge," the details of his interment did not exercise his mind. And thus having long since settled all his personal unentailed property on his heiress and her children, the good old man departed in peace.

The King, doubtless, had less difficulty in obtaining his "heroners" and "buck-hunter" than the Duchess in proving her claim to her father's estate. Her uncle, the heir-at-law, declared himself ruined by the legacies due to her, and threw every

[1] Hist. MSS.: Rutland Papers, "Memorandum of Sir G. Manners," vol. i. p. 492.

possible impediment in her way. The new Earl pleaded that the "burden will be so very heavy by the debts, legacies and charges of my brother, and my own, that I shall not be able to live as I should. I have but the remains of a short time, and but my life in effect in most of the possessions of the Earldom. This life will be miserable and mean if some part of this great load be not taken from me."[1] Katherine was not of a grasping nature, but she was fighting for her children's rights as well as her own. On June the 5th, 1634, with a cold decision, hardly to be expected in "poor fond Kate," she replied: "I cannot forbear any longer, for I see you have no disposition to agree to anything, unless I give away my father's legacy, which he intended for me absolutely. If you have any inclination to agree to this award, I will be at York House to-morrow, and if not, I must go on to the Court of Wards the very beginning of the term." A month later the King intervened, appointing "Sir Henry Hastings, Sir Guy Palmer, and others to report upon what parts of the lands which belonged lately to Francis, Earl of Rutland, in Woolsthorpe, Eaton and Redmill, has descended to Katherine, Duchess of Buckingham in fee simple, and which of them belong to the old entail." And, thanks to their exertions, the dispute was promptly settled in a manner creditable to both parties.

At the Restoration the Duke of Buckingham was accounted the richest person of the kingdom —a position he enjoyed mainly owing to the inheritance for which his mother had so resolutely

[1] Rutland MSS., vol. i. p. 493.

battled. Unfortunately, few of the Duchess's decisions were equally distinguished by worldly wisdom. Charles I. had been sorely displeased with her secession from the Church of England, but he was far more deeply incensed when, in 1635, she elected to marry again; nor did her choice of a second husband commend itself to him.

Randal M'Donnell, Earl of Antrim, a fanatical Papist, exercised considerable influence over his co-religionists in the north of Ireland, where he occupied a position akin to that of a Highland chieftain. He enjoyed the good graces of Henrietta Maria, but Wentworth, Lord Strafford, now the ruling spirit of the administration, regarded him with marked disfavour. The children were consequently yet further withdrawn from their mother's sphere of influence. In 1634, Lady Mary, then twelve years of age, had been solemnly espoused to Lord Herbert, a youth of seventeen. The nuptials, which were of the gayest, were celebrated at York House, on Christmas Day of that year. Shortly after, the boy bridegroom was despatched to Florence to complete his studies, under the auspices of his cousin, that eccentric genius, Duke Dudley. But whilst staying at Olivolo, a Malatesta castle in the Apennines, he contracted small-pox and died, and was buried there.

The tragedy evoked an ode from Massinger. But since the child-widow had openly declared her preference for Philip Herbert, Lord Pembroke's second son, it is possible that her grief was less overwhelming than the poet suggested. Nor, though poor Mall vowed "she was resolved to fall on her knees to the King, that she may live with her mother," [1] did Lord Herbert's death restore her to the Duchess's guardianship.

She returned to Court, where she seems not only to have been happier than she had anticipated, but also to have laid the foundations of a life-long intimacy with Charles II. Indeed the anecdotes of that time show that the discipline of the children was not so rigid as to exclude all frolic and merriment. Mall's chief joy consisted in climbing the fruit-trees in the forbidden ground of the King's private garden. On one occasion, while thus occupied, the Prince of Wales, seeing a mysterious black shape fluttering amongst the boughs in the dim distance, concluded that some strange bird had alighted there, and straightway despatched one of his boy friends, a certain George Porter, with a gun to secure this novel ornithological specimen. Great was the youth's surprise, however, when the supposed fowl resolved itself into little Lady Herbert, whose widow's veil and weeds had caught upon the branches and produced the appearance of wings. Porter had to submit to a pelting before the young marauder would enter into parley with him. But when Mall heard of the Prince's mistake, her amusement and delight were unbounded; nor would she leave Porter any peace till he consented to pack her into a huge covered basket, which was then solemnly carried into Charles's apartments.

Here, Porter told the Prince that he had been fortunate enough to take the "butterfly" alive, and that it was so beautiful he would rather have died

[1] "D.S.P.," Charles I., vol. i. p. 317, 28th March 1636.

a thousand deaths than have killed it.[1] Charles's curiosity was aroused, he raised the lid, the damsel jumped out, and he had—as Mde. d'Aulnoy says—"the agreeable surprise" of receiving an affectionate embrace from his little playmate, henceforward always known at Court as the "butterfly."

This cheerful life did not, however, last long, and, in 1636, Lady Herbert was married to the Duke of Lennox and Richmond, the King's nearest kinsman.

"The nuptials of the Duke and the maiden-widow," writes a contemporary, "were solemnised at Lambeth, honoured with the presence of the King and Queen, and the Royal issue. The wedding dinner at York House; they say there were more cooks than guests—sixty cooks and but six lords; nor the Archbishop who married them, nor the Lord Chamberlain Pembroke."[2]

[1] Mde. d'Aulnoy, "Mems. de la Cour d'Angleterre," vol. ii. p. 59.
[2] Hist. MSS., Rep. IV. : Delawarr MSS.

CHAPTER II

THE CIVIL WAR

THE early years of the Duke of Buckingham and Lord Francis were less eventful than those of their much-married sister. The sole memorial of this phase of their lives is Vandyck's picture, at Windsor, of the two handsome lads, in trunk hose and gorgeous mantles, standing side by side. They grew to boyhood sharing the instructors and lessons of the Prince of Wales and the Duke of York.

The Duke of Newcastle we know, through the quaint biography of his eccentric Duchess, to have been a high-minded gentleman, well worthy of being entrusted with the supreme direction of the heir-apparent's training. The same might be said of his fellow-governor, Lord Hertford.

Lord Berkshire was a far less happy choice, but the actual education of the boys rested more with Brian Duppa, Bishop of Salisbury, than with his nominal trustees. This prelate is praised by Wood, chiefly for the grace of his deportment and the comeliness of his person, and he was eventually promoted by his Royal pupil's gratitude to the See of Winchester. Charles I., however, must have discovered other and less mundane qualities

The Duke of Buckingham and his Brother.

in Duppa, for he made "much use of his pious conversation" when imprisoned in the Isle of Wight.¹ And it speaks highly in his favour that the cynical Charles II. so respected him that, "when the worthy prelate lay on his death-bed at Richmond, he craved his blessing on his bended knees by his bedside."

Yet it is curious to remember that no other than John Hampden was at one time proposed as tutor to the Prince. Between him and these excellent mediocrities the contrast is great indeed.

College life began betimes in the seventeenth century, and at an early age the brothers were despatched to Cambridge. Here they were entered at Trinity College, and George Villiers laid the foundation of a lifelong friendship with Abraham Cowley. No one who has seen Lely's portraits of Cowley, whether clad as an Arcadian shepherd, or wearing the flowing lovelocks and lace collars of the typical cavalier, can fail to understand the fascination that the gentle poet exercised on his contemporaries. If his lyrics, though less ephemeral than many of the verses of that day, do not appear so "incomparable" to us as they did to Mr Evelyn, yet the high estimate that good man formed of his character has never been disputed. Indeed it was an opinion in which so dissimilar a person as Charles II. concurred, for at his death he "was pleased to say that Mr Cowley had not left a better man behind him in England."² Little as there was in common between such a nature and Buckingham's, their mutual affection never wavered;

---
¹ Harris, "Hist. of Charles II.," vol. i. p. 5.
² Echard, "Hist. of England," vol. ii. p. 208.

and when Cowley was carried to his grave in the Abbey, it was the Duke who not only defrayed the cost of the pompous funeral, but also placed a tablet to his memory close to the tombs of Chaucer and Spencer.

When the storm that had been brewing for so long broke at last, and the Standard of the King was raised at Nottingham, the cult of the Muses proved ineffectual to restrain the noble students from seeking other laurels. They contrived to evade the vigilance of the College authorities, and rejoined the King at Oxford. They elected Prince Rupert and Lord Gerard[1] to initiate them into the art of war, and under these two leaders they saw some very sharp service in the storming of the close at Lichfield.

Naturally, this premature campaign did not commend itself to the Duchess of Buckingham. She bitterly reproached Lord Gerard "for tempting her sons into such great danger." But she got scant consolation from the boys' military tutor, for he only replied, "that it was their own inclination, and the more danger the more honour."

Apparently, Charles I. did not endorse Lord Gerard's Spartan maxim, for after this feat of arms the Duke and his brother were promptly sent abroad, whilst the Parliament, which at first had confiscated the Villiers' estates, on consideration of the delinquents' extreme youth, generously consented to restore their possessions.

For the next few years, therefore, under the guardianship of the Earl of Northumberland, and accompanied by a certain Dr Aglionby,[2] the

[1] Brian Fairfax, "Life of G. Villiers."
[2] Nichol's "Leicestershire," vol. ii. p. 213.

brothers wandered through France and sojourned in Italy, "where they lived in as great state as some of those sovereign princes."[1]

Considering the state of affairs in England, no better means could perhaps have been devised to complete the education begun at Trinity College, and continued, as the fighting slackened, at Christ Church, Oxford. During the most receptive period of their life the young men were brought into contact with the leading personalities of the day, and could study on the spot the art and architecture of Europe. Yet the loss of College discipline was an incalculable misfortune to the Duke, whose brilliant cleverness too often degenerated into mere dilettantism for want of exact training. Nor were Florence and Rome, where they spent most of their time, to be recommended as schools of morality. It is true "they brought their religion home with them again," but Buckingham's marked indifference, if not hostility, to orthodoxy, may have originated in his early experiences and observations in the city of St Peter. There were not wanting those who declared that the poisonous effects of the "Italianate" education were already discernible in the Duke, when, in the year 1645, he paused in Paris, on his return from his travels. Here he met his former schoolfellow, the Prince of Wales, and, Bishop Burnet solemnly assures us, "having already got into all the impieties and vices of the Age,"[2] deliberately set himself to corrupt his future King. According to

[1] Brian Fairfax.
[2] Burnet, "Hist. of his Own Times," edited by O. Airy, vol. i. p. 218.

this authority, he set about his wicked design "by possessing the young Prince," not only with "very ill principles both as to Religion and Morality, but with a very mean opinion of his father, whose stiffness was with him a perpetual subject of raillery."[1] "And to compleat the matter, Hobbs was brought to him (Charles) under the pretence of instructing him with mathematicks; and he laid before him his schemes both as to Religion and Politicks, which made a deep and lasting impression on the King's mind, so that the main blame of the King's ill principles and bad morals was owing to the Duke of Buckingham."

It is difficult to reconcile this cold-blooded and systematic depravation with the assertion of one who knew him far better than the gossiping bishop. Brian Fairfax says that "His Grace was always pleased to express a love for good men and good things, how little soever he was able to live up to what he knew." The truth seems to be that the two young men, with the associations of their early boyhood in common, unrestrained by the presence of the "stiff" Royal father and guardian, naturally found in each other's congenial company, "much pleasure, frolick, and extravagant diversion." That stern moralist, Lord Clarendon, strikes a truer note than Burnet, when he writes, "that there are some actions of Appetite and Affection committed, which cannot be banished from the age of twenty-one. Kings are of the same mould as other men."[2]

---

[1] Burnet, "Hist. of his Own Times," edited by O. Airy, vol. i. p. 90.
[2] "Clarendon Papers, Cal.," vol. ii. p. 133, No. 724.

Enamoured as the Duke might be of the pleasures of Paris and the mathematical lessons of Mr Hobbes, he abandoned both with alacrity at the first opportunity which enabled him to prove his devotion to the Royal cause in England. This was in the year 1648, when the fortunes of the Cavaliers might well appear desperate. Charles I. was already a prisoner in the Isle of Wight, which he was only to leave for the final scene at Whitehall. Humanity and common-sense alike prohibited any further struggles on the part of the King's decimated followers. Nevertheless this was the moment chosen by the Duke and Lord Francis to join a forlorn attempt of Lord Holland's at Reigate. Misfortune attended them from the very outset. Goring, who should have seconded the rising, was blockaded in Colchester by Lord Fairfax, and one troop of horse under Colonel Gibbons proved sufficient, as the Parliament had anticipated, to disperse the conspirators. At Nonesuch the Roundheads overtook their ill-matched antagonists. The skirmish took place in the old Royal burgh of Kingston and the outskirts of Surbiton Common. It was short and sharp. "My Lord Francis at the head of his troop, having his horse slain under him, got to an oak tree in the highway about two miles from Kingston, where he stood with his back against it, defending himself, scorning to ask quarter, and they barbarously refusing to give it; till, with nine wounds in his beautiful face and body, he was slain. The oak tree is his monument, and has the first two letters of his name F. V. cut on it to this day."[1] Thus in his twentieth year died Lord Francis Villiers,

[1] Brian Fairfax.

making a willing offering of his life for the king to whom he and his owed so much. Forty years elapsed between his untimely end and the death of the Duke himself in the lonely farmhouse at Helmsley, yet the latter's thoughts may well have reverted with something of envy to the happier fate of the brother who had been taken in the first bloom of his chivalrous loyalty.

That the gallant boy had not plunged into danger imperfectly realised, is proved by the fact that he had scrupulously set his affairs in order before embarking on the ill-fated expedition. In fact, so well had he contrived to make his estates responsible for his "just debts," that Parliament, when it seized on them, was compelled to discharge his obligations. The occasion of these "just debts" is not difficult to surmise. Young as he was, he had already conceived a violent passion for the beautiful Mrs Kirke. Before he rode to Reigate he made her a farewell gift of plate valued at £1000, and after his death a "lock of her hair sewed in a ribbon" was found next his heart.[1] The body of the heroic youth was conveyed by water to York House, passing, doubtless, under the very watergate adorned with the Villiers escutcheon, which still surmounts the archway leading into the Embankment Gardens, near Charing Cross Station. The vault in Henry VII.'s Chapel, which had received Felton's victim, opened anew for the son. Lord Francis' tomb, unlike his father's, is marked by no monument, and the comparative terseness of

---

[1] "Ludlow Memoirs," vol. i. p. 255.

DEPOSITUM.

Illustrissimi domini Francesci Villiers, ingentis specie juvenis, Filii posthumi Georgii Ducis Buckinghamii, qui vicesimo aetatis anno pro Rege Carolo, et Patria, fortiter pugnando nonis horem honestis vulneribus acceptis, Obiit VII die Julii Anno Domino, 1648.[1]

After the disastrous fight at Kingston, the Duke with Lord Holland, and the shattered remnant of the cavalier force, made their escape to St Neots, "They took up inns, were very quiet and sleepy; like young soldiers, though chased from Kingston, yet set no guards. Colonel Scroope with seven troops followed them, entered the town on Monday morning about 4 of the clock, took Holland in his chamber, and about eighty prisoners."[2] Fortunately for Buckingham, though he had been equally remiss in placing scouts, his lodgings were more capable of defence. The gates of the house and courtyard were closed, and this lucky accident gave him time to muster his servants and get to horse. The barriers were then flung aside, and the intrepid little band, led by their young master, charged straight at the troopers. They had a desperate fight, the Duke killing the Roundhead commander with his own hand, but they cut their way through, and reached the seaside in safety, where they found means to embark and to join Prince Charles, who was then with the fleet in the Downs.

That Buckingham had reason to congratulate himself on his escape was shown by the tragic fate of his fellow-conspirator Lord Holland — shortly

---

[1] Manning and Bray's "Hist. of Surrey," vol. i. p. 348.

[2] Historical MSS., Lord Montague of Beaulieu, p. 162, 12th July 1648. Robert Barnard to Lord Montague.

after beheaded in London. Yet George Villiers must have commanded considerable influence at Westminster. For in spite of the provocation he had given to the Parliament, they once more offered, on his submission within forty days, liberal terms of composition. Nevertheless, to use his own words in later years to his forgetful sovereign, he chose "rather with the hazard of my life to endeavour to wait upon Your Majesty in the Fleet, where I found you, than to stay, possessed of my estate, upon condition of having nothing more to do with Your Majesty's fortunes."[1]

Not unnaturally, when confronted in so defiant a manner, Parliament retaliated by confiscating the entire Villiers property. "A few friends still laboured much in the procuring an act of indemnity,"[2] but for the moment with little hope of success, and from this time forward the Duke shared to the full the miseries and vicissitudes of the Stuart exile.

Happily for him he was still able to rely on the fidelity of his servants, whom, indeed, throughout his strange career, he inspired with singular devotion. As at St Neots, the courage of his attendants had saved him from his brother's fate, so now he would have landed in Holland a penniless outlaw but for the foresight of a trusty steward. This excellent old man, Mr John Trayleman by name, contrived to smuggle out of England the pictures and gems which had

---

[1] "Fairfax Papers," vol. iv. p. 252. Letter of Duke of Buckingham to Charles II.

[2] MSS. Clarendon, No. 2833, Bodl. Mr Woodhead to Mr Denham, 14th July 1648.

made York House the finest museum in the land.¹ Under the pass of the States-General, sixteen cases of art treasures found their way to Antwerp to be coined into daily bread for Steenie's son. When we remember that a single picture, the great "Ecce Homo" by Titian, was now disposed of for no less than £5000 to the Archduke Leopold of Prague, we realise that George Villiers must have had no inconsiderable resources. But for a nobleman of the Duke's rank, the expenses of exile were heavy. In spite of the notorious laxity of his theological views, etiquette required that even he should have a private chaplain, and the rest of his establishment was on an equally magnificent scale, the horde of impecunious adherents who surrounded him being no small drain on his pocket. At no time was the Duke noted for wise administration of his patrimony, while, like all spendthrifts, he was possessed with the desire to arrive at wealth by short cuts. Had he lived in these days he would without doubt have promoted many a wild-cat company, and financed speculations of the most hazardous description.

In the seventeenth century, however, noblemen afflicted by these propensities did not frequent 'Change. They engaged an alchemist. "For some years," says Burnet, "Buckingham thought he was very near discovering the philosopher's stone, which had the effect that attends all such men as he was, when they are drawn in to lay out for it."² Charles shared to the full the Duke's passion for

[1] Warrant States-General, Bodl. Cal. MSS. 2732.
[2] Burnet, vol. i. p. 182.

chemistry, and it was in the hours they spent together over the retort and crucible, that George Villiers acquired his great ascendency over his youthful sovereign. But these sedentary pursuits did not deter Buckingham from forming other projects. Adventures are to the adventurous, and Madame d'Aulnoy has strange tales to relate of the Duke of Buckingham's doings at this period.

Undeterred by the severity of the Home Government, he sometimes ventured back across the Channel. On such occasions his talents as an actor and mimic were invaluable ; and in the character of a Jack Pudding[1] he was able with comparative safety to instal himself under the very windows of Whitehall. Beneath the costume Buckingham assumed, it would indeed have been difficult to identify the graceful cavalier of the Stuart Court. His little hat was adorned with a fox's brush and cock's feathers, he either wore a mask or besmeared his face with flour, and the rest of his attire was equally fantastic. Thus transmogrified, he erected an open-air stage at Charing Cross, and hired a certain number of fiddlers and mummers to assist in the entertainments. He speedily drew large audiences, for the ballads he improvised on the current topics of the day were immensely popular, and thus easily defrayed all the expenses connected with this new venture.

But while he played the fool, he kept a strict watch on passing events, and was soon rewarded

---

[1] "Mems. de la Cour d'Angleterre," par Madame d'Aulnoy, La Haye Ed., 1695, vol. i. p. 20.

by learning that his sister, the Duchess of Richmond, who had been imprisoned at Whitehall, was about to be transferred to Windsor. Affection apart, it was of the highest importance to both that he should communicate with her, and he was convinced that the journey would afford the only opportunity of doing so.

Consequently, when the Duchess's coach and escort appeared at Charing Cross, they found their way blocked by an impertinent buffoon bent on making fun, for the benefit of the expectant mob, of the great lady and her family, especially her " good - for - nothing brother," the Duke of Buckingham.

For all their austerity, the dour troopers did not feel it inconsistent with their principles to countenance a show on which the crowd had evidently set its heart, and which, moreover, involved the humiliation of an impenitent malignant. The procession halted, and Mall was obliged to sit at the carriage window and listen with what indifference she could affect to the offensive doggrel reeled off by the minstrel.

When the performance was concluded, Buckingham remarked "that it was only proper the Duchess should possess those Ballads she herself had inspired." The populace shouted for joy at the notion, and Buckingham descended from the trestles, bearing a bundle of caricatures and songs, amongst which some important papers were secreted.

It now became necessary that the Duchess should be acquainted with her persecutor's identity. As he neared the carriage, he therefore raised for a brief second the black vizard he wore over his eyes, and Mall instantly recognised her brother. She behaved with admirable presence of mind, made no sign, and quietly accepted the packet. The carriage then drove off, pursued by the jeers of the actor and the spectators, and Buckingham was able to congratulate himself on having carried out his purpose with absolute impunity.

Successful as the masquerade had been, it was, however, impossible to continue it indefinitely, and eventually Buckingham had to retreat once more to Holland. Here the question of ways and means was again a foremost consideration. In the April of 1649, he confided to Mr William Aylesbury that "though he wished to compound for his estates, such base submissions are required of him in his applications as he cannot submit to. He is resolved to follow the King into Ireland, and wishes to obtain the command of the King's Guards."[1] Dazzled by the vision of martial glory which his ingenious fancy so easily evokes, he charges his correspondent not to dream of selling any more pictures or agates. But four days later his confidence has evaporated. Facts were not to be juggled with, and he reluctantly authorises Aylesbury to pledge the remnant of the pictures and valuables "in the house of Mr Justus Colinaar at Antwerp, to Colonel Robert Sidney in consideration of the latter giving bail for his appearance in a suit owing by the Duke to Charles Valois."[2]

As we know, Cromwell's successful campaign in Ireland speedily put an end to the designs of

---

[1] Clarendon MSS. 44, 16th April 1649. Duke of Buckingham to Mr. W. Aylesbury.
[2] Clarendon MSS. 45, 20th April. Hague Draught of Bond.

Charles II. on that island. Of all torments, the most intolerable to Buckingham was inaction; moreover, the treasure store at Mr Justus Colinaar's was fast dwindling. Under this double stress the Duke's thoughts gravitated towards a composition with the Home Government. In May he threw himself on the kindness of a relative, whose nice sense of honour would, he knew, forbid any counsels of "base submissions." Basil Feilding, Earl of Denbigh, to whom he now addressed himself, was the son of Steenie's favourite sister, "Su," who had brought him up to worship her brother. Her teaching bore good fruit, for once when assassination was in the air Basil gave a signal proof of his devotion by offering to impersonate his uncle. Sir Henry Wotton tells us that although Steenie refused to take advantage of the proposal, he was moved to tears by his nephew's generosity; and the incident must have endeared the youth to the Duchess, for we find her cordially corresponding with him after her husband's death. At the outbreak of the Civil Wars, Basil, Lord Feilding, as he then was, embraced the Parliamentary side with the same ardour which his father and mother displayed for the King. The old Earl met with his death in a skirmish near Birmingham, in 1643. In a touching letter, Susan besought her beloved son to sever his connection with his father's murderers. But Basil's convictions were of the order which are not affected by personal considerations. He remained an adherent of the Parliament, in spite of the lamentations of the poor countess, who regarded his political views as the only flaw in an otherwise faultless character and judgment.

The following letter, written at this time to his cousin by Buckingham, is still extant:[1]—

My Lord,—I should not venture to write to Your Lordship for fear of doing you prejudice, being an excepted person, unless the matter I am to solicit you about, and my present resolutions were such as would not be displeasing to the place where you are. I am now, My Lord, endeavouring all I can to make my composition and knowing noe man that I can rely upon in this businesse but your Lordship I have taken the boldnesse to troble you about it, and to desire you to employ all the interest you have in England, to bring this to passe. I cannot thinke myselfe a fitt judge at this distance to know what is to be done about it. However I should much preferre your opinion before my owne, wherefore I doe wholly resigne the entire conduct of it to your Lordship desiring you to act for mee in this businesse all that you thinke is fitt to be done, assuring you my Lord that you cannot oblige anybody in the world that shall express more gratitude and thankfulnesse for the favours you shall lay upon him than myselfe. There is one thing more I must needs enquire of your Lordship, whether it bee possible to transport monie over out of England, in case I should take conditions here or somewhere else abroad being resolved not to goe into Ireland. If that could be done, I could perhaps provide for myselfe till my composition were made, which would bee noe small advantage to mee in this my present condition. I hope you have soe good an opinion of mee as to believe without much paynes that I am truly, my Lord,—Your Lordship's most humble and most faithful servant, G. Buckingham.

Paris, 19th May.

---

[1] Newnham MSS. Duke of Buckingham to Earl of Denbigh, Paris, 19th May. This letter was not calendared by the Hist. MSS. Comm.

George Villiers did not content himself with making a direct appeal to his cousin. He enlisted the ready sympathies of his aunt, who, from the following letter of Lord Denbigh's in answer to hers, must have warmly pressed the young Duke's claims on her son.[1]

MADAME,—I esteeme it the greatest of my misfortunes to be divided att this distance from the more frequent occasions of expressing my duty to Your Ladyship. It will be noe difficult matter to awaken in your Ladyship a beliefe of my hearty endeavours to compose my Lord of Buckingham's differences here, but the streame runs soe high against him that the issue is much to be doubted, and if the Parliament will incline att all to receive him his composition will bee raised to a greate summe. The enclosed to my Lord Duke will give him some further accompt of that businesse. In the meantime I shall humbly recommend to your care, as your Ladyship tenders the happynesse and being of the family, that the only two branch that is left of my deare unckle be not further exposed to the unnecessary disadvantage of future engagements, which will only serve to render his condition here altogether desparable. You will give mee leave to begg the favour of your blessing upon—Your Ladyship's most dutiful and most obedient sonne,
BASIL DENBIGH.
BROOK HOUSE,
  25*th July*, 1649.

Not in Parliamentary circles alone did the stream run high against Buckingham.[2] Charles's

---

[1] Newnham MSS. Earl of Denbigh. Basil, Earl of Denbigh, to his Mother.
[2] Clarendon.

"very melancholy little court" was as much distracted by the claims of rival personalities as ever his father's had been in the heyday of Stuart prosperity. A subject who had relinquished five and twenty thousand a year at the call of loyalty, had surely some claim to gratitude. Yet, when in September, 1649, Charles bestowed the Garter on Buckingham, this somewhat barren honour aroused the dormant jealousies of his courtly competitors. The Duke's careless association with doubtful characters gave his enemies a weapon which they were not backward to use against him. Before long, Breda was ringing with the report of a desperate conspiracy organised by him and Lord Gerard. According to the gossips, the new Knight of the Garter aimed at nothing less than the forcible seizure and abduction of his monarch, at dead of night, to the high seas. Once on board, the king's destination was unknown. There is no sign that the plot found credence with those in authority, but it is the first of a long series imputed to the fertile imagination of Buckingham. The scandalmongers notwithstanding, in April 1650, the Duke, with the Marquess of Newcastle and the Duke of Hamilton, was admitted to the Privy Council.[1] Undoubtedly, this promotion was mainly due to the fact that, in the autumn of 1649, Sir Edward Hyde, the representative of the old-fashioned, respectable section of the Royalists, had retired to Spain under the excuse of a special mission. His departure left the coast clear to Buckingham, and he had scarcely reached Madrid

---

[1] Clar. MSS., vol. ii. p. 38. Breda, 8th Dec., R. Watson to Edgeman.

before he learnt that the king had conferred the command of the prospective regiment of Horse Guards on his young and ambitious friend.[1]

In 1649-50, the question which called most imperatively for settlement was the policy to be adopted by the youthful sovereign towards the Scottish Covenanters, who were now practically supreme in the North. Treacherous as had been their past conduct towards Charles I., on his death they had immediately proclaimed Charles II. king.

Montrose, indeed, had never relinquished the hope of reducing his stubborn countrymen to their allegiance by force of arms, and he was even now engaged on the Continent recruiting volunteers and funds for a fresh campaign. But few, even amongst his warmest supporters, were sanguine of his success. In Ireland, Cromwell was marching from victory to victory. And the Scilly and Channel Islands, the last Cavalier strongholds, were on the point of hauling down the royal ensign.

The Stuart fortunes seemed to have reached their lowest ebb, and when Argyll, the leader of the Presbyterian party, made formal advances to Charles, there were not wanting councillors to urge the acceptance of the terms, however onerous. Amongst these advisers, the foremost were the Queen mother and the Duke of Buckingham. Henrietta Maria had a personal grudge against the gallant Marquis of Montrose which inclined her to compound with his enemies; and, since she regarded all Protestant denominations as alike beyond the pale of salvation, she had no greater

[1] Clar. MSS., vol. ii. No. 73. Paris, 3rd Dec. 1649.

objection to the Presbyterian than to the Episcopal form of Church government. A Gallio in matters ecclesiastical, an opportunist in affairs of State, Buckingham naturally ranged himself with Argyll, who alone had anything to offer.

But although Sir Edward Hyde was absent, there were many worthy gentlemen who considered that the Crown itself would be dearly purchased at the price demanded by the Scots, and that these terms—repudiation of the loyalists, disavowal of the peace with the Irish, and the subscription of the Covenant—would simply dishonour the King without effecting his restoration.

One of Cromwell's spies, in his " Brief Relation," has left us his impression of the hopes and intrigues which occupied the exiles at this juncture—a picture which corroborates the lamentations of the soberer Cavaliers such as Nicholas and Lord Hatton.

It appears that the man had gone to Beauvais to witness the meeting between the young King and his mother, and to see "what face of a court" was there.

The policy affected by the Queen and Lord Jermyn was an open secret, so that when, after a three hours' interview, Henrietta Maria emerged "red with anger" and forthwith drove away, there could be little doubt that her arguments had not vanquished Charles's lingering scruples. It was indeed surmised that the King hesitated to entrust himself to Argyll's faction without hostages being given for his security. And even if this question was satisfactorily settled, he was reluctant to revoke Montrose's commission.

Much of this was, of course, pure guess-work on the informer's part, but when it came to describing the manner and morals of the Court he was on firmer ground. "I had full satisfaction," he writes, "from my view, and so I think any looker-on would have had, and if these be still the counsellors and this the company, a man that is no witch may foretell the issue; the discourses, councils, projections, and hopes speake such ridiculous follies, and such extream debauchery is amongst them, that you will hardly believe the relation."[1]

The Scots commissioners had undoubtedly a staunch advocate in George Buckingham. But it was the abject condition of the royal finances which most effectually seconded his arguments. Mismanagement and peculation aggravated the original penury. Sir Henry Wood, Henrietta Maria's treasurer, assured Lord Hatton, "that when the Queen and Prince had 4000 pistolls a month allowed them, 2500 of them were misspent upon the expenses of one man, and allowances for his creatures."[2] The "one man," Jermyn, was the bugbear of the little band of Royalists. To his nefarious influence every ill-judged action of the Queen's was ascribed, whilst many of Charles's shortcomings were traced to the same source. In the universal ruin, the Crown jewels were the one resource still left to the impecunious monarch. Yet even with these, the "Baal of the Louvre, which is the idol that ruins our Israel,"[3] contrived a "notable juggle." "Divers

---

[1] "Charles II. in Scotland," by S. R. Gardiner (Scottish Hist. Soc.), p. 29, 16th March, 1649-50.
[2] "Nicholas Papers," vol. i. p. 97.
[3] *Idem*, p. 204. Lord Hatton.

of the Crown jewels were free when the King was last here, and some time since, now, very lately (as they say from advertisements given to the Lord Jermyn from Jersey), he hath taken up divers of the Queen's owne jewels, that were pawned for her owne and particular occasions, and Lord Jermyn hath layed newly to pawne in their room the Crowne jewels,"[1] and as long, adds the secretary's irate correspondent, "as he may be bold and shelter himself by the Queene, expect nothing but these tricks."

In England the plate-chests of the faithful had long since been rifled of their last tankard and flagon. In France the civil dissensions of the "Fronde" diverted public compassion; and amongst the nobility, few were moved to imitate the generosity of the Princesse de Conde. This was that Charlotte de Montmorency, who in the flower of her beauty had been the adored of Henri IV. Now, in the eventide of life, it may be that her mind reverted, not unkindly, to the stormy wooing of the *roi-vert-galant.* Perhaps her own sorrows had taught her sympathy. But whatever the cause, she welcomed the opportunity of serving her royal lover's daughter, and never can gift have been conveyed in more quaintly delicate a fashion.

"She sent an extraordinary fatt mutton to the Queene, as a kind of monster for the fatness of it and in the belly of the sheepe were 2000 crownes. Notice being given of it before, it was at the Louvre carried into Sir Henry Wood's chamber and there anatomised before it was shewed anywhere else. I doe not believe you (Nicholas and

---

[1] "Nicholas Papers," p. 153, Nov. 1649. Lord Hatton to Sir Edward Nicholas.

the King) shall have any of these mutton pyes in Jersey."[1]

Whether in Jersey or in Holland, "mutton pyes" were indispensable. And as this became apparent, Charles inclined more and more to follow Buckingham's advice, and cast in his lot with the Presbyterians.

The Scots believed Montrose's invasion of their shores to be imminent, and consequently, in reply to Charles's invitation, despatched a fresh commission to treat with their young monarch at Breda, whither, in January 1650, he bent his footsteps.

During the journey a little incident must have brought home to him the falseness of his position. Nor can it have failed to add weight to Buckingham's entreaties, rather to hazard himself in the Scottish adventure, than to loiter from one small Continental city to another. When Charles arrived at Ghent, the burghers declined to assign any lodgings for his use, remarking that he could take his choice of inns.[2] Moreover, they added insult to injury, by offering the equivalent in money for the wine which it was their custom to present to any guest of distinction. The young King and his hot-headed friends took this well-meant, if tactless, suggestion in bad part, and angrily rejected the dole. The pipe of Rhenish accordingly arrived at the "Golden Apple," and served to drink not only "cares, but wits away." Indeed, under its influence, so shameless and insolent

[1] "Nicholas Papers," vol. i. p. 160, Nov. 1649, Paris. Lord Hatton to Sir E. Nicholas.
[2] "A Brief Relation," quoted in Gardiner's "Charles II. in Scotland," pp. 33-34, 14th March 1649-50.

was the conduct of the English Royalists, that it "could only be hoped that the Flemings would not take their measure of our nation by their debauched and drunken behaviour." However, in the end, the townsmen scored, for when the bill was handed in it amounted to 1,800 gelders, or £180—200 gelders being charged for such trifles as salt, vinegar, and butter. The courtiers had much ado to pay. But remonstrance was vain, since it was useless to hope for redress from the affronted citizens.

This was only one amongst many petty vexations which probably inclined Charles to lend a willing ear to the Prince of Orange, when he insisted that "as Henri IV. used to say the Kingdom of France was well worth a Mass, Scotland is worth but little if it be not worth the covenant."

In the end of April there was some talk of sending Buckingham as special Ambassador to Germany. It was hoped that his noble presence and fluent address might induce the Diet to vote Charles a substantial subsidy. Yet, finally the scheme was discarded, for Buckingham had found grace in the eyes of the Argyllians, who recognised his value as an ally. Almost alone of the English Privy Councillors, he was invited to accompany the King to Scotland; and the Covenanters, although strenuous in rejecting all "priests," granted the Duke a passport for his chaplain, Dr King, on condition that the reverend gentleman should figure in the official list as His Grace's private secretary. At this juncture George Villiers must also have stood high in Charles's favour, for he had once more refused to make terms with the Parliament, though they offered him his composition for the moderate sum of £30,000, which barely represented a year of his vast income. Before the Royal party embarked for Scotland, they received the news of Montrose's defeat at Carbisdale, and his subsequent death in Edinburgh. It must have needed all the Duke's cheerful optimism and want of principle to encourage Charles, not only to proceed, but to assure the Scottish Estates that he "was not accessory in the least degree" to Montrose's action. In spite of the ominous intelligence, however, the King set sail in the beginning of June, to join the executioners of the great Marquis.

The expedition to Scotland marks a turning-point in Buckingham's career. Those who imagined he was "too young for to take much on himself"[1] had been indeed strangely misinformed. The Duke of Buckingham was never wanting in daring or initiative. But circumstances had hitherto denied him the opportunity of proving his capacity. In any case his high rank, and intimacy with the King, made preferment a certainty; and now that the Presbytery had banished all "prelatical" persons, he had no rival to fear amongst the more experienced councillors. Henceforth, he stands revealed as we shall always know him, daring, unscrupulous, a skilled manipulator of other men's foibles. Burnet tells us "that he took all the ways possible to gain Argyll and the ministers. Only his dissolute career of life was excessively scandalous, which to their great reproach they connived at, because he advised the King to put himself wholly into their hands."[2]

[1] "A Brief Relation."
[2] Burnet, vol. i. p. 93.

Certainly they owed no small measure of gratitude to the adviser who, whilst Montrose's head yet adorned the Tolbooth, could bring Charles Stuart to subscribe the Covenant and the "Act of Classes," which proscribed his most faithful adherents. The "dreary little court" at St Johnstone's should have been more intolerable, one thinks, to the volatile Duke, than the Bohemian existence he had led in Holland.

The interminable prayers and sermons, which replaced all courtly revelry and pageant, must have been a grievous trial to him, only less detestable indeed than to his master, who frequently had to endure the eloquence of six successive preachers on the fruitful theme of his parents' idolatry and sinfulness. Naturally, these spiritual pastors did not make a favourable impression on either George or Charles. "The Puritans breake downe the hedges and then bid the cattle not to wander,"[1] was the caustic comment of the Duke; and again: "They must have a new Religion, and who but the Clergy? Who but Aaron to make the calfe for 'em?" No moment of the day was free from the ill-bred intrusion of these Genevese inquisitors. Though "the table was well-served, and the King sat in Majesty waited on with decency,"[2] the least affliction was the lengthy grace which heralded and concluded the repast. "At dinners," George Villiers says, "they lay as fiercely about 'em as in the Pulpit." Certainly ambition like poverty makes strange bed-fellows, and never in all his versatile career did Buckingham

---

[1] *Quarterly Review*, No. 373, p. 90, Jan. 1898. "George, Duke of Buckingham."

[2] Clarendon, "Hist. Rebellion," vol. v. p. 147.

give stronger proof of his marvellous adaptability than in those weary months in which he identified himself with the party of the godly. The ascendency the Duke possessed over Charles was doubtless strengthened by his appointment as Secretary of State, in place of Long, who had nominally held that post, but had been summarily dismissed with Sir Edward Walker, Clerk of the Council, by Argyll on landing. Nevertheless, if we are to believe Clarendon, the Duke was not at all trusted by the King,[1] who looked upon him as the ally of Argyll —Argyll who had reduced him to the condition of "having nothing of a Prince though he might very well be looked upon as a Prisoner."

The battle of Dunbar, on September the 3rd, 1650, proved a mitigation of the young monarch's bondage, and was indeed as great a subject of rejoicing to Charles as to the victorious Cromwell. The sequestered servants, who had been removed from the Royal service, began to intrigue and agitate. A certain Dr Frazer, the King's body physician, became the intermediary between Charles and the Royalist party, who, under Duke Hamilton and Lord Middleton, were watching the course of events, securely entrenched in their Highland fastnesses.

Encouraged by their assurance of support, Charles appointed a rendezvous, and drafted a declaration denouncing Argyll and the bad treatment he had received at his hands.

According to Clarendon,[2] the proposed meeting-place and proclamation would have remained

---

[1] Clarendon, vol. v. p. 187.
[2] *Idem*, p. 187.

unknown if Buckingham—always the most curious of mortals—finding the King's "cabinet," or strong-box, unlocked, had not perused the correspondence, and imparted the information it contained to Argyll. Clarendon, however, was not only the Duke's bitterest enemy, but he received the details of the Scottish intrigues from highly prejudiced witnesses, writing after some lapse of time.

Henry Nash's contemporary narrative provides a different, and probably more correct, version of the episode known in history as the "Start." According to him, Charles had previously given a hint of his intentions to Lords Lauderdale and Wilmot, as well as to Buckingham. They all opposed the project, and the King appeared to yield to their arguments. But some fresh grievance caused him to revert to the notion, and then, "only when putting his foote in the stirrop as to ride a huntinge, did he imparte his minde"[1] to Lord Lothian and the Duke. Lothian seems to have been struck dumb with astonishment, for he made no reply to the King's hurried assurances that he merely purposed to unite all parties against the common enemy, and that he would faithfully observe the pledges he had given to the Covenanters. Having made this announcement, Charles rode away, and Lothian immediately informed the Committee of what had taken place, while Buckingham, as in duty bound, threw himself on horseback to follow his sovereign. The King, however, travelled fast, Buckingham missed him, and

[1] Clarendon MSS., No. 457, 12th Dec. 1650. Henry Nash to William Edgeman.

returned to St Johnstone's, to find that meanwhile the Committee had despatched a party of twenty horse, under a Colonel Montgomery, in pursuit of the fugitive. After a stiff forty miles' journey, they overtook him in the wild country beyond Airlie Castle. Here a parley ensued, and on the condition that Dr Frazer and his other attendants and friends were allowed to depart in safety, Charles agreed to go back to St Johnstone's.

Buckingham may have been justified in discouraging a scheme which so easily miscarried, but if his real feelings are expressed in a letter to the Marquis of Newcastle, written about the same time, the difference between his policy and his master's does not seem irreconcilable—

"I shall not trouble your Lordship with any relation of our affayres here, since this gentleman will bee able to give you a very particular account of them, only I can but observe to you as a happy omen of our future goode success, that our losses begin to grow lucky to us, for Lambert has lately fallen upon the western forces and routed them, which next to Cromwell was the greatest enemies wee had in the world. I hope now we shall agree and joyne to make a considerable army since they are defeated that were the greatest hindrance to it. If we can but unite among ourselves I am confident we shal yet make as brave an army as was ever raysed in this kingdome, but whether wee shall bee soe happy as that comes to or noe, God knows. For my owne part I am soe weary of ill-fortunes, and the miserable condition we are in heere that I doe wish for some happy occasion of losing my life honourably in the King's service, and in the meantime all I desire is but to be well thought on by my friends, among whom I doe reckon Your Lordship as one of the first and therefore doe beseech you that you will continue me in your good opinion."[1]

Meanwhile Charles's revolt from the overbearing dominion of the Argyllians had a salutary effect on those worthies. After his escapade he was allowed to preside at the Council, and to exert some authority over his subjects. Later he was crowned at Scone, and summoned a Parliament from which his adherents were not excluded.

Before leaving Holland, Buckingham had been appointed General of the Eastern Division of England, and during the winter of 1650-1651 he was in active correspondence with the Royalist leaders in the South, but whilst Cromwell's army blocked the roads to England, opportunities for action were limited. During this weary period, which lasted till the summer, the Duke seems to have had little other occupation than the making and unmaking of plans. In February he contemplated a journey of discovery to the capital, for he writes to a certain Mr Cooke [2]—

SIR,—Since I sent to you last, we have received assurances out of Lancashire from all the considerable men in that County, that they are ready to rise for us and do only expect a party of 1500 horses from hence to countenance their rising ; being confident within ten days after they are up to be able to fight with Cromwell without any other assistance.

[1] Hist. MSS : "Welbeck Papers," vol. ii. p. 137. Duke of Buckingham to Marquis of Newcastle, 5th Dec. 1650. St Johnstone's, Perth.
[2] Cary's " Memorials of the Civil Wars," vol. ii. p. 418. Duke of Buckingham to Mr Cooke (in cypher).

Upon this, the Marquis of Argyll, David Lesley, and some other lords of interest in this kingdom have sent them back word that upon the first drawing together of our army, 2000 of our best horse and as many good Highland foot shall be sent under the command of Massey and the Duke of Buckingham. In the meantime they have given the Duke of Buckingham leave to raise a troop of English horse; which in ten days will be another two hundred good men. I have chosen to go this way into England, believing that I shall be able to do the King more service so than if I went in disguise anywhere to stay about London. This bearer, Captain Birkenhead, will give you a particular account of the whole business and I shall desire you to give entire credit to what he shall say, for he hath been the main negotiator of the Lancashire business. I am, etc.,

BUCKINGHAM.

FROM THE COURT OF SCOTLAND,
25th February 1651-1652.

The Duke's troop of horse do not seem to have been always amenable to discipline.[1] Divers complaints of great disorders reaching him, he begs their colonel "to exhort them by the respect they have to themselves as Gentlemen and souldiers and ye regard they have to ye honour and reputation of theyr countrye that they endeavour to prevent by their good demeanour in all particulars theyr own disgrace and my trouble." And should this pathetic appeal fail, he was to remind them that Buckingham had "power to execute Martiall Law, and to punish all offences and offenders by Death, and otherwise, according to ye Nature of theyr faults."

[1] Cod. Th. Tanner, fol. 65, vol. 54. "George Villiers, Duke of Buckingham to Sir William Blakiston, 17th May 1651."

George Villiers, like all imaginative persons, was essentially an optimist. For one plan that failed he had ever a dozen in reserve. His robust cheerfulness was specially remarkable when the news arrived of the severe defeat inflicted by Lambert on the Royalists in Fife. On this occasion Charles lost two thousand devoted partisans, whilst fifteen hundred more were made prisoners by the Parliamentarians. It was impossible to conceal so great a catastrophe from the English Cavaliers, and Buckingham was entrusted with the duty of announcing it to the gallant Earl of Derby.[1] But, judging by the confident tone of his laconic note, his sanguine spirit remained unaffected by the ill augury.

My Lord,—This bearer is so well able to give Your Lordship an account of the condition of our affairs at the present that I shall not trouble you with it in this letter; only, I shall say thus much concerning our last misfortune in Fife, that it is not so considerable as to hinder our march many days towards England. But I hope very shortly to have the good fortune to see Your Lordship there and to give you thanks myself for the obligation I shall ever owe to you for having been pleased to express so much kindness to my lord,—Your Lordship's most obedient, humble servant and cousin,
Buckingham.

Stirling, 24th July.

In July, 1651, Cromwell's manœuvres left the route to England free. Charles instantly marched southwards in spite of the remonstrances of Argyll and Lesley, who realised that Cromwell had been

---

[1] Cary's "Memorials of the Civil Wars," vol. ii. p. 283. The Duke of Buckingham to the Earl of Derby.

checkmated hitherto only by the difficulties of transport in Scotland. At Warrington in Lancashire the Earl of Derby rejoined the King. Great, however, as was his influence in the north-west, the country gentlemen showed but little inclination to follow his example. Indeed the King's march was so rapid that it did not give them time to prepare for a fresh campaign; whilst nothing could be more repugnant to them than the acceptance of the Covenant, which the Committee of Ministers paraded on every possible occasion. Moreover, stout-hearted as they were, their former sufferings were too recent to be forgotten. This, according to Clarendon, was the moment selected by Buckingham "to administer mortification to the King."[1] The army had barely crossed the Border when Buckingham came to the King with the specious argument that "he ought now to do all things gracious and popular in the eyes of the English Nation, and nothing could be less so than that the army should be under the command of a Scotch general; that David Lesley was only a lieutenant-general, and it had been unreasonable whilst he remained in Scotland to have put any other to have commanded over him; but that it would be as unreasonable, now they were in England, and had hope to increase the army by the access of the English, upon whom his principal dependence must be, to expect that they would be willing to serve under Lesley, and that it would not consist with the honour of any peer of England to receive his orders; and he believed that very few of his rank would repair to his Majesty till they were secure from that apprehension."

[1] Clarendon, vol. v. p. 204.

When Charles enquired who the Duke proposed to substitute for Lesley, Buckingham, no wise abashed, answered that "he hoped the King would confer the command on himself." Charles subsequently assured his Chancellor that he had met with few experiences more startling than this suggestion of his Secretary of State. He sought to put the proposal by, but, on rare occasions, Buckingham could be dogged. "The next day on the march, he renewed his importunity." He told the King "that he was confident what he proposed was so evidently for his service that David Lesley himself would willingly consent to it." Charles said good-naturedly "that his youth made him unfit for the charge." But Buckingham "as readily alleged that Harry the Fourth of France commanded an army and won a battle when he was younger than he; so that in the end the King was compelled to tell him he would have no generalissimo but himself, upon which the Duke was so discontented that he came no more to the Council, scarce spoke to the King, neglected everybody else and himself, insomuch that for days he never put on clean linen, nor conversed with anybody, nor did he recover this ill-humour whilst the army stayed at Worcester."[1]

The Duke's indifference to his personal appearance did not extend to that of his soldiers. At the Restoration, ten years later, the Company of Drapers in the City of Worcester petitioned the King for repayment of £453, 3s. requisitioned and expended on red cloth, by George Villiers, for his regiment of Guards. The unhappy City Fathers had apparently engaged to raise the money by means of a tax on

[1] Clarendon, vol. v. pp. 205-206.

the city,[1] but before they could get any return for their outlay, the King's army was routed and they themselves miserably plundered by the victorious Roundheads. Whilst Buckingham's attention was divided between private grievances and military finery, Cromwell was rapidly approaching. On September the 3rd, 1651, was fought the battle of Worcester, an event which must have recalled the Duke to the stern realities of the situation. All through the long hot day, to the rallying word of "the Lord of Hosts," the godly Parliamentarians [2] beat Charles's ill-disciplined recruits "from hedge to hedge." The defeat grew rapidly to a rout. Buckingham, who behaved throughout with great gallantry, remaining by the King's side under the hottest fire, was one of the small party who finally escorted the defeated monarch out of the town by St Martin's Gate to Barbon's Bridge. Here a brief council of war decided that further resistance was impossible. "Whereupon his Majesty resolved . . . to march with all speed for Scotland, following therein the steps of King David, his great predecessor in royal patience, who, finding himself in circumstances not unlike to these, said to all his servants that were with him at Jerusalem, 'Arise and let us fly; for we shall not else escape from Absalom: make speed to depart, lest he overtake us suddenly and bring evil upon us.'"[3]

At Buckingham's request, a scoutmaster in Lord Talbot's troop undertook to direct their way north-

[1] Dom. State Cal., Charles II., 6th June, 1660.
[2] Oliver Cromwell's "Despatch."
[3] Boscobel, "The Complete Hist. of the most Miraculous Preservation of King Charles II. after the Battle of Worcester," printed in Bohn's Ed. of Grammont's "Memoirs."

wards, but the soldier had promised more than he could perform, and night surprised them lost on a great heath. Men and horses were alike wearied, and it was necessary to call a halt. Another member of the party, a Mr Giffard, suggested they should seek food and rest at Whiteladies, once an ancient Cistercian nunnery, and now in the possession of his family. Dawn was breaking as the doors of the old convent were unbarred to the fugitives, who, whilst they thankfully partook of sack and biscuit, "held a sad consult how to escape the fury of bloodthirsty enemies." Charles undoubtedly owed his preservation to his determination of conducting his flight apart from his followers. He was, moreover, exceptionally fortunate in finding two such splendid fellows as the brothers Penderel to guide and conceal him. They also procured the necessary articles for his disguise, a green suit and leather doublet and a "noggen coarse shirt"—no slight irritation to his delicate skin. Having assumed this disguise, rubbed his face and hands with soot, and distributed the ornaments, which might easily have betrayed him, he bade his friends farewell. His "George" he entrusted to a certain Colonel Blague. It was the self-same jewel which his father had sent him as a last token from the scaffold. Nor was its value merely sentimental. Set in diamonds, it was dangerously conspicuous, and must have severely handicapped its fugitive possessor. Nevertheless Colonel Blague was so well acquainted with the neighbouring country, that three or four gentlemen elected to share his fortunes, amongst these the Duke of Buckingham and Lord Newburgh.[1] They

[1] Ashm. MSS., 1115, fol. 86.

reached unmolested the house of one George Barlowe, who lived at Blorepipe House, about two miles from Eccleshall Castle in Staffordshire. Here Colonel Blague confided his precious trust to Mrs Barlowe, who eventually succeeded in transmitting it to the King. The Colonel was less happy as regarded himself, for that very night he was seized by the pursuers. Buckingham would undoubtedly have shared his fate, but that, with unusual prudence, he had followed his host's advice, and consented to lie in the woods hard by till the search was over. Nor did daylight bring safety. For six days he was forced to remain concealed in a poor cottage till his protectors judged it possible to smuggle him away. He then contrived to reach Nottinghamshire in safety, where he found a refuge with his sister, the Duchess of Richmond, till the search for malignants slackened.

CHAPTER III

EXILE

THE Duke did not linger with his sister in England. At the end of October, accompanied by Ellis Leighton, he landed at Rotterdam, and at first—somewhat to the annoyance of Mr Secretary Nicholas [1]—refused to see any but his intimate friends.

At this time the little knot of faithful Royalists were still in dire incertitude as to the whereabouts of Charles II., and, indeed, many asserted that he must have perished in the rout of Worcester. Buckingham's mysterious return to Holland gave rise to the widely accepted idea that he was none other than the missing prince;—an impression not discouraged by the old councillors, who thought it might be of service in assisting the King's own escape from England.

Nicholas was not the only one anxious to see the Duke. Ormond, also, lost no time in seeking him out, hoping to obtain some clue to Charles's movements from the newcomer. Awed by his visitor's unaffected anxiety and loyalty, Buckingham seems to have answered truthfully and discreetly "that the King is secure, but whether in France, Flanders, or Holland, he cannot or will not say." [2]

[1] "Nicholas Papers," vol. i. p. 278.
[2] *Idem*, p. 278.

It would have been well had he refrained his lips on other occasions. But, if the rancorous memory of James II. is to be credited, his public utterances at this time were the reverse of seemly. He freely proclaimed that the King "had ill-behaved himself in the battle, and that he lay now hidden in some gentleman's house, and was happier in his own opinion, than if he was upon the throne."[1]

Naturally these charges did not pass unheeded. The King's sister, the Princess of Orange, retaliated by forbidding him her Court. Yet more deplorable than Buckingham's incorrigible license of speech, however, was his choice of friends and advisers. And of these none was more universally condemned than his late companion, Mr Leighton.

Elisha, or Ellis, Leighton was the son of the Dr Leighton notorious rather as the mutilated victim of Laud's bigotry, than as the author of "Zion's Plea against Prelates." Ellis had nothing of his father's fanaticism. He was, according to Pepys, "a mad freaking fellow," and "one of the best companions at a meale in the world."[2] Clarendon, on the other hand describes him as a vicious atheist, while Burnet hints that his religion was not the least useful part of his temporal stock-in-trade.

Extremes of character met in the Leighton family, for Robert Leighton, eventually Archbishop of Glasgow, was perhaps the most spiritual personality of his time—"liker a fair idea than a man set in flesh and blood." But great as was the gulf fixed between the prelate[3] and his brother,

---

[1] Sir J. Reresby's "Memoirs," p. 73.
[2] Pepys, vol. iv. p. 341, 178.
[3] Burnet, vol. i. p. 242.

the dissipated worldling's intercourse was not without charm even for the gentle ascetic.

This was also the bond of union between Leighton and Buckingham, for, unlike many brilliant conversationalists, there was no gift the Duke more appreciated in his companions. No sooner did they meet in Scotland than "his Ready Wit and Promptness of Speech immediately gained much"[1] on George Villiers; and the intimacy contracted there survived all the chances and changes of their eventful lives till, in 1682, Sir Ellis was laid to rest beside his saintly brother in the peaceful little Sussex church of Horsted Keynes.

Leighton was not the only soldier of fortune who counted on utilising his talents in the murderous conspiracies then daily concocted at Breda against the Protector. Colonel Silas Titus, the author of "Killing no Murder," was another dashing young blade whom Buckingham honoured with his confidence. Doubtless it was in Scotland that they also had become acquainted, for we know that Titus was the envoy despatched thence to plead with Henrietta Maria on behalf of the projected marriage between Charles II. and Argyll's daughter. To the grave and reverend signiors of the Privy Council the plans of these adventurers were as distasteful as their conduct. To Ormond the crushing defeat of Worcester appeared the natural retribution for the unholy alliance with the Covenanters, the direst foes of the Royal Martyr, and he was filled with amazement that, after his recent experiences, Buckingham should still look for salvation from that quarter. "The

[1] Walker's "Historical Discourses," p. 177.

Duke," he writes, "and all the Presbyterian gang in these parts are very eager that when the king appears, he should walk in entirely the same steps of Presbytery as formerly, as well as in the exercise of devotion as in all his negotiations."[1]

When the King did appear, Hyde instantly rejoined him in Paris. The Presbyterian gang found in the future Chancellor an able and convinced opponent, whilst the fact that his predictions had been verified gave him unprecedented authority. But his chief auxiliary was to be found in the bitter recollection Charles himself cherished against the Saints. Not in vain during these miserable months in Scotland had the iron entered into his soul. It was the one impression fated to be durable on his light fleeting nature.

Between Chancellor Hyde and Buckingham there was as much sympathy as between light and darkness. Secretary Nicholas, indeed, who owed his earliest advancement to the first Duke of Buckingham, was not unkindly minded towards his patron's son; but even he was greatly under the influence of Sir Edward Hyde. He writes regretfully to the latter: "Some of those about His Grace make him believe he is already wiser than his father.[2] I wish he may be half so wise when he doubles his age. But indeed he hath wit enough, but I doubt he wants ballast."

In these circumstances, Buckingham seems to have given himself leave from his close attendance on the King; and, never an easy person to daunt, it

---

[1] "Nicholas Papers," vol. i. p. 278, 16th Oct., 1651. Marquis of Ormond to Nicholas.

[2] Secretary Nicholas to Sir Edward Hyde, Hague, 7th March, 1652.

is immediately after the Princess's rebuff that we find him hovering about her person. Mary Stuart, Princess Royal of England, had now been a widow close on two years, for her husband, William the Prince Stadtholder of Holland, had died of small-pox a few days before the birth of his heir, the future William III.

Undoubtedly, that heroic monarch derived some of his fine qualities from his mother. "A very discreet and virtuous lady," says Nicholas, "and if she had not the natural imperfection of her family, an unwillingness to think of business, she would appear an excellent princess."[1] Never was there a better daughter or sister, and though habitually led in all things by her mother, when the interest of the Protestant religion, or the welfare of her family were at stake, she could find courage to expostulate respectfully but firmly with Henrietta Maria. Discreet and virtuous as she was, the Princess, was, however, no precisian. This, in fact, considering the love she bore her royal brother, would have been somewhat difficult; and it is interesting to note that she carried toleration so far as to describe Lucy Walters as "your wife" in her letters to Charles.

Rake though he was, Buckingham was not unwelcome at her Court. And in the austere atmosphere of Batavian Society, where the most innocent dance was denounced by the chaplains as a sin past redemption, the gaiety, the wit, the mimicry of the brilliant young exile must have made him a welcome guest.

The Princess's gracious hospitality soon encouraged Buckingham to form other schemes.

[1] "Nicholas Papers," vol. i. p. 293.

Like his father before him, blood royal was no barrier to his ardent courtships, and he undoubtedly entertained the hope of becoming his sovereign's brother-in-law. But the fact that Charles II. himself was a humble suitor for the hand of Hortense Mancini did not reconcile him to a *mésalliance* for his sister. Both he and Henrietta Maria, who was herself by this time secretly wedded to Jermyn, were unequivocal in their declarations on this subject.

The King, indeed, contented himself with remarking to the Chancellor, that he abhorred "the wild pretence of the Duke of Buckingham." But Henrietta's anger knew no bounds—in speech, at any rate; for she vowed, "that if it were possible for her daughter to entertain so base a thought, she would tear her in pieces with her own hands."[1] Such frantic protestations inevitably suggest the suspicion that the Princess may not have been absolutely indifferent to the wooing of the seductive cavalier. But however that may have been, the Queen-Dowager—happily for the peace of the Royal family—was more successful in this instance than when dealing with the love-affairs of James of York and Anne Hyde. In fact the Princess seems to have been nervously anxious not to give occasion for any further homilies, as two months later her Secretary Mr Oudart writes from the Hague:[2]—

"I may in confidence, and with Mrs Howard's permission, and upon presumption that she will

---

[1] Clar. MSS., No. 672. Hyde to Nicholas, 2nd Mar. 1652.
[2] Peck, "Desid. Curiosa," p. 460. Nicholas Oudart to Mr Harding, 30th May, 1652.

not communicate it beyond the King and Queen, acquaint you with My Lord Duke of Buckingham's repair hither on Saturday last upon business (as his Grace said) and in the end too that it was to take leave of our Princess. Who (well remembering what reports had been formerly raised to her prejudice, upon the civility His Highness attributed to his quality) thought fit to send him a message by Mrs Howard, to this effect.

"2. That he should tell His Grace that he could not be ignorant, how from the malice of some persons she had suffered much for those civilities which she conceived convenient to a person of his rank. And that (fearing this, his suddain return to this place might soe far revive that malice, as to accuse her of consent) she desired him to understand her most confident that he neither could nor would take it ill if she entreated him as she did to forbear making visits to her.

"3. His Grace was not pleased nor edify'd with this mesage. But resenting it as an affront, labour'd to clear himself of all suspicion of pretence of any kind. But, finding Her Highness fix'd in a resolve to be, on her part, free from giving the least occasion to envy or malice on this subject; His Grace as suddenly withdrew from hence as he came unexpected."

George Villiers had been unmistakably dismissed. But even in the prudent Princess the curious vein of romance latent in the Stuart nature eventually asserted itself, and in the end, after having refused the Duke of Buckingham, she contracted a secret marriage with the younger Harry Jermyn, who, despite an ungracious person and a profound nullity of mind, was the recognized ladykiller of the period.

At this juncture Buckingham was certainly in

no enviable position. The Court at the Palais Royal was no more inclined to welcome him than was the Princess at the Hague. But this was not the most trying feature of the situation. For three years after the battle of Worcester, none of the King's attendants received their wages, so that the Duke was not the only sufferer; but want of ready money must have pressed him sorely at this time, and he was reported to be very angry with the King, because the latter would assist no one except those in actual waiting on his person.

Undoubtedly, few of the exiles had sacrificed so splendid a revenue in their sovereign's service, but as every other record of the erratic Duke's presence is dated from a different town, Charles had perhaps some excuse for his niggardly conduct. However, if Buckingham had remained in Paris, he might not have fared better, for the management of the united royal establishments, which rested entirely with the Queen's servants, gave little satisfaction to most of Charles's followers.[1]

Nor would the mental tone have been more to the liking of the Duke, who ever judged "it barbarous and ridiculous to go about to convince a Man's judgment by anything but Reason"—a view certainly not shared by the then dominant Anglican faction, who could not contain their joy when Hobbes, the "grand Atheist," was summarily dismissed.

Under the circumstances, it is not unnatural that the Duke should have desired to make his peace with the Home Government. The terms which had been offered to him in 1651 were

[1] Clarendon, "Hist. of the Rebellion," vol. v. p. 367.

however no longer available. Nor was he as well inspired in his choice of a mediator; for instead of applying to the universally respected Lord Denbigh, he preferred to address himself to John Lilburne.

This man, one of the most singular figures of the age, was now an exile in Holland. Originally an obscure bookbinder, he drifted into public notice through the persecution of the Star-Chamber, and, in November 1640, found himself the subject of Cromwell's first public utterance in the Long Parliament. Nor did Oliver's protection fail him in the succeeding years. In 1647, John Lilburne still regarded the Lord General as the "most absolute single-hearted, great man in England, untainted and unbiassed with ends of his own."[1] But, as the trend of events inevitably placed greater and greater power in the hands of Cromwell, Lilburne's eulogies of his patron turned by degrees to stern denunciations. By 1648, he had impeached his former idol of high treason. In 1651, as the advocate of the Levellers, he was rapidly forming a cave, where the discontented of every section congregated. Imprisonment was worse than useless in the case of this new David. Each fresh conviction added to his popularity, until at last juries refused to find him guilty. His fervid eloquence, his trenchant pamphlets, made him a serious menace to all constituted authority, and in December, 1651, the Parliament having in desperation passed an Act for his banishment, he took refuge in Holland.

Among the crowd of adventurers who, during the Stuart exile, frequented the Dutch maritime

[1] Firth's "Life of Oliver Cromwell," p. 147.

towns, a certain Captain Wendy Oxford had established his headquarters at Amsterdam. Here he seems to have practised the not unlucrative business of procuring passports for banished gentlemen, in which trade his wife, who remained in England, was, thanks to her questionable intimacy with the officials, an active partner. It was Captain Oxford who first introduced the jolly Duke of Bucks to the pious field-preacher, and, strange to say, the unlikely pair at once became staunch allies. The Duke, according to Lilburne, "craving my best advice how he might the most rationall, expeditious and honourable way he could, make his peace in England and returne hither to breath the aire of the land of his nativity, which he avowed he loved above all the places in the world, and was ready and willing to do anything that the present power in England could require of a man that had a grain of honour or honesty in him, and to give them any security to the utmost of his power, for his quiet and peaceable living under their Government."[1] Lilburne answered sensibly enough that his only way was to make a sure and firm friend of His Excellency the Lord General Cromwell.

But this was more easily said than done; for it soon appeared that Mrs Wendy Oxford, who had undertaken to obtain a pass to England for the Duke, had over-estimated her powers or her attractions. Leighton was then despatched to plead the Duke's cause with His Grace the Lord General, and had many debates with His Excellency and the Council of State. But magnanimous as Cromwell was, his spies served him too well

[1] Lilburne's "Defensive Declaration," pp. 15-16.

not to have reported that Lilburne had offered "through the Duke of Buckingham to bring in the King again, if he had but £100,000."[1] All Leighton's pleading was therefore useless. In June, 1653, Lilburne, wearying of exile, and doubtless alarmed by "the complotted designs" of the desperate cavaliers in Amsterdam, who could never forget or forgive his early career, boldly returned to England. Here he was immediately arrested and put upon his defence, and his intrigues and conferences with George Villiers, which had continued till the moment of his embarkation at Calais, furnished one of the principal accusations against him.[2]

Since London had beheld Charles I. in the dock, no trial had so strongly aroused public feeling. Lilburne could count equally on his old friends the Levellers and on Cavalier sentiment, ever ready to flame up in opposition to Government. Sympathy with the agitator was therefore universal, and the rhyme so famous in 1688 at the Trial of the Seven Bishops may conceivably owe its origin to the "tickets" sown broadcast on this occasion with the inscription:

"And what! shall honest John Lilburne die?
Three score thousand shall know the reason why!"

Cromwell himself, "thought the fellow soe considerable, that during the time of his triall he kept three regiments continually in armes about St James'." When the jury threw out the Bill, the joy of the populace was expressed in a shout

---

[1] Cal. Clarendon MSS., vol. ii. fol. 1232.
[2] *Idem*, vol. ii. fol. 1231.

which was heard an English mile off[1]—a demonstration in which the very Guards appear to have joined.

During the five days in which Lilburne harangued the Court of Justice,[2] the Duke's name was freely bandied about. Lilburne, indeed, had testified to the Duke's character in a manner of which there are unfortunately few other instances. Not only did he owe his life, he said, as much to Buckingham's powerful influence as ever David owed his to Jonathan, but he could not sufficiently admire his "reason, sobriety, civility, honour and conscience."[3] Indeed he called his countrymen to witness that "if ever it should lye in my power to do him any personal service, without detriment to my native country (which I am confident he would never desire of me) I judge myself bound in conscience and gratitude to travel on his errand a thousand and a thousand miles upon my feet."

Such a declaration from the man who had just inflicted a severe defeat upon the Government, was hardly calculated to advance Buckingham's interests with the Protector. Yet this was the moment chosen by the Duke to revisit his native land. The adventure was rash, but George Villiers may have counted on disarming Oliver's hostility by presenting himself as a suitor for one of his daughters. That such an alliance would prove the surest means of retrieving his fortunes must certainly have occurred to him. Clarendon con-

[1] Thurloe, vol. i. p. 442.
[2] *Idem*, p. 367.
[3] Lilburne, "Defensive Declaration."

temptuously declared that Buckingham was ready to marry Cromwell's daughter or be Cromwell's groom to save his estates.[1] The Protector, like Napoleon, fully grasped the advantages to be gained by rallying the old nobility to his Court, but in the marriages of his children he was moved by other than mere political considerations. If he judged "the King of Scots too damnably debauched" to be a fit husband for the future Lady Fauconberg, he was not likely to welcome George Villiers as a son-in-law. Indeed, he is said—though on prejudiced authority — to have dismissed the proposition with the remark, "that he would never give his daughter to one who could be so ungrateful to the King, he owing all he had to the family."[2]

Many years later, in the time of the Merry Monarch, when the name of England's great Puritan ruler was never heard without an accompaniment of ribald jests, Buckingham told Mde. d'Aulnoy some strange anecdotes of his connection with the Cromwells. Nothing, apparently, seemed incredible to the historian of "L'Oiseau Bleu," though Buckingham had long earned a doubtful reputation for veracity. He was indeed, as Grammont said, the father and mother of scandal; but it is more than likely these reminiscences were not altogether purposeless, since by imparting the aspect of an intrigue to serious designs he contrived to escape the suspicion of having courted the Usurper.

One of these episodes—to which, it is true,

---

[1] Clarendon MSS., vol. ii. 1199.
[2] "Macpherson's Original Papers: Life of James II. by Himself," vol. i. pp. 46-47.

Mde. d'Aulnoy assigns an earlier date than the year 1653—is perhaps worth recording.

It will be remembered that Buckingham, in his love of adventure, not unfrequently donned the sock and buskin as a disguise. During one of his theatrical performances the handsome player attracted the notice of Mistress Ireton, who straightway commanded him to her presence. The Duke, bent on discovering her husband's secrets,[1] gladly accepted the invitation. He laid aside his mountebank's costume, cast a cloak over his magnificent apparel, retaining, however, though with great reluctance, a black patch over one eye.[2] But had he appeared without any such disfigurement, he could not have met with a warmer welcome. In fact, the lady showed so little austerity, that could Buckingham have forgotten her detested parentage, there seems little doubt he would have responded to the fair Puritan's advances, even at the cost of revealing his identity. As it was, in order to explain his inconsistency, he boldly declared himself a Jew, and therefore forbidden by the law from any dalliance with the daughters of the Gentiles. Mistress Ireton was not so easily defeated. The next time he was bidden to Whitehall, he found a Rabbi awaiting him to absolve his religious scruples. Buckingham was

---

[1] As I have already said, I do not suggest that this incident actually took place at this date (if ever), since Ireton died of the plague in Ireland in 1651, and the strongest inducement, to see more of the lady, was, therefore, wanting; but it is a good example of the romances Buckingham loved to spin for the benefit of a credulous audience.

[2] "Mems. de la Cour d'Angleterre" (pub. at the Hague, 1695), p. 147.

painfully conscious of an absolute ignorance of Talmudic lore. He dared not engage in controversy, and had no other resource but to postpone the theological conference for two days, during which breathing-space he contrived to escape from the capital.

At the end of July, 1653, Hyde writes mournfully from Paris: "The Duke of Buckingham is here at the old rate and is good for nothing."[1] Since the Duke's ample leisure was mainly devoted to thwarting Sir Edward's policy, the latter's dislike was not unnatural. Victory, however, eventually rested with Hyde, although Buckingham's faction included the Queen-Mother, Jermyn, and Prince Rupert; for, in the course of 1654, Charles quitted the Palais Royal and Sir Edward went with him. Henceforward the royal residence was fixed at Aix or Cologne, where the exiled monarch was far more amenable to his Chancellor's counsels, and the volatile Buckingham seldom intruded on the even tenor of his sovereign's way. Nor is the Duke's absence wholly inexplicable when we read the reports of Cromwell's spies. These gentlemen were hard put to it to justify their salaries. A visit to the Cathedral to inspect Charlemagne's relics, in which — strange irony — Charles Stuart measured his rapier against the mighty Kaiser's blade. A hunting expedition with greyhounds and hawks, lasting eight hours, and yielding the magnificent bag of one hare and four partridges, such were the rare, the "great divertisements" of life at Aix or Cologne, where the King

---

[1] Clarendon MSS., vol. ii. 1284. Paris, 25th July 1653. Hyde to Nicholas.

sought occupation in studying French and Italian, whilst his minister composed meditations on the Psalms.[1]

Undoubtedly there were many points in common between the King and George Villiers, but, unlike his sovereign, Buckingham could never have "betaken himself with great cheerfulness to compose his mind to a manner of life"[2] so monotonous. He was probably wisely inspired when he enlisted as a volunteer in the French Army.

In truth the war between France and Spain afforded an opening for many a banished Cavalier. In 1653, Buckingham was present at the siege of Mouzon, though it cannot be said that fortune favoured him, as he was prostrated by fever during the greater part of the operations. Next year, undeterred by this experience, he joined the little band of Royalists, who, under the Dukes of York and Gloucester, were learning the art of war with Turenne, and on this occasion his desire to see active service was fully gratified.

The Spaniards would have had small chance of success had they not been commanded by the Prince de Condé, whom the miserable divisions of the Fronde had ranged against his gallant countrymen, and even Condé's talents were neutralised by the jealousy of the Spanish generals. However, he succeeded in establishing so complete an investment of Arras, that it appeared extremely doubtful whether the French relieving force under Turenne could succeed in breaking through his lines.[3]

[1] Clarendon, "History of the Rebellion," vol. v. p. 397.
[2] *Idem.*
[3] "Memoirs" of Comte Grammont, p. 85.

Turenne was, however, determined neither to abandon the garrison, nor to forfeit an important fortress, and on the day of St Louis, the patron saint of France, with an army numerically inferior, he forced his rival to raise the siege. It was during this action "that Buckingham signalised his courage, being much regarded by all the great officers," and especially by the victorious Marshal who remained his life-long friend.[1] The slaughter on both sides was terrible. Condé himself charged furiously twelve times, "wishing and seeking for death," and only retreating step by step when abandoned by the Spaniards. The English volunteers bore the burden and heat of the day, and Jermyn had good cause to write proudly of his countrymen's achievements. "None did their duty better than the Duke of York, if any so well. He believes that of the volunteers the English had the best share; among them the Duke of Buckingham, Lord Gerard and Charles Berkeley behaved so as none are better spoken of, and he cannot omit to tell that little Mr Harry (the Duke of Gloucester) held now and then his part well."[2]

In adopting a military career, the great nobles of the seventeenth century did not relinquish their accustomed pomp and luxury, and costly as was their habitual existence, it was far exceeded by their life in camp. At this very siege of Arras, M. le Prince entertained his former friends and actual opponents at a magnificent banquet; and Lockhart, the English Ambassador, informed his Government

---

[1] Brian Fairfax.
[2] Clarendon MSS. 2001. Paris, 19th Sept. 1654. Lord Jermyn to the King.

that he could not afford to join the Royal army without an increase of pay to meet the extraordinary demands of the situation. It was therefore lucky for Buckingham that, in her passage through the Netherlands, the fantastic Queen of Sweden had purchased some of his remaining pictures. He had thus been temporarily furnished with the sinews of war, but when he returned to his normal life in Paris the financial outlook was blacker than ever. From his sister, the beautiful widowed Duchess of Richmond, he could expect no assistance, for on her husband's death she had rejoined Henrietta Maria, and shared the penury of her mistress's Court. And very real poverty it was, when the king's chief ministers wanted shoes and shirts, and "not a servant of his hath a pistole in his pocket."[1] The Duchess, however, seems to have borne the common privations with a light heart, since she vowed that of all the afflictions of that time, the most grievous was the want of gloves; old ones she would not wear, and new ones she could not buy.

As a Gentleman of the Bedchamber, Buckingham had hitherto owned a lodging at the Palais Royal, but on account of his "extravagant carriage" towards the King, he was now deprived of his apartment. Indeed, during the Arras campaign his strictures on his master had been unmeasured.

Lord Hatton declared that "his ink was not black enough to express the base and horrid language Buckingham did belch out concerning our Master."[2] Nor did the Duke confine himself to

---

[1] "Clarendon Papers," 101, 120-124, 174. 27th June, 1653, and 3rd April, 1654.
[2] "Nicholas Papers," vol. ii. p. 9, 1654. Lord Hatton to Nicholas.

generalities. He told a person of quality that Lord Fairfax had promised to join the Royalist cause, on the condition that all transactions should pass through his hands. As the request was refused, the general declined to take any further steps in the matter, and so Charles lost a valuable adherent. Had this been true, Buckingham's indignation would not have been altogether unreasonable; but according to Nicholas, there was not a particle of evidence to support the contention. Indeed the Secretary asserted that the most careful investigation did not disclose any offer or promise on the part of Fairfax, to throw in his lot with the Cavaliers. It was far more likely that the origin of the tale was the casual suggestion of some kindly mortal, that the King should send the Duke to sound, and if possible, to gain, Fairfax. Nicholas certainly had cause to exclaim, "These great wits are none of the best servants or friends. They may be good company for the time, but they are uneasy to live with."

On his side the Chancellor promoted to the utmost the estrangement between the King and his former playmate, and solemnly protested against his being restored to favour.

Bearing the Duke's future career in mind, none can blame Hyde's severity. Yet at this stage, remembering how much George Villiers had sacrificed for Charles, it is impossible not to feel some pity for the Duke. The old story of his intended marriage with the Protector's daughter was not the only accusation his opponents brought forward. He was actually charged with keeping Cromwell informed of the Royalist conspiracies, in order to make his own peace with the Commonwealth, and his continual wanderings, "passing by creekes toe and froe Callais,"[1] were invested with sinister intentions towards the King. That the Duke himself was painfully alive to these reports is proved by his conduct on meeting Ormond during one of these expeditions. He conjured the Marquis not to mention having seen him; for although he admitted that he had a pass from Cromwell to procure himself some means of subsistence in England—a step the King's "unkindness" had made urgent—he was yet returning to Paris without taking advantage of it.[2]

The situation was not without its ridiculous side; for, while the Royalists denounced Buckingham as a traitor, Cromwell's agents accused him of plotting the assassination of the Protector. A certain Colonel Bampfylde, once a staunch Cavalier, and a man of some intelligence, since it was he who had managed the Duke of York's escape from England, had secretly become a recruit of Thurloe's. It was probably through him that the exile's secrets were revealed to Oliver, those mysteries, at least, which were not betrayed by their own folly and indiscretion. In November, 1656, he warns his employer :—

The Duke of Buckingham is very busy, to what end I cannot yet discover. The condition he is in here (Paris) the persons he converses with, together with some other circumstances which have fallen under my observation, brings that fresh into my memory and apprehension which I am not certayn

---

[1] Nicholas, vol. ii. p. 320.
[2] *Idem*, p. 335.

whether I have informed you or not. You may call to minde that about this tyme twelve month I wrote to you,[1] that he was much discontented at a letter he had received from a friend of a very severe character that the Protector had given of him, a part of which letter I tore off and sent you enclosed in one of mine. Upon this information he began to despayre of doing any good with the Protector, and swore a desperate oath that if he could not make himself well with him, he would kill him. Since I now believe him off from all correspondence with you, and paste hopes of the Protector and that I know that he hath been twice with Charles Stewart and that I now observe desperate persons about him as Major Ascott, who has murdered three or four; one Shelden, one Colonel Tuke who has killed four in duel, who is using all the arts he can to get leave to goe into England; one Captain Man and another whose name I have forgotten, and who was one of those who killed Dorislaus, whoe are as desperate in their souls as in their fortunes, and are fit instruments for such a designe.

Political assassination has always been particularly repugnant to Englishmen, but, unhappily, amongst the ruined and broken Cavaliers it was not regarded as a serious breach of the code of honour. So respectable a member of society as the venerable Nicholas describes the abominable murder of Dorislaus, "as the deserved execution of that bloody villain."[2]

When Ascham's murderers were lodged in the Madrid gaol, they were fed and maintained by Colepepper and Clarendon; and if Charles's ministers

[1] Thurloe, vol. v. p. 511. Paris, 2nd Nov. 1656.
[2] Carte's "Letters of Ormond," vol. i. p. 291.

did not openly proclaim their sympathy with the cut-throats, and ascribed their ministrations to Christian charity, this was only in deference to the susceptibilities of the Spaniards. A higher standard of morality than that professed by these worthies can hardly be expected in George Villiers. Yet for all his desperate oaths there is no proof that he attempted the Protector's life. Had such an idea formed part of his programme, there is little doubt that some authentic traces of the plot would be found in the correspondence of the period.

The Duke spent the summer of 1656 as a volunteer in Turenne's army, then besieging the Spaniards in Valenciennes. The defeat of the latter seemed a foregone conclusion. But La Ferté, who commanded under the marshal, committed the fatal mistake of separating his forces, by disposing them on different sides of the river. Don John, the Spanish general, took advantage of the weakness of the position, and fell unexpectedly with all his forces on the isolated corps. The townspeople, moreover, strengthened the natural division by opening the sluices and making the stream impassable. In the dawning of the Sabbath morn the French troops found themselves cut off. At the third charge they broke and were utterly routed. La Ferté was taken prisoner with most of his men and all his baggage, and Turenne himself was constrained to retreat with his division to Quesnoy. The English were loud in thankfulness that the Duke of York had not been involved in the disastrous action, and Buckingham must have returned to Paris a sadder man than after the engagement at Arras. Ill-luck in matters great and small dogged his footsteps at this juncture, for it is recorded that one night after his arrival in the capital, "His Grace goeing late from Monsieur Schomberg's lodging in a chaise, was saluted by some Filous, who taking his hatt band and feathers with thirty pistolls in gold, gave his Lordship the bonsoir."[1]

The Declaration of War between England and Spain, and the alliance each day closer drawn between Cromwell and Mazarin, were productive of great changes to the Royal Exile. To a state at enmity with the Commonwealth, Charles was a personage of no slight importance. Not only was he useful as a means of fomenting discord and civil strife in Great Britain and Ireland, but thousands of Irish and Scots were eager to take service with any Continental Power which counted him as their confederate. Buckingham consequently found a fresh outlet for his energies. With Spanish gold at his disposal, he could kindle rebellion at home, and attract many a stout soldier from the mountains of Scotland and the bogs of Connaught to the standards of Castile. Once more he began to engross the attention of Thurloe's spies, who were quick to note the value set by the Spaniards on a nobleman credited with far-reaching influence over the Presbyterian faction.

Unfortunately, Charles II. did not share the exalted estimate entertained by his allies for Buckingham. In truth, the King received his vagrant subject so coldly as to stifle any thought of the venturesome expeditions to England on behalf of the Cause, which the Duke had lately

[1] Nicholas, vol. ii. p. 335.

been meditating. If he went there at all, it became clear to Buckingham that it must be on his "own score."

Under the new order of things, the English Court had been invited to take up its abode at Bruges in the Spanish Low Countries, and the repose of the slumbrous mediæval city on the canals was soon rudely disturbed by the northern levies of the King of Scots. The streets swarmed with Gaels in their "right Highland apparel, which is no small subject of admiration to the people of Bruges." Unfortunately, the manners and morals of the clansmen did not appear equally admirable to the law-abiding Flemings.

Indeed, when one of the richest churches of that town of fanes and shrines was plundered, the inhabitants made no secret of their conviction that the sacrilegious act was the deed of Charles's heretical followers. On their side, Thurloe's correspondents were equally scandalised by the fact that Charles had not only engaged a company of French players for the entertainment of his sister and guest, the Princess Royal, but that "the most solemn day of acting is on the Lord's Day."[1] The Sabbatarian spy cannot contain his reprobation of such doings, which he characterises in language of Biblical directness. "I think," he concludes, "I may truly say that greater abominations were never practised among people, than at this day at Charles Stuart's Court. Fornication, drunkenness, and adultery are esteemed no sin amongst them, so that I persuade myself that God will never prosper any of their attempts."

[1] Thurloe, vol. v. p. 645. 2nd Dec. 1656.

It was probably less the dissipations at Bruges, than the opportunities for intrigue which attracted the Duke to his master's side. Circumstances appeared propitious. Every banished Cavalier had long desired to make an auxiliary of Spain. Bruges was a splendid base for a raid on England, and if the King proved amenable to his influence, the Duke might yet find compensation in a thousand fertile projects for exile and poverty. But Hyde was determined not to allow the recapture of his royal pupil, and Buckingham vainly enlisted every influence which he could call to his assistance. And from Don Alonso, the Spanish Governor to the Abbess of the Benedictines at Bruges, all were pressed into the service. But neither Don, courtier or nun, could disarm Hyde's inveterate hostility. At every turn he barred the way, until stung by the King's unkindness, the Duke abandoned all hope of reconciliation, and turned elsewhere to retrieve his fortunes.

CHAPTER IV

BUCKINGHAM'S MARRIAGE

THE year 1657 witnessed a great change in Buckingham's career. Parliament had granted General Fairfax,[1] a distant relative of the exile, part of the Duke's possessions—about £5000 a year—in quittance of his arrears of pay. They gave him also, "as a salve for a bad wound" he had received in their service, York House in London, and the Manor of Helmsley, a Yorkshire property which had been brought into the Villiers' estate by Katherine Manners.

Lord Fairfax was one of the noblest characters of his heroic generation. His strong convictions had from the beginning ranged him on the side of civil and religious freedom, but he was no more a democrat than were the other sturdy country gentlemen who followed in his wake. To reform he was no enemy; indeed the efficiency of the New Model Army was largely due to his personal exertions. Like Cromwell, he had first made his reputation as a cavalry officer, and Old Noll himself did not inspire greater personal devotion in his troopers than did Black Tom Fairfax.[2] When the King was brought to judgment, Fairfax's abstention was made memorable

[1] Brian Fairfax.
[2] See Firth's "Life of Oliver Cromwell."

by his wife's dramatic protest; but he did not then sever his connection with the regicides. In 1649 he co-operated with Cromwell in crushing the formidable mutiny of the Army. And it was not until 1650, when the invasion of Scotland was determined upon, that, being unable to reconcile his conscience to an offensive war, he laid down his commission. Thereafter he lived on his estates in Yorkshire, infinitely respected by men of all shades of opinion. Though he could not claim the soaring genius of the Protector, it is owing to men of his stamp that the Great Rebellion remains the most self-controlled, awe-compelling revolution known to history.

After his stay in Bruges, when Buckingham realised that he had nothing to expect from Charles, he began seriously to consider the expediency of addressing himself to Fairfax. To quote his own words, written some years later, he was aware that the Republican General had—

" . . . neither Wealth nor Places sought,
He never for himself but others fought,
He was content to know,
For he had found it so
That when he pleased to conquer, he was able
And left the Sport and Plunder to the Rabble." [1]

The generous veteran had never accounted the Villiers property his own. When Buckingham therefore presented himself in England, he was met by Fairfax, eager to recall their common ancestry and to make ample restitution.

Attraction by opposition—and many friendships

[1] "A Pindaric Ode on the Death of Lord Fairfax," by Duke of Buckingham. Duke of Buckingham's Miscellaneous Works.

Lord Fairfax and his Wife.

and passions have been due to nothing else—can alone explain the affection Fairfax instantly conceived for Buckingham. No two men can be imagined more dissimilar. Fairfax was a truthful, honest, modest gentleman, somewhat taciturn, only losing his stammer when heading a charge with "brutish valour." Versatile, brilliant, the slave of his fleeting loves and shifting ambitions, Buckingham's essential differences supplied the necessary contrast. Such, at any rate, was his power of fascination, that from the first moment of their meeting, he made an enduring conquest of this Puritan Cincinnatus.

It was probably Lord Fairfax's kindly welcome which encouraged the Duke not to limit his pretensions to the recovery of his alienated heritage.

Mary Fairfax, the General's only child by his wife Anne Vere, was a great heiress, and George Villiers had no sooner arrived in London than he saw the wisdom of securing her for his wife. To achieve this end he laid his plans with unusual prudence. For five long months his whereabouts was shrouded in mystery, and to all enquiries his servants replied that he was confined to his bed by illness. Even Bampfylde, that acute sleuth-hound, was thrown off the track; for although he opined "he could not have layne a quarter of that time in the disease is pretended," he made no guess at Buckingham's real occupation. He believed him, indeed, to be in England bent on "some desperate designe either for a risinge in the city, or some attempt upon the Protector's person . . . he swore once to me that since he could not obleidge my lord Protector, he would venture hard to destroy him. I told him it would be a great adventure indeed; that all had miscarried who had attempted it. He replied t'was because they had attempted it foolishly."[1]

The amusing part of Bampfylde's gloomy prognostications is that, at the time he wrote, the missing Duke was more often to be found at Whitehall than elsewhere. It is true that his venturing across the Channel was a bold move. He had no reason to be assured of his liberty, or even of his life, when he came to England, and indeed so far was he from having rendered a considerable service to Cromwell, as the angry Royalists suggested,[2] that the Protector, who enjoyed a larger share of the Buckingham estates than Fairfax, and had himself daughters to marry, seems to have mistrusted such a "conjunction of Mars and Mercury," and would, if he could, have forbidden the banns.

Nevertheless, when the Duke arrived in London, if we are to believe an anonymous correspondent of Fairfax, Oliver would not permit the rigour of the law to be invoked against the suppliant Cavalier.[3] In fact, according to this gentleman, the great man gave his word that the Duke should not be molested. Nay, more, he promised, if it were necessary, that an act of indemnity should be passed in his favour. It might have been supposed that his Highness would refuse to see Buckingham, but as a matter of fact, on more occasions than one, he went out of his way to appoint a time for an audience, and though this

---

[1] Thurloe, vol. vi. p. 363. June, 1657.
[2] Brian Fairfax.
[3] Thurloe, vol. vi. p. 616. Anon. letter to Lord Fairfax.

never actually took place, it was only prevented by stress of business or indisposition.

But disappointed as the Duke must have been when he failed to get speech with Cromwell, he was not entirely to be commiserated. On such occasions he could always count on a cordial reception from the sons and daughters of the Protector. Nor was it only his wonderful versatility that enabled him to adapt himself to the tone pervading that family circle. None of Oliver's children affected the sour austerity associated with the typical Roundhead. Indeed, as we know, his Highness himself had his moments of mirthfulness, and enjoyed a practical joke as much as Mrs Cromwell did the pleasures of the table.

Mrs Claypole's Royalist proclivities were surmised from her close intimacy with the episcopal chaplain, Dr Hewet, who, in spite of all her entreaties, finally paid with his head for his treasonable conspiracies against her father.

As for Richard Cromwell, he was a true country gentleman, with the sporting instincts of his class and age, who infinitely preferred the company of racing and fox-hunting Cavaliers, to the exhortations of the godly. Neither was Henry Cromwell, Lord Deputy of Ireland, though a man of far greater ability, less cheerful and debonair than his easy-going elder brother. Dorothy Osborne's would-be lover, scouring his province for a boar-hound worthy of that charming lady's acceptance, was no pragmatical fanatic. And it is amusing to read of the young man's frank delight when his illustrious father half-jestingly presented him with a gorgeous scarlet cloak, and gloves from his own hands, in which

Harry proudly displayed himself to the gaze of the House of Commons.[1]

Thus in the private apartments of Whitehall, there was no need for the Duke to assume the hypocritical severity of mien and conversation that the Scots ministers had once exacted from him and his master. The ordinary decency of well-bred society amply sufficed. And, judging from the singular absence of coarseness in his commonplace book—a volume intended for his private edification only—such an attitude may not have been as alien to his true character as one might imagine from the blatant ribaldry of his talk in Stuart circles.

Buckingham's past course of action, which might have proved a more serious stumbling-block in his intercourse with the Cromwells, appears rather to have been a help than a hindrance. The loyalty he had displayed for an "insensible" monarch only made him more admirable in the eyes of his romantic and kindly audience. They found a generous satisfaction in consulting with the best lawyers on his behalf. And when the men of law pronounced favourably on the exile's suit, declaring that he lay under no attainder, the jubilation of his new allies was unfeigned, while, moreover, they vowed, "that if they were Christians," he should have a free pardon under the Great Seal. Indeed, so enthusiastic was the zeal the ladies displayed for the handsome youth, that the reflection, that pity is akin to love, was unavoidably suggested to more than one cynical onlooker.

But in spite, or perchance because, of the

---

[1] Thurloe, vol. vi. p. 21. Mr V. Gookin, 1656.

cordial reception extended to Buckingham at Whitehall, Fairfax must have realised the risks he incurred in giving his consent to the proposed alliance. The Protector might be wisely inspired in showing clemency to a suppliant and repentant exile, but the Duke of Buckingham, restored to his heritage, and backed by his illustrious father-in-law, was a different, and even a doubtful object of favour; and the sympathy expressed by the Protector's family for the attractive cavalier, might well be transformed into pique and dislike for the husband of Mary Fairfax. Great, however, as were the obstacles, Buckingham was not without substantial auxiliaries. The Presbyterian party were far from hostile to him, and then, as ever, he contrived to enlist a vast amount of feminine influence on his side. None, indeed, proved a more ardent advocate on his behalf than Lady Vere, the bride's aunt. So fervid was the zeal of the good lady, that she actually carried four Presbyterian ministers in her coach, all the way from London to York, to second her representations in favour of the seductive Duke.

But it was in Mary Fairfax that George Villiers found his best ally. It is recorded by Brian Fairfax, that the young lady could not resist the charms of the "most graceful and beautiful person that any Court in Europe ever saw. All his trouble in wooing was, he came, and saw, and conquered." Nor did the miseries the Duke subsequently inflicted on his unhappy wife ever destroy the glamour wherewith he was invested in those early days of courtship. And to the end she lived on terms of affection with him, patiently bearing with those faults which she could not remedy.

Unluckily, this excellent Griselda had one failing. She was extremely plain. With her father's fidelity and unselfishness she had also unfortunately inherited his dark complexion. Catherine of Braganza's marked predilection for the poor Duchess was said to be due not only to their community in conjugal misfortune, but to their remarkable resemblance. And we must remember that Charles's consort was not beautiful. Even Mr Pepys' moderate panegyric of "her good modest and innocent look which is pleasing," seemed excessive to the majority of English people, the consensus of opinion being rather with Charles II., who, on first beholding his bride, exclaimed, "they had brought him a bat instead of a woman."[1] Not only was Mary Fairfax's skin, like Catherine's, extremely swarthy, but she, too, was short-legged and awkward—a "little round crumpled woman,"[2] and yet so fond of finery, that even when in mourning she would contrive to wear a loose over-robe all edged and laced with gold. Pious and virtuous as she was, she shared readily in the harmless frolics of the Queen's circle.

We hear of her with the royal party who, on one curious occasion, masqueraded as country lasses in red petticoats and waistcoats at Saffron Walden Fair. But having none of her husband's genius for travesty, she and the others had "so overdone their disguise that they looked so much more like antiques than country volk, that as soon as they came

---

[1] "Lord Dartmouth's Note to Burnet," vol. i. p. 307.
[2] Illustration to Bohn's Ed. of Grammont's "Mems.," 405.

to the fair, the people came to goe after them; but the Queen going to a booth to buy a pair of yellow stockins for her sweetheart and Sir Bernard (Gascoigne) asking for a pair of gloves sticht with blew for his sweetheart, they were by their gebrish found to be strangers, which drew a bigger flock about them."[1] Eventually the Queen was recognised, and hemmed in and jostled by the mob, they had to make such haste as their cart jades would allow back to Audley End, escorted to the palace doors by the gaping crowd.

All this, however, took place in 1670, and in 1657 Buckingham was as much engrossed in courting plain Mary Fairfax as if she had been the Goddess of Love.

It was through his friend, Mr Robert Harlowe, and in the following letter, that he made his formal proposal to Lady Fairfax for her daughter's hand:—

MADAME,—I shall hope from the intercession of the person that does me the honour to deliver this to you, what I could hardly have expected upon any other account: that your ladyship will be pleased to pardon me the boldnesse of writing lately to your daughter. Mrs Worsnam was the first that gave mee the confidence of makinge my addresses to her, and it was by her meanes only that I had the happines of wayting upon her, and if that interview has made mee soe little master of myselfe as not to be able to refrain laying hold of an appointment offered to me of letting her knowe the paine I endure for her sake, I hope your Ladiship may be persuaded to make a true interpretation of it, and to believe it cowld

[1] Mr Henshaw to Sir R. Paston, 1670. Ive's "Select Papers," 39.

proceed only from an excesse of that respect and devotion I ever shall beare Mistris Fairfax (whom if my fortune were in any way proportionable to my affections) I should have the impudence to pretend to deserve at least as much as any person whatsoever since I am sure it is impossible to love or honour anything more than I truly doe her and to wish for anything with greater longing or impatience than I doe for some meanes of giving both her and your ladiship undeniable proofs of it, being confident that if your ladiship knew the nature of the passion I have for her, you could not be soe ill-natured (however averse to mee soever she might bee) as not to pitty my condition or to refuse the endeavouring to further mee by your favour to the enjoying of what only in this world can make mee perfectly happy. That is Madame, the honour of being your Ladyship's most dutifull son as I shall forever (whither your Ladiship will or noe) challenge eternally that of being Madame,—Your Ladiship's most humble and obedient servant,

BUCKINGHAM.[1]

Strange to say, of the many *billets-doux* which Buckingham must have indited in his long career of gallantry, the following is the only one traceable—a note it is just possible may have been intended for transmission to Mary Fairfax.[2]

The little Ribbon I received from you last night instead of binding up my wound, has made it greater, and though I have kept it ever since as neere my heart as I cowld, I can finde noe other

---

[1] Hist. MSS., 15th Rep. Part II. p. 48, 25th Aug. 1657. M. Eliot Hodgekin.
[2] Brit. Mus. Add. MSS. 27,872.

Madame.

I shall hope from the intercession of the person that does mee the favour to deliver this to you, what I could hardly have expected upon any other account, that your Ladiship will bee pleas'd to pardon the boldnesse of writing lately to your daughter. Mrs Worsnam was the first that gave mee the confidence of making my addresses to her, and it was by her meanes only that I had the hapines

of wayting upon her. and if
that interview has made mee soe
little Master of my selfe, as
not to bee able to refraine the
Laying holde of an oportunity
was offered mee, of letting her
know the paine I endure for
her sake, I hope your Ladyship
may bee perswaded to make
the true interpretation of it
and to beleeue it could proceed
only from an excesse of that
respect and deuotion I euer
shall beare Mistris Farfax.

whom (if my fortune were in any kinde proportionable to my affections) I should have the impudence to pretend to deserve; at least as much as any other body whatsoever. since I am sure it is impossible to love or honnour any thing more then I truly doe her. or to wish for any thing with greater longing or impatience, then I doe for some meanes of giving

both her and your Ladiship
undeniable proofes of it.
being confident, that if
your Ladiship knew the
nature of the passion I
have for her, you could
not bee soe ill natured (how
averse to mee soever thee might
bee) as not to pitty my
condition: or to refuse the
endeavouring to further mee
by your favour, to the
enioying of what only
in this world can make

mee perfectly happy,
that is Madame the honour
of being your Ladiships
Most Dutifull Son. as I
shall howeuer (whither
your Ladiship will or noe)
chalenge eternally, that
of being

    Madame

        Your Ladiships
        Most humble and
        most obedient seruant

           Buckingham

August. 25

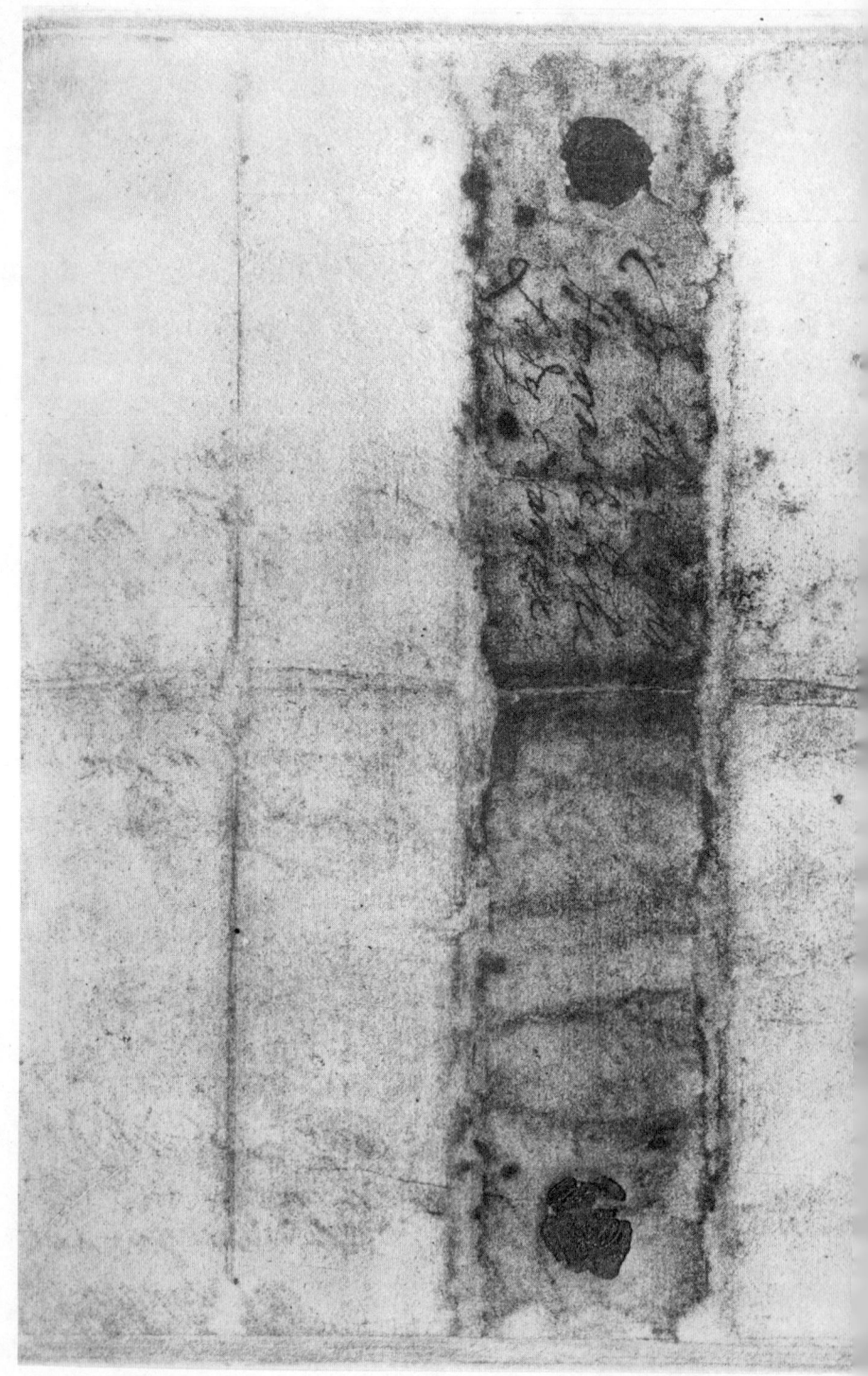

effects by it, then the being much lesse at my ease then I was before. I have not slept one wink never since I saw you, neither have I beene able to thinke of any other thinge, then how to finde the meanes of speakinge to your Deare Mistrisse, for I dare not without her leave presume to call her myne, though it bee already owt of my power ever to call justly soe anybody else. If I were lesse concerned I showld perhaps bee more successful in my endeavours to wayte upon her, but the truth is I am not in a condition to designe any thing well myselfe, seeing her running soe in my head that it does not give mee leave to contrive a way how I should bee able to compasse it. I doe therefore most humbly beg your assistance, since I am utterly unable to afford any to myselfe and doe hope that if your good nature bee not sufficient to persuade you to doe it, at least your curiosity will to see what a change it will bee in your power soe suddenly to worke upon mee, for one minute's conversation with that deare mistrisse of yours (if you could order it soe too as that her answer would not absolutely make mee despaire) would from as troublesome an estate of minde as ever creature was in, settle mee in a condition not to envy the happiest man living. This is the only request I have to make in this world, the gaining your Deare Mistrisse good opinion being the utmost ambition of Your most humble and obedient fellow-servant,

BUCKINGHAM.

Let us hope that it was at this period also, and in his betrothed's honour, that he composed the most respectable of his poetic effusions. As he could never have been so infatuated as to mistake his lawless passion for Lady Shrewsbury for "true love founded on esteem," so possibly his virtuous and amiable wife may claim the dedication.[1]

> "What a dull fool was I
> To think so gross a lie
> As that I ever was in love before!
> I have perhaps known one or two
> With whom I was content to be
> At that which they call, keeping company;
> But after all that they could do
> I could still be with more;
> Their absence never made me shed a tear,
> And I can truly swear
> That till my eyes first gazed on you,
> I ne'er beheld that thing I could adore.
>
> "A world of things must curiously be sought,
> A world of things together must be brought
> To make up charms which have the power to move
> Through a discerning eye, true love;
> That is a master-piece above,
> What only looks and shape can do,
> There must be wit and judgement too
> Greatness of thought and worth which draw
> From the whole world respect and awe.
>
> "She that would raise a noble love, must find
> Ways to beget a passion for her mind,
> She must be that which she to be would seem,
> For all true love is grounded on esteem.
> Plainness and truth gain more a generous heart,
> Then all the crooked subtleties of art.
> She must be—what said I?—she must be *you*
> None but yourself this miracle can do.
>
> "At least I'm sure, thus much I plainly see
> None but yourself e'er did it upon me,
> 'Tis you alone that can my heart subdue,
> To you alone it always shall be true."

---

[1] Walpole's "Royal and Noble Authors," p. 305.

Whether he wooed in prose or verse, the Duke was not long fated to remain in what he is pleased to call as troublesome an estate of mind as ever creature was in. On the 7th of September, 1657, a fortnight after his formal proposal, the nuptials were celebrated at Nun Appleton, near York. They were married by one Mr Vere Harcourt (Sir Simon Harcourt's brother), a great Presbyterian, who, it seems, fell as much a victim to the Duke's charms as Lady Fairfax or Mary herself,[1] for he told the bride's mother that he saw God in the Duke's face. Nor were the clergy alone to indulge in happy auguries. Abraham Cowley burst into verse:

> "Love his gross error saw at last,
> And promised large Amends for what was past,
> He promised, and has done it, which is more
> Than I, who knew him long, e'er knew him do before.
> He has done it nobly, and we must confess
> Could do no more, tho' he ought to do no less.
> What has he done? He has repaid
> The Ruins which a luckless War did make.
> And added to it a Reward
> Greater than Conquest for its share could take,
> His whole Estate could not such gain produce
> Had it laid out a hundred years at use."[2]

The bliss of the newly-married pair was, however, short-lived. No sooner did the news of the marriage reach London than a troop of horse was instantly despatched to seize the Duke and

---

[1] Hist. MSS., App. Rep. V. p. 177, Duke of Sutherland's MSS. Mr Dugdale to J. Langley, 24th Oct. 1657.
[2] Cowley, vol. ii. p. 787, ed. 1707. To the "Duke of Buckingham upon his marriage with the Lord Fairfax his daughter."

convey him to Jersey, there to be confined. But George Villiers was not an easy bird to cage, and when the troop of horse arrived at Nun Appleton, Lord Fairfax assured them upon his honour that the Duke was not there. Still there was cause enough in the wrecked honeymoon for the young lady to be "transcendentally pensive." Mary Fairfax, however, had been reared amid war's alarms. As a child of five, carried on her mother's saddle-bow, she had shared in the headlong flight from Bradford. She had a full measure of her father's stout spirit, and her presence of mind more than once proved invaluable to her adventurous spouse. Stimulated by her, Fairfax threw himself into her husband's cause in his usual whole-hearted manner, and instantly went up to London to intercede for his son-in-law.

The General had not much cause for complaint in the audience which Cromwell immediately granted him. It is true that Oliver bluntly told Fairfax he would have done better to consult "with his old friends that had wente along with him in all the wars."[1] Had he done so, and refused to listen to false advisers, enemies both to his honour and interest, it was obvious he would have been spared the humiliation of his present position. Yet the homily was not an unfriendly one; and the great Dictator listened readily enough to Lord Fairfax's defence of himself and of the son-in-law whom the General pathetically "laboured to prove a better man than the world took him to be."

[1] Thurloe, vol. vi. p. 580, Whitehall, 27th Oct. 1657. Letter of Thurloe to H. Cromwell.

In fact, Cromwell was far more placable than many of his advisers. And we must remember that while some of his officials undoubtedly held that, having inherited the royal prerogatives, no nobleman should marry his children without the Protector's consent, he may also have had to contend with adverse influences nearer home—members even of his own household—who may not have been best pleased at the Duke's sudden marriage.

After the interview, however, it was soon apparent that His Highness was chiefly concerned in doing a favour to an old comrade. The "bawling" that it was a Presbyterian plot was disregarded, and the obsequious Privy Councillors who divined their master's wishes, set to work to facilitate them.[1]

Buckingham, consequently, was not kept long in durance. The Council, with their civil respects to his Lordship's own person, sent Lords Mulgrave, Fleetwood and Strickland to confer with Fairfax, and Buckingham speedily received permission to live at York House with his bride.

No man could well have desired a fairer prison. York House, once the town residence of the Archbishops of York, with its gardens sloping down to the Thames, occupied the ground now covered by the Adelphi Terrace and the adjacent streets. Less ornate outwardly than some of the neighbouring mansions, the interior was noted for its sumptuous decoration. Every chamber was adorned with lions and peacocks, the arms of the great families of Villiers and Manners.[2] A truly royal suite of apart-

---

[1] MSS. Rawl. A. 55, pp. 295-296.
[2] Brian Fairfax.

ments, hung in green embroidered velvet, had been specially designed for the reception of Charles I. when he condescended to stay with his favourite. And even the critical Pepys cannot contain his admiration for the palace, "where the remains of the noble soul of the late Duke appears in his house in every place, in the door cases and the windows!"[1]

But, in spite of its perfections, it was not long before Steenie's son felt cribb'd, cabined and confined in his splendid abode, and, relying on his power of disguise, broke bounds and went off to visit his sister at Cobham. At a later period he proved himself an adept at eluding and defying Government messengers; but the Protector was better served than the second Charles, and the Duke had scarcely quitted the capital before a warrant was launched for his arrest and as quickly executed. We have Colonel Gibbon's letter detailing the event:

RIGHT HONOURABLE,—I this day coming from Canterbury one the road within three miles of Sittingbourne, I mett with three or four men; and finding one of them to shunne me, I thereupon suspected the sayde person and rode up to him, examened him who he was. At the last I came to be assured he was the Duke of Buckingham, knowing hem to be a person serched for, I have secured hem, so as to bring him with me to my house near Rochester, where I shall detayne hem till I know His Highnes pleaser concerning him. He tells me he was goeing to Sir G. Sandes to the Countes of Pemb-

[1] Pepys, vol. iii. p. 160. 6th June, 1663.

rock about the busines of reconsileing her to her lord.

I humbelly desyre that I may as soon as possible know His Highnes Pleaser concerning hem. As yett it is not knowen whoe he is that I have secured.[1]

His Highness's "pleaser" was that the Duke should forthwith be committed to the Tower. Doubtless, recollections of the "desperate designes" against his person, so often imputed to Buckingham, contributed to this severity, and that the Duke should run such risks, for the purpose of reconciling Lord and Lady Pembroke, or visiting his sister, probably seemed puerile excuses. At any rate, Cromwell's anger was now so thoroughly aroused that the consternation of the Duke's family was not ungrounded. The rapidity with which events had succeeded each other added to their embarrassment. Indeed they appear to have been almost as distracted as the unfortunate groom, who had shared his master's unsuccessful expedition, and whom Lord Oxford found "in as much disorder of head as his mare, who was sicke of the staggers . . . for he had soe perplext his brain to imagine why he was left behind, that the people beganne to beleeve him some highwayman's servant that was in great disorder for some accident happened to his Master : he was pleased at my telling him his lord was well, but noe whit less at my taking him with me."[2]

[1] Thurloe, vol. vii. p. 344. Colonel Gibbon to Secretary Thurloe, Aug. 1658, Rochester.
[2] Rawlinson MSS. A. 55, pp. 311-312. Earl of Oxford to Major Harley.

Cromwell's irreconcilable attitude was evidently well-nigh inexplicable to Fairfax, who once more went to plead Buckingham's cause with him. But on this occasion he was less fortunate. The Protector was thoroughly angered. Lord Fairfax's arguments only further exasperated him, and at last he turned from him in the Gallery at Whitehall, "cocking his hat and throwing his coat under his arm, as he used to do when he was angry. Thus," says Brian Fairfax, "I saw Lord Fairfax take his last leave of his old acquaintance, Cromwell, whose servants expected he would be sent to bear the Duke company at the Tower the next morning, but the Protector was wiser in his passion." Buckingham himself believed that he never was in greater danger than at this time. In an autobiographical fragment, he ascribes Cromwell's anger against him to an alliance with Fairfax, "who had a still greater share in the army than Oliver himself."

His treatment in the tower certainly justified the most gloomy anticipations.[1]

"As soon," he says, "as Oliver was dead, they proclaimed his son Richard Cromwell, Protector of England, with the same solemnities that ever Kings of England were proclaimed Kings. I was then close prisoner in the Tower, with a couple of Guards lying always in my chamber and a sentinel at my door. I confess I was not a little delighted with the noise of the great guns, for I presently knew what it meant, and if Oliver had lived for three days longer I had certainly been put to death."

[1] "Fairfax Papers," vol. iv. p. 253.

His commonplace book also contains a few lines on the Protector's death :—

> "Deepe in his flesh, deep stuck th' Almighty's dart,
> The terrors of the great one storm'd his heart.
> Thus in his hight of sin and shameless pride,
> Thus by God's hand the British Gracchus died."[1]

Richard Cromwell's accession produced a relaxation of the Duke's confinement. Yet the Lieutenant of the Tower, Colonel Barkstead, could not immediately forget the strict injunctions of the late Protector with regard to his dangerous prisoner. When it was determined to transfer Buckingham to Windsor, he wrote anxiously to Thurloe, saying, that although the Duke and his lady had earnestly entreated permission to spend a few hours with their parents, at York House, on their way to Windsor, he had refused to accede to the request, reasonable as it appeared.[2] Nor would he consent, unless the Secretary assured him it would not prove in any way "prejudiciall to the publique."

Buckingham's conduct at Windsor certainly justified Colonel Barkstead's suspicions that his most trivial demand might cloak some very different design. Under Richard's mild sway, all discipline was now relaxed; and Windsor, state prison as it was, soon became a rallying point for the crew of reckless conspirators, who ever gravitated towards the Duke. The Government were informed that Buckingham openly boasted that if his petition for release were not

---

[1] *Quarterly Review*, p. 42.
[2] Thurloe, vol. vii. p. 370.

granted, "he would endeavour his escape, and the designe is soe well layde it cannot well miscarry."[1] It was not his own liberty alone at which he aimed. He and his friends had devised a bold stroke with no less intention than that of making themselves masters of Windsor Castle. In truth, the Duke did not wile away the hours of captivity solely in discussing art and literature with his constant companion, Abraham Cowley.[2] His mood was probably more attuned to that of his fellow-prisoner Lauderdale, with whom he must have become intimately acquainted during this winter. But even this semblance of captivity did not last long, for on Monday the 21st of February, 1659, Lord Fairfax preferred a petition to the House of Commons on behalf of the Duke of Buckingham for his enlargement, offering to be personally responsible for his safe custody. All the leading members took part in the ensuing debate, which was opened by Mr Onslow. The "old fox of Surrey" characteristically favoured the suit of the General, who might so soon decide the country's destinies. He urged that since Fairfax "has been trusted with three nations, he may very well be trusted with a single person."[3]

Not the least noteworthy feature of this debate is that it witnessed the commencement of those relations between Buckingham and Sir Anthony Ashley Cooper, which, at a later date, were to make their names inseparably connected. And well-known as is the character of the master

---

[1] Thurloe, vol. vii. p. 715.
[2] Brian Fairfax.
[3] "Parliamentary Diary of John Burton," vol. ii. p. 378.

spirit of the Cabal and the Popish Terror, it may not be amiss to recall the differences and the points of contact which existed between the future Shaftesbury and George Villiers.

At this juncture, Cooper's sympathies were assuming a royalist direction, so that his support was acquired to the Duke. Nor was it of small moment, for the wise Achitophel already loomed large in the public view. Even under Cromwell, who by force of sheer greatness created a desert around him, the Dorsetshire squire had made his mark. Indeed, it could not be otherwise with the man who, as a mere lad, had, by dint of energy and tact, himself rescued his heritage from the clutches of a fraudulent guardian. The experience must have been profoundly instructive. Yet at years so tender, it is not good to look too nearly on human baseness. It was perhaps the worse for England that the iron should so early have seared the soul of the one great man in the pinchbeck age of the second Charles.

Nevertheless, the sordid struggles of Cooper's youth did not dim the unconquerable cheerfulness, the gaiety, the wit, that were fated to survive ill-health and carking care. Fond wife, erudite philosopher, rakehelly courtier, all witnessed to his fascination.

The learned Lord Chancellor, mirror of judicial probity in a corrupt generation, could bandy quips and jests with a facility that rivalled George Villiers. "I believe thou art the wickedest dog in England, my lord," cried the delighted monarch. "May it please your Majesty, of a *subject*, I believe I am!" flashed the retort.

But if Ashley manipulated the vices and foibles of mankind with a cunning hand, he was too much an artist not to understand and value true goodness. Let him who doubts read the touching lines on the death of the first Lady Cooper. Isaak Walton could not have penned anything more exquisitely tender. Naturally, this appreciative faculty vastly enhanced Shaftesbury's power, for it is hard to influence that which we do not apprehend. Indeed, throughout his career he used loaded dice, since it was with the best feelings of a race, its patriotism and its faith, that he risked stakes with fortune. Yet in a character so complex it is hard to disentangle the genuine convictions of the statesman, the innate loathing of oppression, the passionate love of freedom, from the profitable moral stock-in-trade that the arch-plotter of his time did not scruple to profane to personal ends.

Scruples and Shaftesbury were indeed never well acquainted, for perhaps no Englishman has more absolutely incarnated the axioms of Machiavelli. The man's astounding mental span, his unholy gift of prescience, bordering on divination, his God-given memory, must have inspired even the Florentine Secretary with awe. Shaftesbury did not, however, escape paying toll to the superstition of the age. Napoleon himself was not a more devout believer in his "star," than this disciple of the Puritan Sanhedrim. The "dotage of astrology" was upon Shaftesbury even as upon Buckingham. In fact, Cooper carried it a stage further than George Villiers, since he believed "that in a future state our souls went into stars and animated them."[1] And it may be acknowledged that the planet Mars might be no unmeet habitation for that insatiable and militant spirit.

In 1659, Sir Anthony Ashley Cooper probably rather resembled John Greenhill's painting than Dryden's famous description of "the pigmy body fretted to decay." The picture in the National Portrait Gallery shows a countenance, not only pregnant with intellectual force and alert observation, but singularly refined and well-favoured. The nose is delicately chiselled; the upper lip short and formed like Cupid's bow. It is, in fact, a charming, seductive mouth, but freed from all suspicion of effeminacy by the firm, the implacable character of the lower jaw and chin. The eyes are as almond-shaped as those of Mary Stuart, but their colour is the peculiar steely grey, associated in the East with cruelty, and in the West with the dominant races. In truth the world can have held few mysteries which that piercing gaze could not penetrate; few obstacles, which the serene determination imprinted on those features ought not to have surmounted.

On this particular occasion, it was to the more timorous section represented by Colonels Clark and Mildmay that Cooper addressed himself. These worthies would have sheltered their responsibilities behind committees, but the future Shaftesbury disposed of this suggestion, by contemptuously remarking, that "one person cannot do much harm by his liberty"; and, as far-sighted as Onslow, he harps on what is indeed the dominant note of the discussion: "it must not be thought whatever

[1] Foxcroft, "Supplement to Burnet's Hist.," p. 58.

is in our hearts, that we shall have ingratitude to that person that offered the petition. The care that Lord Fairfax will have of him in his family, will be beyond all security you can care for." Sir Harry Vane joined his plea to Ashley Cooper's. His sense of justice was outraged by the notion that the House of Lords could become a respecter of persons. He pointed out that there were others at liberty, such as the Marquis of Worcester, quite as dangerous as Buckingham. Finally, the Solicitor-General speaking for the Government, joined in the universal testimony to Lord Fairfax's high reputation. "When the noble Lord Fairfax says he will engage himself, it is more than £20,000."[1]

Every action of the old General's was indeed calculated to inspire absolute reliance on his integrity and honesty, for, anxious as he was to obtain his son-in-law's freedom, he would not compass it by an equivocal declaration. "When I engage my estate," he proudly said, "I know what I do, but when I engage his honour, I engage what is not in my power."

This straightforward truthfulness did not injure Buckingham's cause, since it was promptly resolved that "George Villiers, Duke of Buckingham now a prisoner at Windsor Castle, upon his engagement and upon his honour, at the Bar of the House, and upon the engagement of the Lord Fairfax in £20,000, that the said Duke shall peaceably demean himself for the future, and shall not join with nor abet or have any correspondence with

[1] "Parliamentary Diary of Thos. Burton," vol. iii. p. 370. 21st Feb. 1658-59.

any of the enemies of the Lord Protector of this Commonwealth, in any the parts beyond these seas, or within this Commonwealth, shall be discharged of his imprisonment and restraint, and that the Governor of Windsor Castle be required to bring the Duke of Buckingham to the Bar of this House, Wednesday next, to engage his honour accordingly."

Two days later, on the 23rd of February, 1659, the Duke presented himself at the Bar of the House, the Sergeant-at-Arms and a deputy of the Governor of Windsor waiting close by.[1]

The gracious task of conferring liberty on the young Duke fell on the Speaker. He informed Buckingham that "though the House had taken into due consideration his demerits which had been very great to this Commonwealth," yet, they "overbalanced them with the high merit of his Relations; and of their goodness had ordered that, upon his own engagement upon his honour, and of the Lord Fairfax in £20,000, that he should not abet any of the enemies of this commonwealth, either at home or abroad, he should have his enlargement." Buckingham could not have been better inspired in his reply. He gave the House his humble thanks for their favour towards him. He touched on the great happiness it was to come before this assembly, and not content with the formal engagement "upon his honour, to behave himself peaceably and quietly, he professed he should be ready to lay down his life and fortune for their service."

[1] "Parl. Hist. of England," 1763, vol. xxi. p. 291.

CHAPTER V

THE RESTORATION

For the first and last time in his chequered career, Buckingham now tasted the blessings of peace and contentment. This, says the faithful Brian Fairfax, "was the happiest time of all his life, when he went to his father-in-law's house at Nun Appleton, and there lived orderly and decently with his own wife, where he neither wanted nor so abounded as to be tempted to any sort of extravagance as he was after, when he came to possess his whole estate." It must have been in these brief halcyon days that he acquired so strong a hold over his poor wife's affections, that, at a later period, as she sorrowfully admitted, she could never free herself from its tyranny.[1]

"This life of regularity and domesticity—no courtships but to his own wife, not so much as to his after-beloved and costly mistress, the philosopher's stone,"[2] proved, however, somewhat fleeting.

Buckingham's long residence abroad had not affected his truly British devotion to field-sports. Hard riding specially appealed to him, and even the attraction of chemistry paled by the side of fox-hunting, probably because he found it no in-

[1] Mde. d'Aulnoy.
[2] Brian Fairfax.

adequate substitute for the dangerous intrigues which had hitherto furnished his chief occupation. Nowhere could he have better gratified this new pursuit than at Nun Appleton. It soon became an infatuation, and he was wont to tell his half-scandalised steward that he would gladly barter his fattest flock of sheep for an equal number of foxes.[1]

As we have seen, the attraction between Lord Fairfax and the Duke was mutual, and it is unfortunate that Buckingham did not carry out his intention of writing his father-in-law's life. Such a production would have been a valuable addition to history, whereas the Ode, which he subsequently dedicated to Fairfax's memory, does honour rather to his constancy than to his Muse.

The friendship of the two men was strengthened by the growing similarity of their views on matters political. It was, doubtless, at his son-in-law's instigation that the General returned to Westminster and joined the little band of Republicans who, led by Vane and Hazlerig, strenuously opposed Richard Cromwell's Government. Yet the fall of the Protector, though largely brought about by the intrigues of his new allies, inaugurated a state of affairs even more distasteful to Fairfax. England, indeed, has seldom known such anarchy as prevailed during the year 1659, whilst Rump and Army battled for ascendency.

It was idle to regret the "old comrade," the "British Gracchus," and, prompted by Buckingham, Fairfax began to regard the restoration of the Stuarts as offering the best prospect of peace for the storm-tossed land. But, unlike his son-in-law,

[1] Nichol's "Leicestershire."

the old Puritan had the self-restraint not to move till the hour for action struck.

It was a "maxim" of Fairfax's that no loyalist levies could contend with his old veterans, and that the King's friends showed more affection than discretion in plotting a revolution which was not based on the consent of the Army.[1]

It would have been better for the Cavaliers had they held my Lord Fairfax's doctrines. In August an abortive Royalist rising, under Sir George Booth, took place, which met with some small success in Cheshire, where the leader enjoyed considerable influence. The insurgents possessed themselves of the county town, but their triumph was short-lived. Lambert, with a small force, utterly routed them and took their commander prisoner.

Lambert's victory, however, only accelerated the inevitable breach between the Army and the Parliament. The gathering storm broke in October, and resulted in the vesting of the authority hitherto exercised by the Rump in a military council of safety. This latest revolution met, however, with almost universal disapproval. The promise of a new Parliament did not reassure the civilian population, already greatly alarmed at the prospect of being ruled by the soldiers. And many of the officers were consumed with jealousy of the powers conferred on Major-General Lambert and Fleetwood, the nominal Commander-in-Chief.

In the circumstances, the hopes of all were centred on General Monk, who still remained in Scotland. Not a man of genius, or even of exceptional intelligence, Monk yet brought the

[1] Brian Fairfax.

very qualities which were needed to bear upon the situation. He had secured the confidence not only of his soldiers, but also of the Scots, whom he had governed during the last few years. His forces were well disciplined and united, his treasury was replenished by the grants of the Scottish estates; and while he kept Lambert and his army amused with negotiations in the north of England, in the south the City Apprentices were rising, and Lawson with the fleet was reinstating the Rump at Westminster.

Meanwhile, Fairfax had refused to take sides. He would not stir when Sir George Booth was defeated by Lambert, nor would he intervene till he saw that General "bent on the ambition of imitating Cromwell," and, even then, he would have hesitated to rekindle the Civil War had it not been for Monk's urgent appeal.

The Scottish Commander-in-Chief was aware that no move which did not include Fairfax was destined to succeed. Therefore, towards Christmas-tide of 1659, he contrived to get a letter smuggled across the frontier by a certain Dr Clergis, in which he cordially invited Fairfax to participate in crushing Lambert.

That participation Fairfax did not refuse, but the Border was so closely watched that it was no slight task to acquaint Monk with his decision, and Dr Clergis, having met with an accident, could not repeat his hazardous journey. Meanwhile, time passed, and Fairfax refused to involve his friends in the rising until he and Monk had settled all the details of a scheme, the success of which he knew hinged on co-operation.

At this crisis, Brian Fairfax, the Duke's future biographer, who was then a Cambridge undergraduate, on his Christmas vacation at Nun Appleton, came to the rescue. He volunteered to carry Fairfax's message to Coldstream, passing himself off as a "young country clown," and his services were instantly accepted by his noble relative. Buckingham entered into the business of disguising him with all the zest with which he would have planned a masquerade. So careful indeed was he in ordering every detail of Brian's equipment, that he would not suffer him to carry weapons, judging them incompatible with the costume he had adopted. Had it not been for the Duke's foresight the envoy would scarcely have won through the lines of Lambert's numerous and vigilant patrols. Yet he must have regretted his defenceless condition, when attacked by a notorious moss-trooper, on a lonely moor. But fortune favoured him, and, somewhat to his own surprise, he eventually arrived unscathed at the Lord General's quarters at Coldstream.

Monk bore a well-earned character for reserve, but he received Brian with an effusion which testified to the anxiety which had consumed him whilst awaiting his old comrade's answer. He hastily drew the youth "into a little hole—we must call it a closet"—where the messenger delivered himself of his commission:[1] "Lord Fairfax undertook that he would, on the first day of January, appear at the head of what force he could raise in Yorkshire, and declare against Lambert's army. But he desired him to watch Lambert that no part of his

[1] Fairfax, "Correspondence," vol. iv. p. 161.

army came down on him." Monk was enraptured. He embraced Brian Fairfax, and "vowed that he would watch Lambert as a cat watches a mouse, and that a troop of horse should not move but he would follow them."[1]

So far all had gone smoothly, yet at the last moment the scheme was nearly wrecked by a "false brother," who gave warning to the authorities of their intention. Lilburne's garrison at York was immediately reinforced, and, on St Stephen's night, a company was despatched to arrest Lord Fairfax and the Duke at Nun Appleton.[2] Happily, a friend at York got wind of Lilburne's intention, and when the troopers arrived they found their quarry flown. For greater security, the conspirators agreed to ride to Knaresborough by separate routes, and in the hurry of departure they were divided. Yet even this incident served their designs; for the old General had not gone many miles from his house before he was met by some of Lilburne's horsemen. Had his Cavalier son-in-law been with him, they would certainly have been stopped. As it was, the soldiers did not venture to seize the popular old Puritan, and, after some parley, allowed the coach to proceed. In the darkness Lord Fairfax and the Duke crossed the river by different ferries, thus for two anxious days losing touch of each other. But if Buckingham was lost to Fairfax, his whereabouts were equally unknown to Lilburne; so that, while the commandant imagined the rising had miscarried, and the two noblemen had flown to

[1] Hist. MSS., p. 193.
Hist. MSS., App. Rep. V. Duke of Sutherland's MSS. Th. Gower to Mr. J. Langley, 5th Jan. 1659.

Manchester, Buckingham was undisturbed at Malton, organising and drilling volunteers. Recruits, indeed, flowed in from all sides, amongst others a veteran troop of cavalry under Captain Strangways, a deserter from Lilburne. But with the latter's advent, difficulties arose which must have sorely taxed Buckingham's small stock of patience. Captain Strangways instantly "excepted against a Mr Gower, professing he loved the man but could not be in a design where Cavaliers were parties."[1] Mr Gower, was too public-spirited to risk the success of the undertaking on personal grounds; he resigned his command to Mr Thomas Vavasour and "marched along as a private gentleman to Knaresborough." In spite of his near relationship to the Commander-in-Chief, the same objections were made to Buckingham. Nevertheless, when, after a hard march through deep snow, they reached Borough Bridge, only to find themselves faced by Hacker's regiment of horse, the imminent danger of the situation dispelled all the previous bickerings and jealousies. Buckingham was permitted "to put himself with his sword drawn at the head of Mr Gower's party to lead them, and the old soldiers gave the new party leave to be in the front." Happily Hacker's men were themselves half-hearted. They drew off without fighting, and Knaresborough was safely reached. Here Buckingham found Fairfax still troubled at having brought those gentlemen "that come so willingly to venture their lives, into this danger." Buckingham's anxieties were of a less unselfish nature. Even the remonstrances of the General did not deter the old Cromwellians from

[1] Hist. MSS., App. Rep. v. p. 193.

objecting to his presence ; indeed, they declared, they would not be satisfied till he withdrew. This must have been a bitter moment for Buckingham, since, by directing the whole movement, he had counted on retrieving all, and more than all, his former credit with Charles. Mr Gower had, however, set him an example which it was impossible to disregard, and though chafing at being placed in a subordinate position, he elected to remain with Fairfax.

Meanwhile the immediate prospect of battle had operated a transformation in Oliver's old comrade ; "he became another man, his motions so quick, his eyes so sparkling, giving the word of command like a General."[1]

The hearts of Lilburne's troopers, however, were not in the cause they were called upon to defend ; nor had long years of retirement affected black Tom Fairfax's popularity with the gallant fellows, whom he had so often led to victory. They would not fight their former leader, and the encounter so eagerly anticipated was avoided. Assuredly this bloodless triumph was not the least in his noble career, and he must have felt no little pride as he entered York, a pacific conqueror, to the cries of "Fairfax! Fairfax!"

A few days later he was rejoined by Monk, who was well aware that he owed the peaceful dispersion of his antagonist's forces as much to Fairfax as to his own measures, or the exhortations addressed by the Rump to Lambert's soldiery. Yet when his ally urged the instant proclamation of the King, the politic General was deaf to his advice, and protested that he dared not take such a step in the present temper of his army. In public, Monk was even

[1] Brian Fairfax.

less encouraging. He caned an officer who accused him of meditating the recall of Charles Stuart. Nor would he march southwards till he had received the Parliament's invitation to do so. Fairfax was included in the formal vote of thanks which the House of Commons tendered to Monk, but he did not accompany the King-maker to London, and remained at York, disbanding his volunteers. Buckingham was less easily discouraged. He saw that for all his protestations, Monk's sword must eventually turn the balance. "Where the carcase is, there shall the eagles be gathered together." The national decision must needs be given in the metropolis, and thither he hurried. We know that he witnessed the outburst of popular delight when Monk cast in his lot with the city fathers, and announced his determination to call a free Parliament. Like Mr Pepys, George Villiers saw Cheapside and the Strand alight with bonfires, and "in derision of the present members, the great burning and roasting and drinking for rumps." He never forgot the strange saturnalia; but of his subsequent doings during that time of storm and stress we have no hint, though it is safe to surmise that the "jolly Duke of Bucks" was deep in the plots and counterplots of the succeeding months.

Bitterly must he have regretted his father-in-law's rejection of Monk's offer to take over the chief command of the Army. This he had not been able to prevent, but we can trace his influence in the fact that it was Fairfax who headed the Parliamentary delegates commissioned to wait on the King at the Hague. Charles received so important an individual with marked respect;

but, unlike the future Duke of Albemarle, the old General sought no selfish advantage from the Restoration. When admitted to a private audience, he simply "asked pardon for all his past offences and made a full, voluntary and sincere submission to His Majesty, for the rest of his life. This was all Fairfax had to ask—and this was all he obtained."[1]

As we know, the Duke of Buckingham did not affect such high-minded disinterestedness. Many as were the parts which his versatile talents enabled him to fill, he never aspired to enacting that of a Christian Cincinnatus. During the last two years, he had completely immersed himself in the bucolic occupations of an English Squire— rural pastimes, diversified by music, chemistry, and the wooing of his own wife. But now, with the return of Monarchy, a vision of power, such as few subjects save his own father had wielded, rose before him. Nor were his hopes of such stuff as dreams are made of. His rent-roll, were he reinstated, would be the highest in the kingdom. While the statesmen, who returned with Charles from Breda, had grown grey in an alien land, George Villiers, at Nun Appleton and York House, had learnt to know the best and wisest of that new England, which Hyde and his contemporaries obstinately refused to recognise. Younger, richer, better informed, the Duke did not start ill-equipped in the race. The peculiar circumstances of his boyhood had endowed him with an insight into the second Charles's character possessed by few others. And though the last years of their common

---

[1] Fairfax, "Correspondence," vol. iv. p. 218.

adversity had apparently sapped the friendship of the former playfellows, yet the Duke was confident that his recent services to the Royal Cause must efface any disagreeable impressions concerning him the King might still retain.

On Friday, 25th May, 1660, amidst every imaginable token of popular rejoicing, Charles II. landed at Dover. He had contented himself with assuring Fairfax of his gracious oblivion of former offences. But he received Monk, who knew better how to estimate his own achievements, in a very different spirit; and, not content with giving him every evidence of grateful affection, he called him "Father," and repeatedly pressed him to his breast. Buckingham had not failed to assist at the dramatic scene. Nor did he come unaccompanied, having raised a corps of gentlemen volunteers in Yorkshire; but his reception was in marked contrast to that accorded to the General, who was still the paramount influence with the Cromwellian soldiery. So pronounced, indeed, was Charles's coldness towards George Villiers, that the French Ambassador comments on it in his despatch to Mazarin.[1] When the Lord General was invited to enter the Royal carriage, no such proposition, in spite of the privileges of his rank, was made to the Duke. Had he been of a sensitive disposition, he must have taken offence and, with his illustrious relative, retired to the pleasant orchards and meadows of Nun Appleton. But George Villiers was not lightly to be rebuffed. The boot was still unoccupied, and there he installed

---

[1] Guizot's "Monk," App. p. 373. M. de Bordeaux au Cardinal Mazarin.

himself before any objection could be formulated.[1] Again, when after leaving Dover, the King wearied of the coach, the Duke instantly followed suit, and, bareheaded, rode immediately behind his Sovereign. At the gorgeous ceremony of the King's public entry into London, Buckingham occupied a place directly after the Royal Dukes. He was likewise present at St Paul's Schools when the ministers of London presented the King's sacred Majesty with a handsome Bible—a gift, Buckingham must have smiled to hear his former boon companion receive with the solemn declaration, "that he would make that Book the rule of his life and government."

Meanwhile, both Houses of Parliament busied themselves with the restitution of the Duke's confiscated estates. The actual possessors were immediately warned neither to alienate any portion of the property, nor even to collect the rents. The only opposition to this act of justice came, strangely enough, from a Cavalier. The Earl of Bristol had been entrusted[2] with the care of a bill to repair the losses that he, the Duke, and Lord Newcastle had sustained during the Civil Wars. But, when that brilliant but eccentric nobleman arose to propose the question, he put it, "Whether their Lordships did consent to this Bill in favour of my lord of Newcastle, without exclusion of the other lords. The Duke of Buckingham, judging my lord of Newcastle named and himself not, stepped from his seat, and in some heat more

---

[1] Hist. MSS. Le Fleming Rep. XII. p. 24. 3rd June, 1660. D. F. to Wm. Ambrose.
[2] Duke of Sutherland MSS., App. Rep. V., p. 155. 7th Aug. 1660. A. Newport to Sir Leveson.

than usual asked my lord of Bristol why he named my lord of Newcastle and not him, and pressing him in an extraordinary manner for his reason in soe doeing, my lord of Bristol told him that he thought my lord of Newcastle a man of more merit than him; the Duke said he believed him not and returned in some anger; of which passage the King having immediate notice, they were commanded not to stir out of their lodgings." This was not the sole occasion when the King's intervention was necessary to prevent the hot-headed Duke from plunging into affairs of honour. One night when paying his court to his former love, the Princess of Orange, he and Mr O'Neale, her chamberlain, fell out in her drawing-room. He gave the lie to Mr O'Neale, and cartels would have been exchanged but for the Sovereign's opportune appearance on the scene.[1]

During Charles's triumphal progress to London, Buckingham had doubtless many opportunities for retrieving his credit with the King. Something, too, he may have hoped from the favour with which Charles regarded his cousin, Barbara Villiers, the notorious Lady Castlemaine. For, though later, this "enormously vicious and ravenous woman" honoured Buckingham with one of her furious demoniac hatreds, yet they were at first on excellent terms, and it was at her lodgings that Buckingham was brought into nightly contact with his Royal master. Moreover, both mistress and wit were united by their common detestation of Chancellor Hyde, newly created Earl of Clarendon. It was to his influence, that Bucking-

[1] Duke of Sutherland MSS., App. Rep. V., p. 157.

ham attributed the conspicuous omission of his name from the list of the Privy Council, to which all the former members had been reappointed. His revenge was not far to seek. The convivial gatherings at Lady Castlemaine's gave him his opportunity, and at the little suppers, where Charles sought to drown in wine and ribaldry all recollection of the homilies of his Chancellor, the flippant Duke caricatured to the life the pompous deportment of that austere Minister. In truth, it must have been difficult for the Merry Monarch to repress his amusement at the ridiculous spectacle of the madcap Duke, preceded by his old associate Titus, with a fire-shovel for the mace, and a pair of bellows for the purse, solemnly apeing the portentous gravity of the tedious "Schoolmaster."

Reckless as he habitually was, the Duke did not, however, affront the Minister without safeguarding himself against too critical an enquiry into his own past doings. Already on June the 6th, 1660, he had taken out a pardon under the Great Seal "for all past offences." It is true that this step did not necessarily presuppose an admission of guilt.[1] In fact, at a period when a mere technicality might place the most upright citizen at the mercy of an informer, it was dictated by ordinary prudence. But, on this occasion, the Duke did not prove overhasty, for, but a week after his pardon had been signed and sealed, a warrant was issued against two of his gentlemen, on the ground that they had betrayed the King's secrets to his enemies during the Commonwealth."[2]

[1] Dom. State Cal., 6th June, 1660.
[2] Guizot's "Life of Monk," App. p. 374.

Each "revolving moon" of the Duke of Buckingham's varied career is closely associated with his cult for some woman. Thus his exile in Holland was marked by his courtship of the Princess Royal. His wife was the presiding genius of the years when he lived orderly and decently at Nun Appleton. And now, with the return of the Stuarts, he advertised a mad passion for Princess Henrietta, the youngest member of his Sovereign's family. Nor in this instance was his infatuation astonishing. The testimony of two Courts, the devotion of Louis XIV., every letter, every memoir that survives, carries the conviction that never since her hapless ancestress, Mary Stuart, was royal lady so amply dowered with grace and charm. When Princess Henrietta returned to England, her hand was already bespoken for Monsieur, the Duc d'Orleans, her own first cousin, and the Grand Monarque's only brother. The conditions of this alliance were debated during the following weeks, and in the winter a special embassy was despatched to escort Madame to her bridegroom. The delirious festivities, which had not even been checked by the successive deaths of the Princess of Orange and the Duke of Gloucester, received a fresh impetus from their advent, and nowhere were the envoys more sumptuously feasted than at Wallingford House. Indeed, so splendid were the entertainments of the ducal lover, that he speedily impaired a fortune once judged inexhaustible. His French guests infected him with their mania for high play. "Had he continued," says the faithful Brian, "his estate had not lasted so long." For once in his life, however, he showed signs of self-control, and, alarmed by his heavy losses, he not only resolved to give up gaming, but ever after kept his resolution.

When the Princess left England, with the Queen-Mother, for her future home, Buckingham obtained permission to accompany them. As Charles II. remarked, "Mamie's luck at sea" was proverbial.[1] On this occasion, thanks to the negligence of the pilot, the voyage was inaugurated by the ship running foul of the Horse Sand. This necessitated their putting back to harbour. Nor did their misfortunes end there. Hardly had they arrived at Portsmouth, when Henrietta fell dangerously ill. The fever was of such a nature that the doctors at first diagnosed her malady as small-pox, and even when it proved to be merely the measles, her life, notwithstanding, hung awhile in the balance. Happily she preserved her senses, and obstinately refused to allow the posse of doctors, despatched from London, by Charles II. to bleed her—a resolution to which she probably owed her recovery. During this period of suspense, Buckingham's misery found vent in a furious outburst of anger. Indeed, it is charitable to suppose that solicitude had affected his brain, for his behaviour is reported on all sides to have been that of a lunatic. Nor did Henrietta's convalescence mend his manners. When the Princess was sufficiently recovered to resume her journey to Hâvre de Grace, his preposterous courtship passed all permissible limits. The Queen became alarmed that Monsieur, whose jealous nature was notorious,

[1] "Madame," by Julia Cartwright, p. 81.

would resent his familiarities, and finally commanded him to precede them on the route to Paris. Much as he disliked being parted from the Princess, Buckingham had no choice but to obey. The only vent he found for his ill-humour was in a futile squabble with Lord Sandwich, of which "my lord's" confidant has left us a lively picture. The dispute arose at a game of cards between the Admiral, Lord St Albans, and Buckingham.

"The Duke did to my lords[1] dishonour often say that he did in his conscience know the contrary to what he then said about the difference at cards, and so did take up the money that he should have lost to my Lord, which my Lord resenting, said nothing then, but that he doubted there were ways enough to get his money of him.[2] So they parted that night, and my Lord sent for Sir R. Stayner and sent him the next morning to the Duke, to know whether he did remember what he said last night, and whether he would own it with his sword, and a second, which he said he would, and so both sides agreed. But my Lord St Albans and the Queen and Ambassador Montagu did waylay them at their lodgings, till the difference was made up to my Lord's honour, who hath got great reputation thereby."

The English suite had hoped that the presence of the princely bridegroom would act as a restraint on Buckingham. Philippe, Duc d'Orleans, was not, however, the kind of personage to impress George Villiers, and that nobleman continued to put so little curb on his feelings that the Princess began to fear that she would be held responsible

---
[1] Lord Sandwich.
[2] Pepys, Wheatley ed., vol. i. p. 342. 5th Feb. 1661.

for his follies. Finding her own rebukes unavailing, and alarmed lest Monsieur's displeasure should be aroused, she besought her mother to intervene. But Henrietta Maria now regarded the matter as foolish rather than compromising, and frankly told Monsieur that his bride only tolerated the Duke's attentions because he was her brother's favourite. The excuse seemed preposterous to Philippe: he refused to be pacified, and made a formal complaint of the Englishman's presumption to Anne of Austria. Monsieur had always been his mother's spoilt darling, and had George Villiers borne any other name, he would certainly have incurred the formidable displeasure of the Ex-Regent. But "the passion which his father had cherished in bygone days for the Queen now earned indulgence for the son."[1] She deprecated an open breach, and recommended that after he had remained a short time longer in France, he should be given a hint that his return to England was necessary.

In pursuance of this advice, Henrietta Maria wrote privately to Charles II., exposing the perils of the situation, and the King sent orders, which, though amicably worded, Buckingham could not disregard. It must have been the harder for him to tear himself away, since, with the prescience of a lover, he had already recognised in the Count de Guiche a more formidable rival than the effeminate husband, or the royal brother-in-law. He departed, therefore, but only after a thousand lingering farewells and renewed protestations of love and devotion.

The Duke left the *fêtes* given in honour of the

"Hist. de Mde. Henriette d'Angleterre," par Mde. de la Fayette.

Duchesse d'Orleans' marriage for the festivities of Charles II.'s coronation. After the sober, neutral-tinted pomps of the Commonwealth, the nation hailed with enthusiasm the sumptuous pageant, which marked the restoration of Royalty. The peers vied with one another in magnificence. So gorgeous was the Royal procession, that the beholders complained that their eyes were dazed and wearied by the excess of gold and silver. At the religious ceremony, Buckingham bore the orb, or mond, before the King. And when we learn that the Puritan Lord Wharton had expended £8000[1] on his horse furnitures, and no less than £500 on the mere bridle-bit of the steed he bestrode, it is less difficult to credit the rumour that the Duke had declared "that notwithstanding the malice of cards and dice, he bestowed £30,000 upon a suit to attend His Majesty at his coronation."

In 1661, the King conferred the Lord Lieutenancy of Yorkshire on the Duke of Buckingham. The honour was far from being a sinecure. It entailed not only vast expenditure, but grave responsibilities. For Calcutta is nowadays no further removed from the centre of Government, than was York from London, at that time of slow locomotion. The gentry and nobility of the northern province received the King's favourite with an enthusiasm hardly to be augured from their treatment of him in 1660.

At Doncaster, all the county notables who were warned in time, assembled "to wait upon His Grace, with all the joy and best music they could

---

[1] Hist. MSS. App. Rep. V. Duke of Sutherland's MSS., p. 175. 13th April 1661. William Smith to J. Langley.

make." Nor did the citizens show less eagerness in greeting their new Governor. On his arrival the Mayor and Aldermen feasted him " with good store of wine," and the next day, when the Duke scrupulously attended both morning and evening service, they did not fail to accompany him to church. At York his reception was even more cordial. When he arrived there, escorted by a gallant band of volunteers, he found the way to his inn lined on both sides by the city regiment, under the command of the High Sheriff. Then the bells and cannon took up the tale, and pealed and roared so continuously that there can have been little rest for anyone that night in York.[1]

This exuberant loyalty concealed, however, very genuine discontent. Many persons in Yorkshire had lost Church and Crown lands, allotted to them during the Civil War. Naturally, these were not enamoured of the Restoration. Nor were the evicted Nonconformist ministers alone to be pitied. The old soldiers and officers of the Cromwellian regiments, alike dismissed their profession and deprived of the right to worship God according to their conscience, were in sorry straits. As a rule, they showed their sterling worth by accepting the altered state of things, and proving themselves superior to ordinary civilians in every peaceful trade and industry. But, here and there, some of the fiercer spirits could not contain their disgust at the new *régime*, and this disapproval was adroitly fanned into open rebellion by the cloud of spies and informers, who battened on forfeitures and blood-money. Indeed, it was to

[1] "Mercurius Politicus," York, Nov. 1661.

the machinations of these gentry that the unhappy rising of Rymer and Oates, in 1663, was mainly due.

Two old Parliamentary officers, Rymer and Oates, were no desperadoes. Owning as they did properties valued from £200 to £300 per annum, they held a stake in the country that no middle-aged Englishman lightly imperils. Moreover, they would not have assumed the initiative of revolt had they not in an evil hour confided their heart-searchings to their former comrades, Colonels Smithson and Greathead. To doubt the honour of their brothers-at-arms would have seemed rank blasphemy to these loyal souls. Nor, when they sought their advice, had they formed designs, which even a Crown lawyer could construe into high treason. Smithson and Greathead, burning to curry favour with those in power, at first doubted whether they were not reporting mere disaffected chatter. In some perplexity they consulted Sir Thomas Gower, the Governor of York, who encouraged them to lead their friends on beyond retreat. And, owing to the personal consideration they enjoyed among their fellow-religionists, the task was in no way arduous.

It is only due to Buckingham to state that while Charles's representatives were ingeniously contriving the ruin of his honest but misguided subjects, he himself was absent from the Lord Lieutenancy. Meanwhile, the black work progressed, more rapidly than Sir Thomas Gower can have desired; for when it was known that the conspirators had assembled at Farnley Wood, near Pontefract, the public alarm bordered on panic. It was ascertained that the intention of the rebels had been to raise the countryside, fall unexpectedly on Whitehall, and paralyse Government by the seizure of the heir-presumptive and the principal Ministers. But this somewhat comprehensive plan required no inconsiderable force, and when the trysting-place was reached, the scanty band recognised that with their actual numbers such an attempt was utterly hopeless. They therefore dispersed, but they had scared their opponents, and the reprisals were bound to be savage. We possess an account of the situation in a letter of George Villiers, who had been recalled in hot haste to Yorkshire.

Buckingham to Charles II.[1]

YORK, 12*th October*, 1663.

Though upon the receipt of that paper I sent your Majesty from Royston I rid night and day, the waters were soe up upon the Road, that I could not possibly get to Doncaster before 9 of the clock in the morning of Saturday, when meeting with my Deputy lieutenants and a regiment of foote, which they had drawne thither before I came, I was stayed soe late that I came not hither till Sunday morning, at four of the clock; as soone as I arrived, I sent and enquired of Sir Thomas Goare how his intelligence was of this design, and hee telling mee that hee believed the businesse was blown over upon their seeing the country was in soe greate a forwardnesse to take up armes, I confesse I did not thinke it necessary to put the country gentlemen and Militia to further trouble, and soe left them in

---

[1] Dom. State Cal. Charles II. vol. lxxxi.

their several quarters as they were ordered to be before I came, but receiving at night intelligence from Colonel Chaytor (who is a very understanding as well as a very brave man) that the rebels should be in arms this day or to-morrow at latest, and that he was assured it from an officer, that formerly had beene of their party, who was offered to command them, and refused it, I thought it was not propper to delay any more time and therefore sent orders immediately to draw all the militia together to Pomfret and Fernbridge, except the militia regiment of foote and the volunteer regiment of foote of this town, which I thought better to leave here for the defence of this place. Colonel Chaytor's letter I sent last night to the Generals as soon as I received it, and deferred the giving Your Majesty this account of myself, till the morning that I might not delay that poste. We have howerly intelligence to the same effect from generall hands, so that I do not only believe they have really a designe, but that they are still resolved to make some attempt, to which ende it is not only my opinion, but the opinion of Colonel Trebswell and all the rest of the gentlemen here, *that wee draw out of this towne the troops* of horse and foote of Your Majesty's Guards and joyne them with the Militia. I shall have heere about 1000 foote in the Towne, which will be sufficient for the defence of it, besides that we have reason to conclude theyre rising will be in the west parts, and soe being drawne together in the fields, wee shall bee in a greater readinesse to fall upon them. Collonell could not last night remember who it was that Colonel Chaytor designed in his letter for the man that has given him this intelligence, but this day he tells me it was Colonel Smithson, which makes us more confident of the truth of it, hee being the man in these parts of the greatest

credit among them. Your Majesty may be pleased
to keepe his name private, for hee may be of more
use to Your Majesty than any man in this country,
if I can but engage him to deal truly with us.

I could wish Your Majesty would be pleased
to make me a commission for Raysing a Regiment
of Horse, which I promise not to make use of,
except there be occasion, and when I am sure it
would be for Your Majesty's service that as many
men as could be raysed. I am sure it would be a
great encouragement to a greate manie gentlemen
that are very zealous in Your Majesty's service, and
the sooner we could get into armes the better. I
give Your Majesty the trouble of reading this
tedious letter, having the fortune to have soe many
about Your Majesty that I know will censure
everything I doe, that I am resolved to make
Your Majesty yourselfe the judge of my actions
and the director of them, and I hope Your Majesty
will have the justice to protect mee from the mallice
of my ill-wishers, since I have noe ambition in this
world but to serve your Majesty to the utmost of
my power, and to approve myself, etc., etc.

To this letter Charles ordered Arlington to
reply, acknowledging the Duke's "exceeding care
in his service," but refusing to grant him permission
to raise a regiment of horse. Arlington did not
forget to include in his despatch the latest bulletin
of the Queen, Catherine of Braganza's illness. He
must have known that it was of special interest
to Buckingham, who had completely identified
himself with the party inimical to the Duke of
York, whose hopes centred on the childlessness of
that poor lady.

The Duke's business-like epistle proves that he
could on occasion throw off the indolence which, far

more than the "mallice of his ill-wishers" impeded his ambitions. Buckingham was not over-scrupulous. He was ready at this crisis to make use of Major Greathead or Smithson, but common-sense alone would have forbidden him to foment rebellion in order to destroy possible malcontents. Moreover, his long residence at Nun Appleton had taught him to appreciate the sterling virtues of the Yorkshire Nonconformists. He made no secret of his admiration for them, and much of his unpopularity with the Church Party is to be referred to his strenuous advocacy of the claims of the dissenters. Amongst his constant correspondents was William Penn, the Quaker. When their intimacy provoked comment, the latter replied: "My only business with him ever was to make his superior quality and sense useful to this poor kingdom, that he might not die under the guilt of misspending the greatest talents that were among the nobility of my country."[1]

On October the 17th, Arlington wrote again to Buckingham, saying that there was no sign of a rising in the South, and that if there was any recrudescence of trouble in Yorks, "His Majesty bids me encourage you to be very severe with the beginners, and to be confident that you shall be avowed therein, which he saith is all the directions he can give you, till he hears more from you. . . ." Again, on 20th October, Arlington is commissioned to desire, "that Your Grace should proceed, with the assistance of the High Sheriff and Deputy lieytenants, to cause strict examination to be made of all persons whom you know or suspect to be

---

[1] *Belfast Mag.*, 1812, viii. p. 8, quoted in note to Burton's "Parliamentary Diary," vol. viii. p. 48.

guilty or contributing to the intended rising, that they may be punished by such ordinary or extraordinary course of law as His Majesty shall appoint and they shall appear to have deserved: the originals of which examinations, Your Grace may please to be sent hither by an express, or Copies of them, if they come by the ordinary Post."

When the papers reached Whitehall, Arlington was forced to confess that "most of them related only to what they (the conspirators) said to one another, without being able to give accompt of the bottom and source of this design." Apparently, he judged that more could be extracted from the delinquents by the Council in London, for he ordered several to be sent there under a good escort, and with proper precautions to prevent their having any communication one with another. A certain Mr Walters, who had shown willingness to turn King's evidence, was to be reserved for His Majesty's particular enquiry. Meanwhile, in the hope of a full pardon—for which the Duke had evidently pleaded—Walters was to be urged "to be more ingenuous and more particular than he had been," and Buckingham was assured "that great care should be taken that Your Grace's word be not violated"—not, perhaps, an unnecessary pledge to a man whose acquaintance with the standard of honour at Charles's Court made him profoundly distrustful of vague promises. Moreover, to allay any irritation the Duke might exhibit at the prisoner's removal from his jurisdiction, Arlington reiterates the King's "entire and perfect satisfaction in your carriage and management of this whole matter, of which he promises speedily to give you a particular assurance under his own hand."

The Northern crisis was short-lived, since this letter of Arlington's, dated the 24th of October, closes the series. The Lord Lieutenant's prompt action had, probably, discouraged any further insurrectionary attempts. Nevertheless the plot cannot have been widely extended, since the tryst at Farnley Wood was the conspirators' first and last effort to carry out their complicated and spirited designs. But the public were not easily reassured, and for some time there were recurrent alarms that the disbanded army would attempt another rising.[1] Terror invariably leads to cruelty. All the prisons in the North were so full that it was thought necessary to send down four or five judges to Yorkshire, with a commission of oyer and terminer, specially to examine the whole matter. Material for a miniature edition of the Bloody Assize was evidently not wanting. Happily, Charles differed as much in character from James as the Duke of Buckingham from Colonel Kirke. The Merry Monarch was soon so "wearied with continual discourse of plots and insinuations, he resolved he would give no more countenance to any such information." This was a determination which Buckingham must have hailed with all the greater joy that the one man whom he specially venerated had broken through his rule of silence to plead the cause of the sufferers. Lord Fairfax's letter deserves to be given at length, as characteristic of the man.

My Lord,—When I understood from my cousin

[1] "Life of Clarendon," 1827 ed., vol. ii. p. 280.

General Fairfax.

Brian Fairfax of dangerous designs now in acting,[1] I could not satisfy myself in hope they were but rumours, but should have waited on your Lordship personally, to express a duty every one owes to the King and his country at such a time; but not able to, for want of health, I can pray only for a good success in finding out those that are the cause of these troubles and wish I could contribute anything by my advice in it. But, I hope when you have taken a view of the forces, and put such officers over them, whose discretion and moderation will more sweeten than exasperate the spirits of men and find out the real offenders, rather than suppose them, these distempers will soon blow over, and bring those offenders to light, which now escape away clear under the shadow of some innocent but suspected criminals. There cannot be too much care, I confess, in preventing these mischiefs; and I know nothing will do it better than to have discreet and sober officers; as they are likest to do their own duties, so no honest and sober man but will be ready to do his in giving intelligence, advice and assistance to them on all occasions, when those destroy unity by keeping up distinctions, which both the King and the Parliament, in great wisdom, have thought fit to bury in oblivion, and this I doubt not hath caused many to seem enemies which are real friends. But I shall plead for no man, but leave such to clear their own integrity, which, if they do, your Lordship will do a great act of justice, service to his Majesty, and honour to yourself, not to let them be destroyed and ruined by some men's private passions, under colour of doing public service. Your Lordship may be a good instrument in accommodating many things by your presence here, which your own observations will best direct you in; and though I had not a

[1] "Memorials of the Civil War," vol. ii. p. 221.

talent, I could not withhold my mite from offering it for the peace of my country ; and that your lordship might be a happy instrument of it, is the desire of, my lord, your Grace's most affectionate and humble servant,

THOMAS FAIRFAX.

14*th October*, 1663.

The far more terrible retributions of subsequent years have obliterated the recollection of the Farnley Wood Rising. Yet Fairfax's mite was not uncalled for, since seventeen or eighteen rebels were executed.[1] While some were reprieved, very many were left in prison—a terrible fate, when one remembers the condition of the gaols at that period —to be tried at the next assize.

[1] " Life of Clarendon," vol. ii. p. 415.

CHAPTER VI

BUCKINGHAM AT COURT

THE labours of his Northern administration did not engross the Duke of Buckingham to the exclusion of other interests, and during the next few years he was much at Court. He was aware that, while Clarendon and Ormond were supreme, he himself could never attain to power, and that the sole method of undermining their influence was by making himself indispensable to the pleasure-loving King. This he speedily compassed, for, when he chose, George Villiers was irresistible. It is true that his relations with Lady Castlemaine soon became somewhat strained, but thanks to his boundless versatility he was generally able to dispense with her good graces. "The Lady" could make and unmake Ministers, but an ungovernable temper and an errant fancy caused many a breach between her and the debonair monarch. Indeed, a good judge declared that if the beautiful Miss Stuart, the most formidable of her rivals, had "been possessed of tact, she might have become as absolute a mistress over the King's conduct as over his heart."[1] This was a fine opportunity for those who had experience and ambition. The Duke of Buckingham formed the design of

---

[1] "Memoirs" of Count Grammont, p. 141.

"governing" her, in order to ingratiate himself with the King. "God knows," says Grammont, "what a Governor he would have been, and what a head he was possessed of to guide another; however, he was the properest man in the world to insinuate himself with Miss Stuart; she was childish in her behaviour, and laughed at every thing, and her taste for frivolous amusements, though unaffected, was only allowable in a girl about twelve or thirteen years old."

It was as easy to Buckingham to accommodate himself to these trivial pastimes, as to discourse on statesmanship with Fairfax, or on literature with Cowley. Like the lover in the poem, Frances Stuart might command him anything, and that task became apparently the aim and object of his existence. For her, he constructed, tier on tier, the card-castles which were her special delight; for her, he elaborated the most unheard-of tales; for her, he composed songs which he set to music. In short, never was there such a master of the revels, and it is small wonder that he soon became absolutely indispensable to her, and that if he failed to attend the King to her apartments, she sent all over the town to seek him. Unfit as Grammont judged Buckingham for the post of mentor to the beauty, it is possible that the course of English History might have been different had he remained on the same terms with her. Neither Lord Clarendon nor Lady Castlemaine would so long have enjoyed their different offices and the childless Queen might well have been forced to exchange the throne for the convent.

But, as usual, the Duke's heart refused to

acquiesce in the decisions of his brain. It was impossible for so impressionable a mortal to enjoy the close intimacy of "la belle Stuart" with impunity. He fell in love with her, declared his passion, was severely repulsed, and forthwith abandoned his designs. And, left to her own devices, Frances Stuart preferred the estate of matrimony with the Duke of Richmond, to the precarious glories offered her by the King.

Under the second Charles, Whitehall was said to be as much governed by players and singers as the Escurial by priests and dwarfs. The prevailing fashion was not one to displease George Villiers, for he was no less in his element in the green-room than in Miss Stuart's boudoir. In 1661 he brought out a play—*The Chances*—adapted from Beaumont and Fletcher, a piece with which Mr Pepys was well pleased, when he saw it performed some years later at the King's House, though he may have been prejudiced by the fact that it was his favourite, Mrs Knipp, who "sang very properly and admirably" the air, "All night I weepe."[1]

The Duke of Buckingham was not, however, dependent on theatrical society for his entertainment. The two most noted wits of the time, John Wilmot, Earl of Rochester, and Charles Sackville, Lord Buckhurst, afterwards Duke of Dorset, were his constant companions. Rochester, whose fame has survived that of his brilliant compeers, was not the least curious personality of the day. His career was a round of impish depravity, till the madcap poet, with the face of a St Sebastian

[1] Pepys, vol. vi. p. 162.

and the vocabulary of a fish-fag, died like a saint in the arms of a Broad Church bishop.

Buckhurst, "the best good man with the worst-natured muse," was made of different stuff. Indeed it is difficult to imagine a greater contrast than their several portraits. We see Wilmot negligently wrapped in a scarlet roquelaure, to all appearance the incarnation of pensive grace and aristocratic refinement; while Dorset beams on us in full Court panoply, rubicund, portly, with a stolid face, in which a pair of roguish eyes alone give promise of the mordant sayings, which made his pen so formidable.

Of the two it was, however, Rochester who generally shared Buckingham's adventures. Like George Villiers, Wilmot once assumed the disguise of an Italian mountebank, and, hid in Tower Street, drove a flourishing trade in quack medicines. Other frolics brought him into contact not only with the Law, but with the good-natured Monarch. In 1665 he was sent to the Tower for abducting Mrs Mallett, "the great beauty and fortune of the North." And his scandalous libels, which did not spare the King's Sacred Majesty, not infrequently led to his exile from Court.

All readers of Count Grammont will remember the many anecdotes he tells of the mad pranks perpetrated by the libertine Duke and Earl.

The following tale, however, from St Evrémond, is probably less well-known, and it is not uninstructive as illustrating the moral obliquity of an age in which wanton wickedness was regarded as a fitting pastime for fine gentlemen.

Burnet tells us that, for some years, Rochester

was never sober. But even that miserable excuse cannot be pleaded for Buckingham, and it is indeed difficult to picture a society in which men of such frank immorality were the actual and responsible governors of England.

According, then, to St Evrémond, it occurred to Buckingham and Rochester, during one of their periodical exiles from Court, that it would be a new, and possibly an amusing experience, to take an inn and instal themselves there as hosts. Such a tavern presented itself in the Newmarket Road, and the two scapegraces had no difficulty in acquiring the goodwill of the establishment. In spite of their slender acquaintance with the duties of their new estate, it cannot be said that the custom of the hostelry declined. Indeed, it could hardly be otherwise, as any man who could claim a female relative, with any pretension to beauty, was warmly welcomed at the ducal bar, and royally feasted for next to nothing.

Out of the entire population of the hamlet, however, one damsel alone retained, as well as excited the interest of the friends, and her merits were probably enhanced by the fact that it was next to impossible to come to speech with the lady.

"Phyllis" was the wife of a venerable Puritan, who guarded her youth and loveliness with the same elaborate precautions he exercised on behalf of his beloved and well-garnished strong-box. He was fortunate enough to have found an ideal duenna in the person of his crabbed old sister; and when at rare intervals the good cheer and genial fellowship of the tavern enticed him from home, he felt that he could safely confide both his treasures to her keeping.

But love, or its counterfeit, laughs at locksmiths. Wilmot's sedulous enquiries soon revealed the vulnerable point in the seemingly impregnable fortress. Like her prototype, Cerberus, the sister possessed one weakness—only in her case it was the bottle and not honey-cake.

One fine night, therefore, when the "old miser" was safe at the inn enjoying Buckingham's hospitality, Wilmot, duly provided with the necessary flask of strong waters—which for greater security was drugged—presented himself at his lady-love's door. He had assumed for the occasion, a part made easy by his girlish face and form, the costume of a peasant wench, and with diabolical cunning strove to gain entrance into the well-guarded mansion by simulating a fainting fit at the door.

As he had reckoned, even the dour matron was not insensible to the pleadings of charity. The bolts were speedily withdrawn and the deceiver admitted. Once within, the fatal cordial was produced, and before long, to all intents and purposes, the young lord was enjoying a *tête-à-tête* with the pretty Puritan.

Phyllis did not prove cruel. In fact, the pair were soon on the best of terms, and Rochester readily assented when she begged him to "deliver her from this prison of a place where diversion and comfort were alike denied her." Moreover, as the plucking of "a very Harpagon of Puritans" was a sport that eminently appealed to a fine gentleman's sense of humour, he looked on benignly while the emancipated fair one helped herself to the guineas from her husband's store. Hand in hand, they then left the cottage, narrowly escaping an encounter with the outraged spouse. At the tavern, a council of war was held, and it was decided that Phyllis should go to London, where, being unknown, and with her "dowry" greatly increased by their munificence, the noble patrons held that she would have no difficulty in securing a new partner.

Meanwhile the goodman, "that wretched detestable miser, when he reached home to find the doors wide, his sister a-snoring, his wife eloped and his gold vanished, was overcome by so great a despair that having raved all night, in the morning he went and hanged himself."[1]

The farce being thus played out, the ingenious noblemen hastened off to Newmarket, where the account they gave of their frolic caused so much amusement that they were straightway reinstated in the Sovereign's good graces. Such were the tales that charmed not only the Merry Monarch and his courtiers, but the greatest ladies in the land, when Charles was King.

Seven years had elapsed since Buckingham's marriage, and still no children had come to grace his union with Mary Fairfax. According to the patent granted by James I. to his favourite Steenie, Mary, Duchess of Richmond, held the reversion of her brother's honours. The estates, however, were unentailed, and much curiosity existed as to the Duke's disposition of them. During the Commonwealth, the Duchess of Richmond lost her only boy, and she now betrothed her sole

---

[1] *Revue des deux Mondes,* Aug.-Sept. 1657. "John Wilmot, Comte de Rochester," par. M. E. D. Farques, p. 85.

surviving child, Lady Mary, to Richard, Earl of Arran, son of the Duke of Ormond. Buckingham, who had never been on cordial terms with the head of the house of Butler, did not conceal his dislike of the match. But since he was not associated with his sister in the guardianship of his niece, he had no excuse for interference.

Young and beautiful as she still was, none of her contemporaries anticipated that the Duchess of Richmond would long remain single. Rumour, indeed, had betrothed her to Prince Rupert, but the gossips proved as much at fault as when in her infancy they bestowed her on the elder Prince Palatine, Charles Louis. Twice had Mary Villiers married at her family's bidding. In her choice of a third husband she was entirely swayed by her personal inclination. The bridegroom elect, Thomas Howard, was a younger brother of that stirring politician, the Earl of Carlisle. But while the Earl had been a trusted counsellor of Cromwell, Thomas Howard himself was body and soul with the Royalist faction—the social conditions at the Hague being far more to his liking than the austere atmosphere of the Protector's Court. Thomas Howard did not trouble himself with statecraft, but he was noted as an ardent squire of dames. His desperate encounter with Harry Jermyn, when that young gallant interfered with his courtship of Lady Shrewsbury, caused no slight stir at the time. Such a reputation, however, had nothing alarming to Mary Villiers, who, if tradition is to be believed, had herself fought a duel with a female rival. And though the world marvelled that the Dowager-Duchess should bestow herself on so inconsiderable a personage as "northern Tom Howard," yet it was evident that they were "the fondest couple that can be.[1] The Duke of Buckingham, however, was mightily troubled at the match." Nor was he better pleased when the Duke of Ormond sent him a polite request to settle his estates on the new Lady Arran.

For once, Buckingham had public opinion with him in his contention that if his sister had a son, it would only be reasonable that as this child must succeed to the Dukedom, the Villiers estates should also be his; and the world considered that Lord Arran deserved no pity, since he received £20,000 dowry with a "high-born pritty lady." Unfortunately, as the following letter shows, indiscreet friends were not lacking to widen the breach between the two Dukes, and much of their subsequent enmity was probably caused by the quarrels which took place over Lady Arran's settlement.

My Lord,—I received yours of the 10th of this month, but since my returne to the Fleete,[2] otherwise I should have wayted upon your Grace when I was last in towne to give you myself this answer. First that I wonder very much at the discourse George Porter had with you, since though it had beene all true with you upon his owne knowledge, meethinks hee might have forborne the speaking of it. That I did once make a settlement very much to the advantage of my niece and my lorde her husband, hee did know, but whether I have altered it since I conceive hee does not know, neither doe I thinke myselfe oblidged to give him

[1] "Hatton Correspondence" (Camden Soc.), vol. i. p. 42. Sir Charles Lyttleton to Lady Hatton, 26th Nov. 1664.
[2] Carte, MSS. 34, fol. 160. 26th April, 1665.

or anybody else an account of it. What guesses hee may make either of your Lordship's behaviour to me or my sense of it, I cannot tell; perhaps his kindnesse may make him judge more in my favour than I doe myselfe; for I have beene myselfe soe long accustomed to be ill-used, that I may very well begin to thinke I deserve noe better; and that it is high time for mee to leave off the pursuite of those things I have had soe little success in to looke after the repairing of my owne private fortune. This humble opinion I have of myselfe hinders mee from making any complaints only I shall assure your Grace, that my professions and kindnesse to you were soe reall, that if it layed in my power to doe you service, I should not have left a possibility for you or the world to doubt of my being, My Lord,—Your Grace's Most faithful and obedient servant,

BUCKINGHAM.

Doubtless, much of the discontent apparent in this letter must be attributed to Buckingham's recent experiences. Having assisted at the Council,[1] where the Declaration of War with Holland was drafted, he had instantly volunteered for active service, and requested the command of a ship. All nominations were, however, in the gift of the Duke of York, who never missed an occasion of mortifying Buckingham. The Duke's petition was consequently rejected; James refused to entrust a man-o'-war to a gentleman who, however distinguished by birth, had no experience of naval matters—a doctrine of undeniable soundness, though somewhat opposed to the practice of the seventeenth century. Nothing daunted, the Duke determined "to go as a volun-

[1] 22nd Feb. 1665.

teer, and put himself on board a flagship, the captain whereof was in his favour.¹ Once there, he desired that in respect to his quality and his being a Privy Councillor he might be present in all Councils of War." James replied that he did not consider this reasonable, and that he would not make a fresh precedent in his favour. The fact that George Villiers had frequently amused the King by mimicking ² eminent members of the Council at Whitehall, probably strengthened James's resolution to exclude Buckingham from the Naval Board. He was quite determined not to allow himself to be made ridiculous, and welcomed the opportunity of wiping out the long score of grievances which he and his father-in-law cherished against the waggish Duke.

Yet so unpopular was James, that public opinion would quickly have veered round to the injured nobleman, had that worthy maintained a calm and dignified attitude. Even Lord Peterborough, a staunch partisan of the heir-presumptive, was inclined to think Buckingham ill-used. And the Duke's friends placed his contention on a sound basis in "fixing his pretence not upon a Peerage, but his being a Privy Councillor."³ Unfortunately, calm and patience were not reckoned amongst Buckingham's qualities. Instead of remaining at his elected post on the flagship, he rushed back to Whitehall to see what his persuasive tongue would effect with the Merry Monarch. James had, however, too often suffered from Buckingham's personal

---

¹ "Life of Clarendon," 1727 ed., vol. ii. p. 356.
² Clarendon, p. 342.
³ Dom. State Cal., Charles II., vol. xiv. p. 54. Letter to Lord Peterborough, 16th April, 1665.

ascendency over his facile brother, not to realise that if they met, his judgment stood in danger of being reversed. He took his precautions accordingly, and promptly despatched Harry Killigrew to the Court with letters. Killigrew made such haste that he arrived six hours in advance of the Duke, and Charles had thus ample time to weigh matters before being subjected to his favourite's influence. Consequently, when the latter made his appearance, he was informed that the King perceived that it would be an affront to the Lord High Admiral to override his action, and that Buckingham must owe his advancement—if any—to His Royal Highness.

Buckingham's eloquence being ineffectual, he had no alternative but to return to the Fleet, where he set to work to justify what previously had seemed an unjust and harsh decision on James's part. Lord Peterborough, for instance, writes: "Buckingham's fickleness and uncertainty (for those are the epithets of such as would favour him), gives scandal to every sober thing. He has quitted his ship, sent back his goods, and abandoned to shift several gentlemen (who) came with him, and because of the appearance of her strength and the goodnesse of her defence thrust himself aboard the *Earl of Sandwich* as a private volunteer to the disturbance of that shipp and the dislike of everyone."[1]

On June the 3rd, the battle of the campaign was fought off Lowestoft, but there is no record that Buckingham took any part in this great British victory. In 1666, however, he joined the Duke of Albemarle, and was present at the

[1] Dom. State Cal., Charles II., vol. xiv. p. 95. On board the *Unicorn*, 20th April.

protracted engagement of 1st-3rd June. Never was action more hotly disputed. Since 1665 the Dutch had acquired the assistance of Louis XIV., and it was in pursuit of an imaginary French Squadron that Prince Rupert, with twenty sail, became separated from Monk. Moreover, Albemarle, misled by false reports, and believing de Ruyter and de Witt to be still in Holland, was utterly unprepared when he sighted the enemy's fleet, eighty strong, anchored off the North Foreland.

Surprised, and knowing himself to be numerically inferior, he yet insisted on attacking the Dutchmen. The resolution was foolhardy, and outnumbered and outmanœuvred, it was his bull-dog courage alone that saved the English from annihilation. At the critical moment, indeed, he vowed that, come what might, he at least would never fall alive into the hands of the enemy, or, as Dryden phrases his speech:

> "Yet like an English General will I die,
> And all the ocean make my spacious grave;
> Women and cowards on the land may lie;
> The sea's a tomb that's proper for the brave."[1]

Buckingham, who noticed that, as he uttered these words, he had slipped a loaded pistol into his pocket, was convinced that, sooner than surrender, Monk intended to blow up the ship. Such quixotic resolutions hardly commended themselves to George Villiers, and in his usual flippant style the young Duke announced that he and the other gentlemen on the flagship had formed the "agreable counterplot" of anticipating his action by throwing their

[1] Dryden, *Annus Mirabilis*, Works, vol. ix. p. 122.

Admiral overboard. Happily, at the end of the third day, when matters appeared desperate, Prince Rupert's fleet hove in sight, a circumstance which not only saved the situation, but averted the threatened mutiny.[1] The next morning a thick mist parted the belligerents, who severally repaired home to make good their losses.

On June the 25th, the fleet was once more able to put to sea. Buckingham must, however, have had his glut of fighting, for the next notice we obtain of him is in York, discharging, the duties of his office.

No one acquainted with the country towns of England can have failed to notice the number of handsome old houses that adorn their alleys and Cathedral Closes. Even now, when converted into shops, warehouses, taverns or dissenting chapels they still retain many a trace of their original condition. Exquisite ceilings, heraldic scutcheons on chimney-piece or panelling, shallow oak-stair cases vividly conjure up for us a time when the world was younger and more picturesque. The fact is that when a journey to London was an epoch-making event, a country squire's madam could not dispense with her house in the borough town. Here she attended the assemblies and married her daughters. Here her lord visited the markets and regulated both justice and opinion. Nor were such mansions limited to the smaller gentry of the neighbourhood; great magnates, to whom attendance at Court was a primary duty of life, also passed some portion of the year in the High Street of their local town. Few, however, were so fortunate as

[1] Guizot's "Monk," p. 181.

George Villiers, for, from all accounts, Fairfax House at York was not the least valuable portion of his wife's heritage. An Elizabethan mansion, it occupied by far the best situation in the town, "in the Micklegate[1] with a noble ascent to it, out of Skeldergate and gardens extending to the ramparts of the city walls beyond." From his correspondence with the municipality of York, the Duke seems to have been as eager to enlarge this fine domain as he was in later days to beautify Cliveden or rebuild York house. One addition, however, he might have spared. He erected a laboratory in the grounds where, "if he did not find out the philosopher's stone, he knew a way of dissolving or evaporating gold and other metals quicker than any other man of that age."[2]

Nevertheless, all his researches were not barren. In 1663, he took out a patent for extracting glass and crystals from flint, and, with an energy worthy of a member of the Royal Society, he founded a manufactory at Lambeth, for which he imported Venetian workmen.

In 1676, Mr Evelyn visited this establishment, and highly praises the wares produced there. He was evidently delighted with "the huge vases of metall as cleare, ponderous, and thicke as crystal; also looking-glasses far larger and better than any that come from Venice."[3]

During his stay at York, Buckingham did not confine himself to building laboratories. He also

---

[1] "History and Antiquities of the City of York," by Francis Drake, ed. 1736, p. 269.
[2] *Idem.*
[3] Evelyn's Diary, vol. ii. p. 322, 19th September, 1676.

caused a wooden turret to be erected on the Cathedral steeple with side lights to alarm the country, in case the Hollanders or French should attempt to land upon our coasts.[1] Nor was this the only provision he made for such occurrences. He issued a warrant to the chief constables to watch the beacons, and ordered that on their firing, every man between sixteen and sixty was to appear, with such weapons as he possessed, at the rendezvous fixed in the various hundreds, and to place himself at the disposal of the Deputy-lieutenants.

Mercifully this *levée en masse* proved unnecessary, though Buckingham's next step, the enlisting of a regiment, was warmly applauded. The response to his appeal was highly satisfactory, and Reresby tells us that before the month was out, a full troop answered to the roll-call: "All of them gentlemen and old soldiers, being in number eighty, besides officers, and the servants that belonged to the troop being as many as their masters."[2] The Duke's liberality seems to have been great, deserving the favourable comments of Mr Secretary Williamson's anonymous correspondent, who remarks:

"The prudent managery of His Majesty's affairs heare by His Grace the Duke of Buckingham, hath soe prevailed upon all sorts of persons in this country and city that they shew an inexpresible redinesse and willingnesse to serve His Majesty and the Kingdome under His Grace commande when there shall be occation. His Grace mustered

---

[1] Drake, p. 487.
[2] Sir J. Reresby, "Memoirs," p. 6.

his troop on Wednesday last; which appeared in a very great and good equipage; ther was so many came in hopes to be listed that they very much outnumbered those he entertained, whom he kindly dismissed with a reward of 10s. 6d. a man to defray the charge of their journey."[1]

Amongst the gentlemen congregated at York, was one destined to play a notable part in English History; and it was while drilling their volunteers that Sir George Savile, the future Marquess of Halifax, and George Villiers became acquainted.

A superficial resemblance between the two men, in reality, masked a profound difference of character. Like the Duke, Sir George belonged to a loyalist family, and during his childhood had known the miseries incident to civil war. But happier than Buckingham, he had been spared the degrading shifts of exile, and had grown to manhood amongst his own folk, on his own lands, at beautiful Rufford.

The future King-maker was now thirty-three. Never was there a more loyal friend, a kinder father; while Buckingham himself could not surpass the ready wit, the delicate satire, which made him the brightest, the most delightful of companions. Savile's political tracts rank amongst our classics, and their matchless style makes it a matter of no little regret that we only possess fragments of the great trimmer's speeches. His keen intellect impatiently rejected many of the shibboleths of the day. "He hoped," he said, "that God would not lay it to his charge if he could not digest iron like an ostrich." It would seem that his

[1] Dom. State Cal. to Sec. Williamson, vol. 164. No 24. 21st July 1666.

creeds and his statesmanship were, in truth, reflections of his humane and tender spirit. He was as irresistibly impelled to plead for mercy to his opponents, as to denounce the ruthless doctrine of eternal punishment. It was this attitude which made him well-nigh incomprehensible to the mass of his contemporaries, who perpetually reproached him with being shifty and untrustworthy. Yet no one had, eventually, a larger share in the shaping of England's destinies; and no character, of all that stormy period, has passed through Time's ordeal with a purer and nobler fame than the Great Marquess of Halifax.

In 1666, however, Sir George Savile was merely a promising young country gentleman, and his association with Buckingham was his first introduction to active politics. But their common detestation of the Chancellor's policy formed a bond of union between them, and, henceforward, the two men were much together during the manœuvres, and exchanged various good offices. The Lord-Lieutenant furnished the new recruit with pistols and holsters for his accoutrements, and Savile agreed to act as his second when a duel with Lord Fauconberg appeared imminent.

However assiduous Buckingham showed himself in discharging his duties—and at this juncture he regularly, thrice a week, exercised his troop himself — he had still ample leisure for other occupations. Much of this time he dedicated to music, a taste in which he was not singular; for never was that art more popular than at this period. Many will remember how Mr Pepys remarked, during the Fire of London, that "hardly a lighter or boat that had the goods of a house in, but there was a pair of virginalls in it." The great provincial towns were no whit behind the capital in their enthusiasm. "All the officers at York loved music so well, that the Duke had a set of violins, Sir H. Bellasis another, and Reresby, also, had three musicians that played very well, one on the violin, one on the hautboy, and one on the bass viol."[1]

Thus there was no lack of polite diversions to offer Lady Shrewsbury when George Villiers' evil star led her to York. In an age of scandalous depravity, Anna Maria Brudenell, Countess of Shrewsbury, achieved an evil pre-eminence. Reared amidst the turbulence of civil factions, she had imbibed none of that wholesome terror of the law, which often curbs the impulses of the conscienceless; while, though born and bred a Roman Catholic, no ghostly menace, no dread of death and judgment, could check the primeval vigour of her natural instincts. Even in that coarse and blood-stained time, she seems an anachronism, and we seek her fellows rather in the Rome of the Cæsars than in the Court of the laughter-loving Charles.

As a rule, the portraits of that day afford none of the clues to character, so frequently found in the work of Great Masters. Kneller's Duchess of Cleveland was long mistaken for Rachel, Lady Russell; and, seen through Lely's medium, the virtuous Mary of Modena might well be twin-sister to Nell Gwyn. Yet Lely, who had inherited

[1] Sir J. Reresby, "Memoirs," p. 6.

many of Vandyck's traditions, occasionally emancipated himself from the trammels of his own making. The picture he has left us of Lady Shrewsbury (now in Mr Astor's possession at Cliveden) is one of these happy exceptions. The usual frippery of costume, the hackneyed background are discarded. The lithe figure, draped in the green satin, so dear to Venetian artists, has undoubtedly a certain panther-like grace. The heavy-lidded eyes have a haunting fascination. There is a suggestion of mystery about the brows. According to our modern ideals, Lady Shrewsbury was not beautiful, but, at the same time, she is so little commonplace that it is difficult—having once seen her—to banish the image from the mind.

Truly, "many strong men have been slain by her. Her house is the way to hell, going down to the chambers of death."

In 1666, Lord Cardigan's daughter had already been married some years, and Francis, Lord Shrewsbury, the eleventh Earl of his illustrious race, had hitherto mainly earned distinction as the most long-suffering of husbands. Not even the prodigious sensation created by his wife's amours with Thomas Howard, Harry Jermyn and Harry Killigrew, could rouse him to vindicate his marital authority, and as he appeared contented to be numbered amongst the imperious lady's train of humble adorers, an astonished world concluded that he would always remain quiescent.

Spacious as was Fairfax House, it proved inadequate for the reception of Lord and Lady Shrewsbury, her parents, Lord and Lady Cardigan, and their respective retinues. The Duke, conse-

Lady Shrewsbury.

quently, hired my Lord Irwin's house, where for a whole month he entertained this great company at vast expense.[1] "The days," says Reresby, "were spent in visits and play, and all sorts of diversion that place could afford, and the nights in dancing, sometimes till day the next morning, only the two Earls, not being men for these sports, went to bed something early. . . . The Duchess of Buckingham, good woman, perceived nothing at that time of the intrigue that was carrying on between her husband and the Countess of Shrewsbury. . . . This design (or rather practice) was not, however, concealed to all people, for my Lord Brudenell, brother to the Countess, told me over a bottle of wine, that coming hastily through the dining-room the evening before, he saw two tall persons together, and he thought they looked like the Duke and his sister, but he would not be too inquisitive for fear it should prove so. And one night my Lord Brudenell was sent for from the tavern very late, to his sister's chambers to her and my Lord Shrewsbury's friends, they having had a great quarrel of jealousy concerning the Duke, and yet the Countess had so great a power over her lord, that he stayed some time after that." In the midst of these revels arrived the news of the Great Fire of London. The Duke instantly repaired to the King, but the letter he addressed to his Deputy-lieutenants in Yorkshire, gives a vivid picture of the sensational and alarming rumours which must have materially increased the horror of the situation.

[1] Sir J. Reresby, "Memoirs," p. 6.

WORKSOP, 6*th September*, 1666.

GENTLEMEN,—A servant of my owne is sent to me from London to lett mee know, that in all probability before I cowld receive the letter the whole citty of London within the walls would bee in ashes. This messenger tolde mee that before hee came away, hee saw all Cheapside and Pawls Church on fire. Theams Streete and all that part of the Towne had beene burnt before. Since that, another man is come from London that assures mee Holborne is allso sett on fire, and that aboute threescore frensh and dutch are taken, that were firing of howses; besids this weeke, the posts are stopt, which must either proceed from the burning of the Post Office, or from some insurrection in those parts, it being almost impossible that a thing of this nature cowld bee effected without a farther designe. I am going myselfe imediately to His Majesty, as my duty obliges mee, in the meantime I have sent this to lett you know the state of our affaires, and in case you receive no letters from London at the time that you ought to receive them, by the poste on Saturday night next, that you imediatly summon all the Militia under my command to bee in armes with all the speed imaginable, and to keepe them together till further order from mee or from His Majesty. If I find upon my way to London, or when I am there, reason to alter this order, I shall dispatch one imediatly to you about it, in the meantime I desire you to acquaint the Lords and Deputy Liftenants of the East and North Ryding of Yorkshire with what orders I have sent you, and I doe not doubt but they will follow your example,—I am, Gentlemen, Your most affectionate friend and servant,

BUCKINGHAM.

Since the writing of this letter a Gentleman is

come from London that assures mee almost all the Strand is burnt, and that a great many Anabaptists have been taken setting howses on fire, as well as frensh and Dutch.[1]

The Duke had long watched for an opportunity to attack Ormond and Clarendon. It was therefore with delight that he hailed the turn of affairs at the end of the year. Ireland, then as always, furnished abundant matter for dispute and lamentation. Yet, under the honest old Duke of Ormond's administration, the distressful country was showing signs of reviving prosperity. Her fertile pastures were no mean compensation for her absence of mineral wealth, while industrial England furnished a ready market for the supply of cheap beef and mutton, which she increasingly despatched across the Irish Channel.

But, unfortunately, the thriving cattle trade speedily aroused the ever-watchful jealousy of the English landlords and farmers. With the logic peculiar to their class, they did not fail to attribute the decline in rents and prices to the fact of their being undersold by the sister country. Already, in 1663, their agitation was rewarded by the prohibition to import live beasts, for which the dead meat trade was a poor substitute. Yet, so skilfully was it handled, that in the Oxford Parliament of 1666 a Bill was brought forward by the envious landowners of England to suppress this last remaining outlet for Irish industry. Buckingham's keen intelligence, unobscured as it was by many of the prejudices of his contemporaries, should have

---

[1] C. J. Smith's "Historical and Literary Curiosities."

preserved him from endorsing the faulty economics of the agricultural party. Moreover, the sturdy Protestant settlers—pioneers of civilisation in a semi-barbarous land—were a class of the community, who generally commanded his warmest sympathy. But the Bill was opposed by the Government whom he detested, and he imagined that in the general ruin its provisions would bring upon Ireland, Ormond's fortune must needs be gravely compromised. He therefore flung himself into the promotion of the measure with an energy worthy of a better cause. Nor did he want allies. Two men, whose names were henceforward closely associated with his own—Lauderdale and Ashley, were drawn by similar considerations to Buckingham's side.

Against an opposition so ably generalled, the easy-going King, heavily weighted as he was by financial embarrassment, could not long maintain his own. Neither was the delay in granting the promised subsidies the sole cause of alarm to the impecunious Monarch. After the Cattle Bill had been sent up by a large majority to the Upper House, during the debate there, the monstrous power exercised by "the Lady" formed the subject of caustic criticism.

Before such menaces, Charles, who had hitherto shown more firmness than usual, capitulated, and instructed his adherents to accept the obnoxious Act. Nevertheless, some stormy scenes were enacted before it passed through its final stages.

Other causes were not wanting to inflame matters. On one hand, Lord Ashley's attempt in the Committee of Privilege, "to have all the Irish nobility degraded from taking any place in England"—where hitherto their rank had been recognised—naturally excited much indignation.[1] On the other, Charles's exclusion of Buckingham and Ashley from the joint committee of both Houses, charged with the investigation of the war expenditure, drew down on the Government the "violent fury of the Opposition," and the Commons passed a vote of censure on the unparliamentary conduct of the Lords, for deferring the selection of their delegates to the King.

During the eleven days that the fight over the Irish Cattle Bill raged, Buckingham astonished the Peers by his continuous attendance. Under the second Charles our ancestors were still almost as matutinal as their forbears had been under the eighth Harry. Clarendon went down to Westminster Hall very little later than his predecessor Wolsey. By nine o'clock, Mr Pepys tells us, business was in full swing at the Law Courts. To men, who, like the Duke of Ormond, were in the saddle or at their desk by six, the early sittings of the House of Lords presented no inconvenience; but to Buckingham, who "rises, eats, and goes to bed by the Julian account, long after all others that go by the new stile, and keeps the same hours with the owls and the Antipodes," —which, being interpreted, signified that occasionally he stayed in bed till eleven—the custom was no small hindrance.[2] Now, however, even Charles II. —who vowed that the House of Lords was better

---
[1] Carte's "Life of Ormond," vol. iv. p. 265.
[2] J. Butler, "Genuine Remains of Duke of Buckingham."

than any play—was not a more frequent visitor than the volatile Duke, who may have found in the many opportunities the debates offered for his "unusual and ungrave dialect," some compensation for his enforced attendance.

When the Bill reached the Committee stage the Duke remarked, "that whoever was against it had either an Irish interest or an Irish understanding." The insult was not allowed to pass unchallenged. Lord Ossory, the Duke of Ormond's eldest son, had a thousand gibes and innuendoes against his illustrious father to avenge. He would not trust himself to give an immediate answer, but desired the Duke to come into the next room with him. Here, he told Buckingham, "that he had taken the liberty to use many loose and unworthy expressions which reflected upon the whole Irish nation, and which he himself resented so much that he expected satisfaction, and to find him with his sword in his hand."[1] Different as was the code of the English Parliament, its practice was not remote from that of a Polish Diet. Buckingham had, therefore, few sympathisers in his efforts "to avoid the encounter by all the fair words and shifts he could use." He had none when, having agreed to meet Lord Ossory at Chelsea Fields, he failed to appear there, and instead of His Grace arrived Monsieur Blanquefort with a Guard and a Royal warrant to secure my Lord Ossory.

The following day the Duke addressed a personal explanation to his Peers:

"Although he did not hold himself obliged,"

[1] "Life of Clarendon," p. 714.

he said, "to fight in maintenance of anything he had said or done in the Parliament, yet that it being suitable and agreeable to his nature to fight with any man who had a mind to fight with him,[1] he appointed the place in Chelsea fields, which he understood to be the fields over against Chelsea; whither having only gone to his lodging to change his sword, he hastened, by presently crossing the water in a pair of oars, and staying there in expectation of the Lord Ossory until some gentlemen were sent to prevent his and the Lord Ossory's meeting, whom others were sure to find likewise for the same prevention. Whereupon, concluding that for the present there would be no meeting together, he returned with those gentlemen to his lodging, being always ready to give any gentleman satisfaction that should require it of him."

In reply, Lord Ossory declared that he had grounded his challenge "not on words spoken in Parliament, but for words spoken in other places, and for affronts which he had at other times chosen to bear rather than to disturb the Company."

A wrangle then ensued, in which—if we are to believe Arlington, Lord Ossory's brother-in-law, writing to the Duke of Ormond—Buckingham spoke "very ineffectually, speaking much and often upon the subject matter, but often digressing from it, by endeavouring to show it was not his fault that they had not met; this obliged my lord of Ossory to make a narrative to the House of what passed in the whole quarrel, and my lord of Buckingham pressing the House to ask him what had been

---

[1] Carte, MSS. 34, pp. 459-60. Conway to Ormond, 27th Oct.

the subject of his quarrel, said it was some sharp railleries and unhandsome reflections the Duke had made upon his relations, and called me for a witness, how often he had resented them, and resolved to fight him. I said it was most true, and that I had ever interposed to moderate him therein, having till this occasion been ever an humble servant to the Duke of Buckingham, and for proof of this, humbly besought His Royal Highness to declare whether many weeks ago, I told him I feared much a quarrel betwixt my lord of Ossory and the Duke of Buckingham, upon the occasion aforesaid; His Royal Highness frankly avowed it, and in the whole matter concerned himself, as far as fittingly he could, much for my lord of Ossory."[1]

After hearing Buckingham and Ossory, the Lords required them both to withdraw, while they discussed the grievous misdemeanour of which they had been guilty. That offence being much less injurious to character than the suspicion of evading a duel, the ridiculous spectacle was now witnessed of Buckingham's "better friends" praying that he might be as severely punished as my lord Ossory. Finally, the belligerents were summoned to the Bar. Ossory was ordered to the Tower, and Buckingham was committed to the custody of Black Rod.

A few days later both noblemen were released. But his enforced seclusion had not made the Duke more placable; for he was hardly at liberty before he involved himself in a fresh squabble. The two Houses were sitting in con-

---

[1] "Miscellanea Aulica," p. 424, 20th Oct. 1666. Lord Arlington to Duke of Ormond.

ference in the Painted Chamber, when Buckingham chose to rest his elbow on the arm of his neighbour, the Marquis of Dorchester. Lord Dorchester resented the liberty, remarking that "he ought not to crowd him so much, for he was as good a man as he."[1] "The Duke made some very smart reply, to which the Marquis returned him the Lye, upon which the Duke pulled off his periwigg." A scuffle ensued. The Marquis being considerably shorter and less active than George Villiers, vainly attempted to retaliate in the same manner. Yet, before they were separated, Dorchester could boast that if the Duke had dragged off his periwig, he in return had pulled Buckingham's hair out by the handful. This disgraceful scrimmage naturally aroused much indignation. Indeed, Clarendon remarks, "it was a greater misdemeanour than had ever happened in that place and upon such an occasion."[2] Certainly, no words are too strong to describe so wanton an outrage. Yet the Chancellor must have remembered the scene at the Council Chamber, when Philip, Earl of Pembroke and Montgomery, during an altercation with Lord Mowbray, hurled the heavy silver inkstand at the latter's head. Charles I. had, however, a higher standard of decorum than the Parliament of his successor. Lord Pembroke's fit of temper cost him his Chamberlain's wand. Whereas the two Peers were permitted to purge their offence by a few days' residence in the Tower, which they left on promising to make friends.[3]

---

[1] Echard, "History of England," vol. iii. p. 171.
[2] "Life of Clarendon," p. 719.
[3] Carte, MSS. 46, fol. 428. Lord Arlington to Ormond.

Buckingham's enlargement took place on the 22nd of December, and already by Christmas Day he had plunged anew into disgrace; for, having presented himself at Whitehall, without first observing the form of entreating the King's forgiveness, he incurred the Royal displeasure, and was forthwith banished the Court. Of contrition he showed but little, much to the disappointment of his ill-wishers, who were forced to acknowledge that "he seems not much concerned, knowing the infinite good nature in His Majesty to pardon such offences."[1]

[1] Carte, MSS. 35, fol. 26. Sir Allan Brodrick to Ormond, 12th Jan. 1666.

CHAPTER VII

BUCKINGHAM'S OUTLAWRY

In the year which opened in so inauspicious a manner for my Lord of Bucks, a worse trouble was yet in store for him. Certainly, in his case, the saying held good that a man's foes are they of his own household. Faithful Brian Fairfax loudly laments, that "though the expenses of the Duke's establishment were moderate, he had but few honest servants who never wronged him in his estate, nor flattered him in his faults."

"Beggar'd by Fools, whom still he found too late,
He had his jest, and they had his estate."

In the seventeenth century, the household of a great nobleman still formed a self-contained community; and the amazing number of retainers deemed indispensable in these semi-feudal mansions is proved by the account-books of the Somersets. Including a "master of the fish-ponds," and four squires, who day and night watched the war-horses, Henry, Lord Worcester had in his service no fewer than twenty-four gentlemen and pages of gentle birth, who, in their turn, bore rule over vast cohorts of menials.[1] And in 1666 that puissant and mighty

[1] Hist. MSS., Beaufort, 26th September, 1694, p. 3. "Memorandum of the Household of Henry, Earl of Worcester."

prince, George, Duke of Buckingham, was probably a richer and more important personage than the ancestor of the Dukes of Beaufort. Nevertheless, it must be admitted that, in point of respectability and decorum, the establishment at Raglan must always have contrasted favourably with that at Wallingford House, where Mary Fairfax had conspicuously failed to introduce the "order and good government" that prevailed at Nun Appleton. Indeed, in their degree, the Duke of Buckingham's servants appear to have been as remarkable for turbulent eccentricity as their restless master.

For instance, in 1663, "the Duke of Buckingham's servants fought a set battle in his courtyard; divers of them hurt, and the porter, it is thought, will not recover."[1] On another occasion, a page of the Duke's gave much scandal by eloping with a rich young lady of quality.

Their deaths were in harmony with their lives. In 1681, the corpse of one of these rascals was picked up in the streets of London, having undoubtedly met with his end by violent means.[2] A year later, the Duke's cook was executed for murdering the Earl of Feversham's cook. In fact, it is difficult to understand how that excellent scholar, Bishop Sprat, long the Duke's chaplain, and Abraham Cowley, "the Pindar, the Maro and the Flaccus of his age,"[3] accommodated themselves to this troublous atmosphere.

In such wild and lawless company the Duke

---

[1] Hist. MSS. 15th. Rep. App. Part VII. p. 170. 10th Aug. 1663.
[2] Narcissus Luttrell, "A Brief Relation of State Affairs," vol. i. Feb. 1681-2.
[3] Echard, vol. iii. p. 208.

himself ran some hazards. On one occasion, indeed, as Comminges tells us in a State Paper which deserves to be quoted at length, he narrowly escaped with his life.

"I do not know, and Monsieur le duc de Buckingham does not himself know, what strange whim led him to retire at 9 o'clock and to sup with Madame his wife.[1] His steward's valet, apparently an honest, faithful man, seems to have thought that as the Duke had retired thus early he would certainly be in his chamber by midnight, whereupon carrying a sword, he left his room, to the astonishment of another fellow who slept with him. The latter enquired where he was going and what he meant to do with the weapon. He answered, that he had heard a cry of 'Thief,' and that he was following the direction of the noise. He continued his journey to the Duke's chamber, thinking to find him in bed, but failing to do so, he passed on to the Duchess's apartment. At the door was a servitor, who seeing him with a naked sword in his hand, was coward enough to save his own life by flight, leaving his master in danger. With the blade still in his hand he entered. The four attendants, of whom one only was armed, instantly ran away. The Duke, who was talking with his wife by the chimney-corner, rose and asked him what he sought in such a state. He replied, 'It is thou that I seek! It is thou I will have!' At these words, the Duke seized a knife from the table and was fortunate enough to disarm him. The man was clearly raving mad, and as the Duke tried to reach the door and call a servant, the unhappy wretch essayed once more to lay hold of his master and stab him with a knife he

[1] Wheatley's "Pepysiana," p. 291. Despatches of M. de Comminges, Londres, 2nd Av. 1663.

had in his pocket. In this he would undoubtedly have been successful, had not a scream from the Duchess warned her husband in the nick of time of his fresh danger.

"From this, Monsieur, you can judge of what England is. When I reflect that this land produces neither wolves nor venomous beasts, I am not surprised. The inhabitants are far more wicked and more dangerous than these vermin, and if one had to guard against every possible ill that might befall, it were better to leave the country forthwith."

The "unhappy wretch" was doubtless a certain Abraham Goodman. Mad he evidently was. After his attack on George Villiers he was committed to the Tower, whence he addressed the following appeal to his former Master:[1]—

"It is my hard hap to be held a prisoner by Your Grace's command for attempting to murder Your Grace, which I call God to witness for me that I had not such intent in me neither by the persuasion of any other person. But, only what I did was to inform Your Grace I was hated by your servants for being so strict of my charge committed to me, and if through ignorance I have offended Your Grace, I hope Your Grace will forgive me."

Naturally enough, Abraham Goodman's petition was not granted. Nor can we blame George Villiers for refusing to set a homicidal lunatic at large, though it is impossible not to pity the poor wretch, who, after an imprisonment of several years, was finally hanged, on a charge of plotting

[1] Dom. S. Papers, Charles II., vol. lxxi. pp. 34-35, 7th April, 1663.

the King's death, from the recesses of his dungeon cell in the Tower.

At the Restoration, George Villiers did not break off all intercourse with his Republican acquaintances. Nay more, he had actually appointed one of them, Braythwaite by name, to manage his estates. Braythwaite was a man of conspicuous ability, but as he had once been a confidant of Cromwell's, the Duke's selection of him as an agent, naturally aroused much comment and criticism from the King and Court.

In 1663, when Braythwaite had been threatened with arrest on suspicion, Buckingham had persuaded Charles to grant his *protégé* a personal interview. Braythwaite, a plausible rascal, came out of the ordeal with flying colours. Not only did he captivate Charles by his entertaining conversation, but he received permission to communicate henceforward directly with the Sovereign, should any movement amongst his former associates come to his knowledge. In 1667 he came to the King with a long tale about his benefactor. He vowed that of late His Grace was much altered, and that he had taken to seeking out "men of very mean condition, but of very desperate intentions."[1] Moreover, not content with corresponding with lawless characters, Buckingham actually stole out to meet them "at unreasonable hours and in obscure places." Such conduct in a person of quality was only susceptible of one explanation. And Braythwaite had no hesitation in declaring that the Duke must be engaged in a political conspiracy of one kind or another.

[1] "Life of Clarendon," vol. iii. p. 203.

The moment Braythwaite chose for his denunciation was singularly well-timed to compass his patron's ruin. Buckingham's conduct during the discussion of the Irish Cattle Bill had greatly exasperated Charles. Moreover, had the King himself been ready to forgive the attacks on Lady Castlemaine, that lady would not have allowed him to do so. Nor had Buckingham many friends to plead his cause with the King. To Clarendon, he was no longer merely odious and contemptible; the ability and perseverance the Duke had lately manifested, showed that he could also be formidable. Arlington, whose influence was steadily increasing, saw in him his most dangerous rival, and hated him as much as did the Chancellor. And while, on the one hand, Ormond and the more respectable old Cavaliers abominated his lax principles, on the other hand, courtiers of a less austere type envied him his successes. Ashley was, indeed, a potent ally, but the wise Achitophel was not the man to endanger his own prospects for the sake of a possible competitor.

Braythwaite's evidence was not the sole weapon possessed by Buckingham's ill-wishers. The Duke had long sought his fortune in the stars, as well as in the crucible, a pursuit not uncommon at this time, when astrology had received a powerful stimulus from the recent developments of the mysteries of the Rosy Cross. Amongst these illuminati was a certain Dr Heydon, author of "The Holy Guide," which he had dedicated to the Duke of Ormond. In the Doctor's case, star-gazing had not proved a profitable trade, and his career was a striking refutation of Buckingham's own saying, that, "he could not imagine how astrologers should be miserable, unless the stars are angry with them for revealing theyr secrets."[1] Indeed, anxieties of the most sordid nature had effectually intervened between the seer and the bliss, which on George Villiers' computation should have been his; for, in 1664, he was actually cast into the Gate House for debt, and only owed his release to Buckingham's liberality. The public had, however, some justification for their incredulity, since, according to Sir Allan Brodrick, the Prophet had inaugurated his career "by prognosticating the hanging of old Oliver, to his son Richard Cromwell and Thurloe, who in disguise came for the calculation of nativities to him, like distressed Cavaliers, for which I saw him in Prison (with many wiser and better men on other accounts), sixteen months, whilst Cromwell outlived ye Prediction near four yeares."[2] Nor did Heydon's more intimate acquaintances give him a better general character. "There is no such person," writes one of these, "as Dr Heydon, but there is one Robert Heydon assumes that title, one of no religion, parts or honesty, a very imposter who pretends himselfe to be the Secretary of Nature, and this is the person you mention; two or three yeares since he was conversant with the Duke of Buckingham and then sayd hee kept company with none but Dukes and Princes; hee is a lewd fellow and no Astrologer to any purpose; out of other men's writings he picks up some statements, and prints them for

---

[1] *Quarterly*, p. 96.
[2] Carte, MSS. 35, fol. 329. Brodrick to Ormonde. London, 2nd March, 1666.

his own . . . what his affection is for His Majesty I know not, having for six yeares past refused to see him because of his juggling and lying."[1]

Yet it was to this "poor fellow's poorer lodging at Tower Hill," that the brilliant Duke, masked and disguised, often repaired at dead of night, hoping, perchance, with the aid of the adept, to solve those mysteries which perpetually haunted his imagination.

Heydon was undoubtedly a charlatan, and probably also "of no parts or honesty," yet, when arrested on a charge of conspiracy, he seems to have displayed greater fidelity than the ingenious Mr Braythwaite.

Amongst his papers were several addressed to the Duke, but one only which could be ascribed to the latter; nor can this letter have been actually treasonable, since his bitterest enemy merely describes it as "containing many unusual expressions which were capable of very ill interpretation, and could not bear a good one."[2] But one document of importance rewarded Arlington's eager search —a horoscope of the King's nativity, cast by Heydon at the Duke's request.

That such a proceeding came within the statute of High Treason may very likely have escaped Buckingham's memory. Nevertheless, in the old days, men had paid with their lives for such idle curiosity, and, even in 1667, were the charge in the hands of a clever Crown lawyer, it might well lead to the scaffold. Nor would it be difficult for spies

---

[1] Clar. MS. 85, fol. 37. "Old" William (Lily?) to Sir Edward Walker, Garter King-at-arms, Husham, 28th Jan. 1666-7.
[2] "Life of Clarendon," vol. iii. p. 372.

to unearth other accusations. Indeed one of these gentry, described as "the party brought from Ireland," actually did forward a long, and singularly ill-spelt, memorandum on Buckingham's treasonable projects.[1] According to him, when the Duke was committed to the Tower for his assault on Lord Dorchester, Heydon, at his patron's request, and with the help of the discharged and unpaid seamen who thronged the London docks, intended to surprise that fortress and release the noble captive. They calculated that the sailors would not be difficult to "incense," as they would readily believe the Duke had been imprisoned for pleading their cause in Parliament, and the plot was only relinquished because the prisoner was unexpectedly released.

Ill-considered as were many of the Duke's schemes, he had sufficient judgment not to entrust a plot of this magnitude to so poor a creature as the Secretary of Nature. Nor is it likely that two men as shrewd as Clarendon and Arlington gave much credit to such a mare's nest. Clarendon distinctly says, Charles himself showed him "the examinations and depositions which had been taken; and that letter to that fellow which His Majesty said 'he knew to be every word the Duke's own hand.'"[2]

Then, not too reluctantly, we may suppose, the Chancellor acquiesced in the decision to serve a warrant on the Duke. Such a resolution, however, was more easily formed than executed, and the

---

[1] Carte, MSS. 35, fol. 302. William Leving to Sir George Lane, 7th Feb. (enclosure).
[2] "Life of Clarendon," vol. iii. p. 373.

Odyssey of the unfortunate Serjeant Bearcroft, charged with the mission, proves that the King's writ did not always run in ducal houses.

The worthy serjeant was within six miles of Owthorp, the Duke's seat in Suffolk, when he was overtaken by the Duchess of Buckingham returning in her chariot from a visit to Deane,[1] a house of Lord Cardigan's. In spite of the gathering gloom of the February evening, the gentlemen of her escort instantly recognised Bearcroft, and "withall ridd to the coatchside and told the Dutches that there was one of the King's serjeants at Armes with his mace." The Duchess had none of whom to take counsel, for she had only "her weomen" in the carriage. But she instantly realised her lord's peril, urged her six horses to their utmost speed, easily out-distanced the officer, and arrived at Owthorp half an hour before him.

That half-hour proved Buckingham's salvation. When the wearied messenger dismounted, he found all the signs of a beleaguered fortress about the splendid Tudor mansion, which, in a past century, Charles Brandon had built for his royal spouse. The servants were flocking to the "greate howse," and although one admitted that His Grace had lain there last night, the others were too well indoctrinated to vouchsafe any reply to the officer's questions. The porter was even more impervious to enquiry. In spite of the Royal warrant, he utterly refused to unbar the gate, and only with extreme reluctance consented to acquaint his mistress with Bearcroft's errand. Finally, Mr Fairfax — probably our old friend Brian — slipped through a postern door, which

[1] Clarendon MSS. 85, fol. 96.

was instantly locked behind him, and proceeded to interview the serjeant. A violent altercation ensued, the one exhorting "to show more respeckt to the Howse of the Lord Duke of Buckingham and his Dutches," the other retorting that "he had not found any respeckt that was due to the King's servant being on his duty."

At last, as entrance except by force was impossible, Bearcroft decided to sleep at Stamford, and to postpone his meeting with Buckingham till the morning. Accordingly the next day at eight o'clock, escorted by four justices of the peace, he returned to Owthorp. This time he was admitted, and though somewhat alarmed by the host of servants, "having soards in there belts and the livery men staves in there hands," he formally "demanded in His Majesty's name the Body of My Lord Duke of Buckingham." At these dread words all the company, even the scowling rows of retainers, ceremoniously uncovered, but no one produced George Villiers, or volunteered any hint as to his whereabouts. Neither was Bearcroft more fortunate in his search for compromising documents. He was duly escorted to the Duke's closet, but when the cabinet there was broken open, save for some "tunes prickt on seaverall papers with the Duke's owne hand," nothing was to be found.

Foiled and baffled, the poor serjeant had to renounce his useless quest. Nor was he comforted on the return journey by learning that the Duke had passed through St Albans openly, in a coach and six, having evidently given him the slip during the night he had spent at Stamford.

The expedition had indeed been a complete

failure, and Bearcroft felt he had lamed both his steeds to no purpose. Another time, when sent on such missions to the houses of the great, he earnestly implored that a troop of horse might accompany him to enforce His Majesty's commands, which otherwise had little chance of being obeyed.

Thus once more did Buckingham owe his escape to the devotion of his wife. Nor, impossible as it seems for a fugitive in "a coatch and six and six led horses" long to elude detection, was he recaptured. Vainly did Charles launch a proclamation of the most fulminatory order against his former favourite. Though the King "threatened all severity to those who would harbour or conceal him,"[1] no one gave information of the "places obscure and unknown" to which the brilliant Duke had retreated. Reresby declares that for some time he was concealed at the house of his friend and neighbour, Sir Henry Bellasis in Yorkshire. Later, however, he certainly came to London, and was even, it is said, taken into custody by the watch for rioting in the streets, but, not being recognised, was once more released.

Meanwhile the Duchess of Buckingham removed to town, where she quietly established herself in St Martin's Lane, thence to watch the course of events. It was to her, therefore, that Dr Heydon addressed himself in a letter which, if it reached her, must have given her both relief and anxiety—relief to know he still remained true to his patron, anxiety as to whether readier witnesses might not be suborned against Buckingham.

[1] Bishop Kennet's "Hist. of England," vol. iii. p. 263.

"Mr Montague," writes the prisoner, "my sorrows salute you wishing health.[1] Though false reports raysed against my Lord I will prove to the doings of A. Williams that was hyred to inform against him and my (illegible) correspondence.

"My Lord Duke is wronged and with my life I will let the world know it. I pray let not my lady be affrayed, for when his Majesty hears the truth hee will bee restored to more favour than ever, and his enemies ashamed of their actions. Let me have your answer by this or another faithfull person, for the Duke is most unjustly abused and I am kept a close prisoner, tortured in these dungeons to forward their designs against him, but Death shall close on the scene before I will be found to damn my sowle for a witness to their wicked designs. My last words shall be the Duke is innocent, for I know nothing against him.— Your humble servant,

JOHN HEYDON."

"TOWER, 13*th March*, 1667."

The examination of a certain Mrs Damport confirms Dr Heydon's account of the methods used to construct a case against the fugitive Duke. Mrs Damport deposed that a certain "Middleton did confese that he had received £100 from my Lord Arlington to bear witness against the Duke for having the King's nativity cast by Heydon, and to testify he heard the Duke speake treason against the King and the Government." Mrs Damport had a daughter, to whom Middleton had apparently been making love. This young lady having asked him "whether there was any truth in the matter to which he was to bear witness, he acknowledged

[1] Brit. Mus. Add. MSS., 27,872, fol. 6.

there was none, but that he did it to get money; and that he was to receive £500 more when the businesse was done. That he had also drawn in Fryr, and that Fryr had received £60 for to joyne with him in bearing witnesse against the Duke and was promised £500 more when the businesse was effected." She adds further, "that upon some jealousy or presumption that this wicked designe was discovered, both Middleton and Grice in a very short space and distance of time dyed suddenly not without manifest tokens of being poisoned—to part of this foule practice shee affirmes that my Lord Treasurer and my Lord Buckhurst can bear witnesse."

Mrs Damport's evidence may not have been worth the paper on which it is written; yet a woman in her humble circumstances would hardly evoke the testimony of two great nobles such as Lord Buckhurst and Lord Southampton, if she had not good grounds for her accusation.

Buckhurst, the future Duke of Dorset, a boon companion of Buckingham's, might not indeed inspire unmitigated confidence; but if the Lord Treasurer to whom she refers was the Earl of Southampton, who only died on the 16th of May, 1667, no one in Charles's Court was more universally respected.

Doubtless, Buckingham's wealth was a direct incentive to perjury. Whitehall swarmed with human sharks, watching with unconcealed avidity for the rich Duke's attainder. Such generosity as that shown by Shakespeare's Lord Pembroke, in restoring the grant of Sir Gervaise Elway's forfeited estate to the poor widow, was sadly out of fashion.

If the following letter from the Duke of Ormond to Clarendon came to Buckingham's knowledge, it would have been hard to persuade him that Lord Arran was as intent on "mediation on his behalfe" as on the reversion of the Villiers property. Nor can such a proceeding have further endeared Ormond to him :—

"My sons friends in London," writes the Lord Lieutenant to Clarendon, "trusted with his wife's fortune . . . hold it very necessary he should goe for England . . . as upon this occasion of the misfortune befallen the Duke of Buckingham to discharge himself in those offices which in such cases are allowable and which may be expected from the relation he has to him.[1] It is considered and hoped that if the King shall admitt of any mediation in behalfe of the Duke, my son may, more properly than any man I can thinke of, be allowed to doe it, and that if the offence prove capitall, and be soe pursued and punished in the end, he may then in behalfe of his wife, humbly put His Majesty in minde of her innocence and the merit of her father and his family; Noe man can bee a better judge or a director of the conduct of such an affaire, nor can I doubt but that as you retaine much kindnesse for the memory of the late Duke of Richmond, soe you will not bee the less willing to lett his daughter finde the effects of it for the family shee has come into and to which she is in her single person, as great a blessing as could be wished from any person of her sex."

No one was on terms of greater intimacy with the Chancellor than Ormond. That he therefore

[1] Carte, MSS. 48, fol. 488. Ormond to Clarendon. Dublin, March, 1666.

felt obliged to safeguard his daughter-in-law's heritage proves that Buckingham's danger was not imaginary, and that the Duke was well-advised to remain in hiding for the moment. But as the weeks went by, the King's anger began to abate, and Buckingham grew unutterably weary of his hunted existence. More than once, the Serjeant-at-Arms and other agents employed for his apprehension descended on the lodgings where he was known to have been but an hour before, only to find their quarry flown. The necessity of sleeping during the day-time, and spending the night in rambling from place to place to cheat the pursuers, became after a time intolerable, even to Buckingham, who prided himself on keeping strange hours. Few nerves could stand such a strain, and at the end of June he determined to capitulate; but even then he refused to surrender at discretion, and it is no small tribute to Clarendon's integrity, that it was his mediation and advice that the Duke of Buckingham then invoked. His secretary, Mr Clifford, was charged to go in person to plead his cause with the Chancellor, and to request an interview. Undoubtedly, Clarendon was justified in declining such a proposal; yet, had he adopted a less rigid attitude, it is conceivable that he might have converted a violent antagonist into a useful ally. But it was not to be. He refused to stultify his own proclamation by conferring with an outlaw. Nor would he pledge himself beyond remarking that "the Duke's crimes might not be of that magnitude to endanger his life." And he added, "he was most confident that there was no conspiracy to take that from him and he was sure there was no grant of his estate to any man, which must have passed the Great Seal."[1] Thus repulsed, it is hard to guess what course Buckingham would have adopted, but, at this very juncture he learnt that one of the chief witnesses for the Crown lay at death's door from small-pox, and that the other had retracted his evidence. This was an unexpected piece of luck. He hesitated no longer, and, on June the 28th, entrusted Sir Robert Howard with a letter for the King.

MAY IT PLEASE YOUR MAJESTY—Though I could not but bee afrayd of your Majesty's anger, yet I dare trust your Kindnesse, and now I understand that your Majesty thinkes your honour is concerned with my surrender, I will have noe longer consideration of myselfe, since that comes in question, but as soone as I am in a posture fitt to appeare before Your Majesty I shall come and throw myselfe at your feete to be disposed of as Your Majesty shall thinke fitt, being with great humility, may it please Your Majesty,—Your Majesty's most dutifull and most obedient subject and servant—   BUCKINGHAM.[2]

The King who was "as weary of the prosecution as the Duke was of concealing himself to avoid it," would gladly have granted him the audience he proposed. But the "King's Schoolmaster," as the Duke had aptly dubbed Clarendon, was faithful to his pedagogic functions. He remained inflexible. The Duke was forced to bow to necessity, and finally yielded himself in due

---

[1] "Life of Clarendon," vol. iii. p. 374.
[2] Dom. State Cal. vol. ccvii. 273. Duke of Buckingham to Charles II., 28th June 1667.

form to the Sergeant-at-Arms. Yet the Chancellor's victory cannot have given him unalloyed satisfaction; for, with characteristic maliciousness, the Duke contrived to invest his very submission with the appearance of a triumph.

Indeed, his journey to the Tower partook somewhat of the nature of a Royal progress. Surrounded by a heterogeneous troop of friends, comprising such discordant elements as the Quaker Lord Vaughan and the gay poet Buckhurst, he arranged, on his way thither, to dine at "The Sun" in Bishopsgate. Here, considerable crowds assembled to catch a glimpse of the daring opponent of the unpopular Chancellor—a satisfaction Buckingham did not deny them, showing himself with great ceremony on the balcony of the inn.

No sooner had the gates of the Tower closed on Buckingham, than he straightway appeared to cast off any imaginary fears which might yet possess him. On the 1st of July, the Government sent a select Commission to examine the ducal outlaw. It was composed of Lord Arlington, Sir William Morrice, Sir William Coventry and Lord Clifford; and never, surely, had the grim old walls witnessed such careless levity on the part of a prisoner arraigned for high treason.[1] Had he been brought up before a City Alderman for night brawling, he could hardly have assumed a more farcical tone. Arlington, the spokesman, initiated proceedings by expressing the hope "that His Grace would give a positive answer to some questions commanded by the King." Whereupon

---

[1] Brit. Mus. Add. MSS. 27,872 (7) f. 13.

the Duke responded: "I hope when I answer you'll believe what I say. Otherwise I shall have but an unequall part of this business, if I am not to be believed when I speake truth, and am made speake only that advantage may be taken from what I say; but, however, I promise you I will answer very clearly and positively to any question you aske."

He acknowledged the acquaintance of Dr Heydon and the fact that the latter had been "in the relation of a Domestick Servant to him." But when Arlington enquired, "Did you ever trust him with anything?" he retorted with, "I suppose you have had conversation with him?" Arlington assenting, he proceeded: "Well, my Lord, I don't know what you take him to be, but the first time I saw him, I tooke him to be soe silly a fellow that I would not thinke it fitt to trust him with a tallow candle."

The epistles addressed to him by the Doctor, he described as begging letters, "absolutely unconnected with publicke businesse," and when one of his own to the Secretary of Nature was mentioned, he exclaimed, "I have heard that I writt a letter to him, and that your Lordship has it, but if I were to dy this minute, and were to be forgiven my sins upon condition of speaking truth in this matter, I should sweare that I never did write to him, and I am soe confident of this, that I will lay your Lordship £100, if you please, I never did."

Arlington prudently declined the proffered bet. Instead, he put the last question—"Why did not Your Grace render yourself sooner to the King's proclamation?" But Buckingham, for all his flippancy, was not to be enticed into dangerously indiscreet revelations. He made no reference to conspiracies against his person and estate. In decorous phrases he expressed his fears that His Majesty had been very angry with him, and that he merely desired to probe "what was in the bottom of these designs," before he gave himself up. The Commissioners now judged their task accomplished. They retired, citing Buckingham to appear before the King in council. Here he was confronted with the single piece of evidence the Crown possessed, the letter—for the authenticity of which Charles had personally vouched. The King, however, proved a bad witness; for when Buckingham had seen the document and answered that the letter was not in his hand "but in his sister's, the Duchess of Richmond's, with whom it was known that he had no correspondence," the King, when he had once more examined it, could not refute the assertion. "Having looked upon it he said he had been mistaken and confessed it was the Duchess's hand."[1] Not unnaturally the Monarch appeared slightly "out of countenance," and the Duke was, of course, immediately set at liberty, returning to his own house with the happy consciousness that he had scored another victory against the Chancellor.

[1] Clarendon, p. 280.

CHAPTER VIII

THE TRIUMPH OF BUCKINGHAM

BUCKINGHAM had been acquitted, but he was not straightway restored to favour; though, thenceforward he never seems to have doubted that it was only a question of time before he regained his ascendency over his former playmate. And for the next few years—till confronted by the rivalry of Mademoiselle de Kéroualle — he undoubtedly exercised the power that a stronger nature with better defined aims must always exert over one more indolent and infinitely less enterprising. Indeed, when his fall came, the shrewdest diplomatists refused to consider it as anything but a momentary eclipse, from which he was bound to emerge triumphant.

It will, therefore, be readily understood that Buckingham did not long confine himself to his domestic circle; and no later than the 16th of July, he was admitted, by favour of the lady herself, to kiss the King's hand in my Lady Castlemaine's chamber. The eager courtiers, though unable to follow the conversation, which ensued and lasted half-an-hour, noticed that the King's manner remained persistently cold, not only during the interview, but that, later, in going to bed, he expressed himself somewhat bitterly on the subject of his former favourite. The Royal moods were, however, notoriously variable: Ossory believed that they hinged mainly on the carriage of the Duke towards his sovereign; but, in speaking thus, he forgot that the main factor of the case was the attitude it pleased the imperious Barbara to assume.[1]

Since Frances Stuart, once Buckingham's friend, had forfeited the King's favour by her clandestine marriage with the Duke of Richmond, Lady Castlemaine had become more than ever powerful, and the Duke was well aware that she was the one person whom it behoved him to conciliate. On her side, "the Lady" was ready to forget ancient feuds if she could obtain his assistance in the desperate struggle she was waging with the incorruptible Chancellor. Between Buckingham and his kinswoman a truce was therefore patched up, which was destined to endure as long as they were under the necessity of combating their common foe.

Meanwhile, the stars in their courses fought against the Minister. After a brief illness, his wife, the Countess of Clarendon, died suddenly. She had been a true helpmate to the Chancellor; his companion in all his banishments, who had made —the words are his own—all his former calamities less grievous by her company and courage. Utterly overwhelmed by his loss, and regardless of all else, Hyde shut himself up for a fortnight in his empty house, and refused to be comforted.

[1] Carte, MSS. 220, 259. Lord Ossory to Duke of Ormond. London, 16th July, 1667.

Enemies were not slow to take advantage of the absence of the sorrow-stricken statesman. The awakening was a rude one. At the end of these two short weeks, the King, without further ado, commissioned the Duke of York to require the surrender of the Great Seal. Nor was the avowed motive for this act of characteristic ingratitude reassuring; for the Sovereign declared this to be the only means by which his Minister's impeachment by Parliament could be averted. Clarendon did not submit without a struggle; nor was he without adherents, though it was in vain that the Archbishop of Canterbury and the Duchess of York pleaded his cause with his Royal master. The suspicion that the Chancellor had promoted Frances Stuart's marriage had hopelessly alienated the King's affections from his old servant. When, on the 26th of August, Clarendon sought the Royal presence, his fate was determined. For two hours he spoke, but he spoke to unheeding ears. Charles was resolved to depose him, and since he would not yield to mere persuasion, and resign his office, on the 30th of August Sir Orlando Bridgeman was sent to Clarendon House, to demand the Great Seal in the King's name.

The Chancellor's fall meant the Duke's rise. Already on the 5th of September an "*esclairesissment*" of two hours in the King's closet was noted by the Court gossips, and ten days later the Duke was restored to all the dignities and emoluments which had been his before the late estrangement.[1] Finally, a week later, the " King bid the

---

[1] " Savile Corres.," p. 21. H. Savile to Sir G. Savile, London, 5th Sept. 1667.

Duke of Buckingham ask him what he pleased and he would grant it,"[1] nor, had he asked for Clarendon's head in a charger, would the fickle monarch perhaps have been ill-pleased. And though George Villiers did not himself proffer such a request, he certainly inspired Parliament to do so.

On the 10th of October the Houses met, and promptly voted the King an address of thanks for removing the Chancellor. Charles responded by an engagement never again to employ him in any capacity whatsoever. Thus encouraged, the House of Commons drew up an impeachment under seventeen heads. They charged the fallen statesman with venality and cruelty in his office; with selling Dunkirk; with disclosing State secrets; with unlawfully acquiring vast wealth; with *intending* to introduce military government into England. Had the Upper House concurred, Tower-Hill would certainly have heard Clarendon's dying speech. But, after much angry discussion, the Lords refused to commit him on general charges —a decision the Commons regarded as a breach of privilege—while the Conferences daily held merely aggravated the friction between the Houses without removing their differences. The King remembered the ill-omened precedent of Strafford's trial. He feared a like result, and earnestly advocated the Chancellor's voluntary withdrawal from the country, as the best solution of the crisis.

But the old man's spirit was not quenched.

---

[1] Hist. MSS. 14th Rep. Pt. IX.: Lindsay MSS. Chas. Bertie to his brother-in-law, the future Duke of Leeds.

For a time, the Duke of York was prevented from coming to his assistance by an attack of small-pox, yet during those solitary days, Clarendon remained indomitable, obstinately refusing to listen to the various emissaries despatched by Charles. It was not till his princely son-in-law personally brought him the King's express command to leave England that, on the 29th of November, he crossed to France. But though hounded into exile, he did not abandon his native land without a protest; and in the form of a petition to the House of Lords he left behind him a strongly-worded vindication of his conduct. Doubtless, Buckingham recognised himself in the description of those "of Licentious Principles . . . who took to themselves of reviling all Counsels and Counsellors, and turning all things Sacred and serious to Ridicule." Nor was he the only one likely to take umbrage at the document. The Peers were equally incensed by a passage in which Clarendon announced his intention of deferring his return to a period "when his Majesty's justice may not be obstructed or controlled by the power and malice of those who have sworn my destruction." Their revenge on the fallen Chancellor was a somewhat unworthy one, for they selected his avowed enemy, the Duke, to deliver the fugitive Minister's missive to the Lower House.

On this occasion Buckingham's warmest admirers—if there are such—cannot claim that his conduct erred on the side of generosity. He remarked, "That the Lords had commanded him to deliver to the Commons that scandalous and seditious Paper sent from the Earl of Clarendon; they bid me present it to you and desire you in convenient time to send it to them again; for it has a style they are in love with and they desire to keep it."[1] Party feeling ran so high, that, strange to say, this fashion of "turning the justice of nations into a jest" did not create a reaction in favour of the persecuted fugitive; and, on the 19th of December, Parliament passed a Bill making Clarendon liable to all the penalties of high treason, if he did not render himself before the 1st of February. The unfortunate man immediately set out for England; but at Calais he fell seriously ill, and the time of grace had expired before he could resume his journey.

Henceforth all his supplications and petitions were vain to procure his recall. The rest of his life was spent in the South of France, which he only quitted to die at Rouen, in December 1674.

The power that the Chancellor had wielded now for the most part devolved on Buckingham. Though he held no office till he purchased the Mastership of the Horse from the Duke of Albemarle, for the sum of £20,000, he was practically the Prime Minister of the new administration. It was to him that the foreign Ministers applied "before they were admitted to have audience with the King . . . who consulted him chiefly in all matters of moment."[2] In truth, at this period Arlington was his only serious competitor in the Government.

Harry Bennet, like George Villiers, had graduated for high office by sedulous devotion to the

---

[1] Kennet, "Hist. of England," vol. iii. p. 220, 4th Dec. 1667.
[2] Reresby, p. 76.

Royal pleasures; but save in their general laxity of principle, the two men had little in common. Arlington's countenance, even without the disfiguring black patch which an ancient scar obliged him to wear, would always have been harsh and unpleasing. Nor did the pomposity of his manner, acquired apparently during his embassy at Madrid, make amends for these physical defects. Needless to say, Buckingham never wearied of caricaturing this ponderous gravity for his monarch's benefit; and Bab May, and other ribald courtiers, with sticking-plaster on their noses, and shovel and tongs borne before them to imitate the insignia of office, loved to ape the solemn deportment of the Chief Secretary of State.

In his youth, Lord Arlington had been educated for the Church, but save for a graceful familiarity with the Classics[1]—which he quoted aptly, and without pedantic affectation—he retained little of his early breeding. Nature had intended him for a model head-clerk. He was resourceful, assiduous and methodical in the transaction of business. A ready debater he was not, and public speaking he abhorred; yet, when driven into a corner, no man could make a better defence. Though he had married the granddaughter of Maurice of Nassau, his natural bias inclined him to Romanism. Indeed, before the Restoration he urged Charles II. to declare his conversion to Catholicism, but he himself remained nominally Protestant till the close of his career. This

---

[1] Sheffield, "Duke of Buckinghamshire," Works, vol. ii. pp. 66-67. Character of Lord Arlington. See also Burnet and Thomas, "Lord Ailesbury's Memoirs," Roxburgh Club Ed.

religious ambiguity was reflected in his general course of action. His master's whim, rather than the welfare of his country, was his law ; so that with all his possibilities, he ended by being " rather a subtle courtier than an able statesman."[1] It must be admitted that, unlike the Duke, Arlington was a "civil and obliging husband," a faithful friend and a devoted father. His matrimonial alliances were singularly fortunate. To his wife, Isabella von Beerwaert, a sister of Lady Ossory's, he owed the friendship of the Ormond family. And, in 1672, he consolidated his influence with the King by the marriage of his only daughter and heiress with the latter's illegitimate son, Henry, Duke of Grafton.

Such was the man who by degrees became the dominant factor in the Government, and Buckingham's most formidable rival. And never could the volatile Duke have suffered more by comparison with his industrious colleague than during those first months of office ; for it was at this time that his unfortunate attachment to Lady Shrewsbury first began to bear bitter fruit.

This unfortunate connection was already an open secret for everyone except the Duchess of Buckingham, who, poor, kind soul, long remained on terms of friendly intimacy with her rival. When Serjeant Bearcroft made his fruitless pilgrimage to Owthorp, it will be remembered that he met the Duchess returning from a visit to the lady's father. And, indeed, the reason Mary Buckingham pleaded for not receiving that officer was her extreme fatigue, after a night spent in nursing Lady Shrewsbury.

[1] Duke of Buckinghamshire.

But, after Buckingham's release from the Tower, it became impossible, even for his confiding wife, to remain in ignorance of her husband's infidelity. His lordship's passion was no longer capable of concealment; it dwarfed all other objects. As he himself describes the sentiment, "Like Moses' serpent it devours all the rest."

In July a noisy brawl with Harry Killigrew, one of his mistress's former lovers, made their connection public. The latter, a handsome young scapegrace, had not taken his dismissal in a philosophic spirit. Everywhere he advertised his irritation by startling and indiscreet reminiscences of the Countess, and naturally these revelations did not fail to reach Buckingham's ears. On the 20th of July they came face to face on the steps of the Duke's playhouse. A scuffle ensued, in which "the Duke did soundly beat Harry Killigrew, and take away his sword and made a fool of, till the fellow prayed him to spare his life."[1] Indeed, Killigrew's hurts proved so serious, that though the Lords of the Council had ordered his committal to the Tower, they relented, and allowed him to nurse his wounds at his own lodgings. The culprit seems, however, to have distrusted their tender mercies; for instead of appearing when called up for judgment on the 9th of August, he decamped abroad, with the avowed intention of not returning till he was reconciled to all parties.[2] As the sequel showed, the decision was prudent, for the Countess of Shrewsbury was a dangerous enemy, and from no quarter could he anticipate a favourable verdict. Both sober citizen and

[1] Pepys, vol. vii. p. 33. 22nd-23rd July, 1667.
[2] Hist. MSS. Rep. XII. Le Fleming. Aug. 9, 1667.

Merry Monarch were loud in condemnation of his conduct, Mr Samuel Pepys remarking, "that in this business the Duke of Buckingham did carry himself very innocently and well, and I wish he paid this fellow's coat well." And Charles II. describes his "carriage towards Lady Shrewsbury as being worse than I will repeat, and for his démêlé with my Lord of Buckingham he ought not to brag of, for it was in all sorts most abominable."[1]

The scandal inaugurated by Harry Killigrew did not, however, end with his flight; for, on the 16th of September, "my lady Shrewsbury with only one Chambermaid, took to her heels and they say is gone either into a monastery, or to kill Harry Killigrew herself, since none of her relations will undertake it, but her lord has sent to Dover and Rye to stop her if possible."[2]

Hitherto Lord Shrewsbury had been a byeword amongst husbands for long-suffering meekness. Yet even his patience did not prove inexhaustible. He was too polite, Grammont tells us, to venture on reproaches to his wife, but being resolved on some redress to his injured honour, he, very much to his friends' surprise, finally sent a challenge to Buckingham.

Duels were not an infrequent feature of life under the Stuarts, though they were sternly discountenanced by the Privy Council. But they were never as common in England as in France, where, despite the edicts, nine hundred and thirty gentlemen had met their death in this fashion during

---

[1] Julia Cartwright, "Madame," p. 260, 17th October. Charles II. to his sister, "Madame."

[2] "Savile Corres.": H. Savile to Sir George Savile.

the recent regency.¹ Nor were the conditions here the same as across the Channel, where it was the habit for a large number of combatants simultaneously to engage. Perhaps Buckingham's lengthened exile had imbued him with French prejudices; but, at any rate, in the arrangements now made by him and Lord Shrewsbury, we can trace the influence of those miniature battles which had often strewed the Place Royale with dead and dying. Naturally, an assignation on a scale so considerable—for the partisans each nobleman had enlisted were to take an active share in the fight—could not be achieved in absolute secrecy. Mr Pepys, indeed, declared that the tragedy might have been averted had the authorities bestirred themselves; for "pretty it is to hear how the King had some notice of this challenge a week or two ago and did give it to my Lord Generall (the Duke of Albemarle) to confine the Duke, or to take security that he should not do any such thing as fight, and the Generall trusted to the King, that he sending for him would do it, and the King trusted to the Generall; and so between both, as everything else of the greatest moment do, do fall between two stools."²

The Earl's seconds were his kinsmen, Mr Bernard Howard, brother to the Duke of Norfolk, and Sir John Talbot. Buckingham was supported by a Mr Jenkins and Sir Robert Holmes. The former, who is described in a newsletter as "Lieutenant to Sir Harry Jones," was, according to

---

[1] "Noblesse française sous Richelieu," by Vicomte d'Avenel, p. 273.
[2] Pepys, vol. vii. p. 284.

a Howard tradition, a fencing-master. As for Sir Robert, he was a fast friend of Buckingham's; but he did not bear the best of characters—"first an Irish livery boy, then a highwayman, now Bashaw of the Isle of Wight, got in bonds and in rapine £100,000, the cursed beginner of the two Dutch Wars," writes Andrew Marvell of him at a later period.[1]

The meeting was fixed for Thursday, the 21st of January, in a close near Barn Elms, that suburban mansion of the Duke's where the gentle Cowley had so lately breathed his last.

Never was there a more calamitous encounter. Mr Jenkins' science was of scant avail, for he was killed outright by Mr Bernard Howard.[2] Sir John Talbot and Sir Robert Holmes, who engaged each other, were both wounded, the one very severely in the arm, the other in his hand. Naturally the two principals attacked each other with fatal results to the injured husband, who fell, thrust through and through, the sword entering by the right breast and coming out at the shoulder.[3]

Terrible as was this fight, it has assumed a yet more sinister aspect, in the eyes of posterity, from the well-known anecdotes circulated at the time.

According to Lord Peterborough, the miserable woman, who was the cause of the catastrophe, watched the butchery, disguised as a page, and

---

[1] A. Marvell's "Seasonable Argument."
[2] Carte, MSS. 222, fol. 178. Newsletter to Sir G. Lane, Whitehall 21st January, 1667.
[3] Pepys, vol. viii. p. 11.

holding her lover's horse. Nay more, "to reward his prowess, she went to him in the shirt stained with her husband's blood." And St Evrémond further declares that Lady Shrewsbury had concealed pistols on her person, wherewith she had sworn to shoot both herself and Lord Shrewsbury, should the fortunes of the contest go against the Duke of Buckingham.[1]

Had this been true, it would be vain to seek a greater instance of depravity in that or any age. But on examination it appears to be as unreliable as many another sensational tale; for, when arraigned in 1674 by his Peers, the Duke distinctly stated that, at the time of the duel, the Countess was living in a "French monastery." Nor does this statement appear to have been controverted, though made before an assembly eager to convict him of every infamy. For the sake of human nature, one can but hope that a man who, as we shall see, was reckoned by no less a judge than Louis XIV. to be "the only English gentleman he had ever known," was incapable of the brutality this story suggests.

Meanwhile, the unfortunate Lord Shrewsbury, though sorely wounded, did not die on the spot.[2] His friends carried him to Arundel House, where he lingered till the 16th of March, when he expired. On the 19th, his body was opened in the presence of several noblemen and persons of quality, and the distinguished physicians and surgeons, who were in attendance, formally testified that his hurt

---

[1] St Evrémond to Waller, Lett. IV., quoted in "Rochester, and other Literary Rakes," p. 94.
[2] Hist. MSS., Le Fleming, Rep. XII. p. 24.

was then perfectly cured. Buckingham had not, however, awaited a medical certificate to ensure himself against the penalties attending the "killing or murther of Mr Jenkins, as also all assaults, batteries and woundings, at any time heretofore don, or committed, or procured to be don or committed upon Francis Earl of Shrewsbury and Sir John Talbott, or either of them, whether they be now dead or shall hereafter dye."[1] Probably this dispensation would have been less easily obtained but that "my Lady Castlemaine do rule all at this time as much as ever she did, and she will it is believed, keep all things well for the Duke of Buckingham."[2] Yet, even with her powerful help, so plenary an absolution was not lightly procured. Indeed, the conspirators, knowing that the Lord Privy Seal, who dreaded a Parliamentary enquiry, would scruple to pass it, were forced to elude his vigilance by procuring an immediate warrant for which his assent was not needful. This did not, however, prevent criticism. In fact the business aroused a perfect tempest, as it was recognised to be a greater abuse than any that had occurred in the days of Clarendon.

Charles felt constrained personally to justify his action to the Privy Council by enlarging on "the Contemplation of the eminent services heretofore done by most of the persons who were engaged in the late duel or rencontre"; and he assured his advisers that "on no pretence whatsoever any pardon shall hereafter be granted to any person whatsoever for killing of any man in any duel . . . but that the

---

[1] Dom. St. Cal., Charles II., vol. 223, No. 9.
[2] Pepys, vol. vii. p. 285.

course of law shall wholly take place in all such cases."[1]

That Buckingham was prudent to lose no time in obtaining a full pardon is proved by the curious petition of the Bailiff of Westminster—a document which provides that touch of comedy inseparable from the most tragic episodes. The worthy burgess points out to the King that had George Villiers' estate been forfeit, as it should have been, "a considerable portion whereof... in the citty and liberty of Westminster would of right become due to your servant. But since Your Majesty is gratiously inclined to grant Your Majesty's pardon to the said Duke, before his conviction, by which meanes Your Majesty doth wholly discharge that great fortune and advantage, which otherwise would happen to your servant, therefore your servant would humbly pray that you will be pleased to recommend your servant to His Grace the Duke of Buckingham, to the end he may give your servant some reasonable compensation for soe greate a forfeiture."[2]

Doubtless King and Duke had a hearty laugh together over the honest bailiff's confident simplicity; for now that he was secure of immunity, Buckingham's gaiety showed no diminution. Neither did he assume in public a gravity he did not feel. Only a fortnight after the "rencontre," he was sitting openly in the pit of the Duke's Playhouse, criticising the new piece, *She Would if She Could*, to its author, Etherege.[3] Yet such levity appears

---

[1] Cal. of State Papers, 1667-8, pp. 192, 193, quoted in Pepys.
[2] Dom. St. Cal., Charles II., fol. 223, No. 94.
[3] Pepys, vol. vii. p. 307.

almost decorous compared to his subsequent conduct when the Earl being dead, he installed the "widow of his own making" in his home. And upon his Duchess saying that it was not for her and the other to live together in a house, he answered: "Why, Madam, I did think so, and therefore have ordered your coach to be ready to carry you to your father's"—a speech which Mr Pepys tersely characterises as "devilish."[1]

In spite of the scandal his duel had occasioned, the new Prime Minister presented himself, seemingly unabashed, at the opening of Parliament, on February the 10th, 1668. From our modern standpoint it must, however, be confessed that at this juncture his main policy was as humane as it was statesman-like. He had always felt a profound distaste for religious persecution, and he was now resolved to mitigate the disabilities of the Nonconformist population. It is true he did not propose to extend this clemency to Roman Catholics; but he cannot reasonably be blamed for the exception, since no Government could then have survived the suspicion of Popish proclivities.

Undoubtedly the moment appeared favourable to his scheme: Charles gave it his full approbation; Clarendon, the Church's champion, was an exile; the Conventicle Bill was within six months of expiration. Yet all these considerations proved ineffectual. Vainly did Buckingham strive to conciliate the legislators by permitting a full Parliamentary enquiry into the conduct of the late war. Commissioner Pett, charged with culpable neglect of the British Navy during the Dutch Raid up the

[1] May 1667, vol. viii. p. 18.

The Duchess of Buckingham.

Thames, and Brunkhard, accused of slackening pursuit, after the victory of the 3rd of June, 1665, were both handed over to their tender mercies. The Duke did not attempt to shield Clarendon's officials from impeachment. The Commons had their full glut of prosecution. They wallowed in unsavoury recitals of peculation and jobbery. But such sacrifices could not charm them into compliance with Buckingham's measures. Their behaviour proved it was rather the person than the principles of the ex-Chancellor they had ostracised, and not only did they refuse half the Naval Subsidy demanded, but by an overwhelming majority they rejected the proposed Toleration Act.

Once again had the Church shown herself inexorable, and Buckingham must have recognised that much of the opposition was due to intense suspicion of himself. Indeed, Lord Conway was not alone in his belief that "the Duke heading the fanatics and guided by their counsels, thinks to arrive to be another Oliver."[1] Such a suspicion was wide-spread, and the notion was undoubtedly assisted by the report that immediately before the fatal encounter at Barn Elms, the would-be murderer "had celebrated a day of humiliation and seeking of God at Wallingford House, in the manner and as zealously, as ever Fleetwood performed his exercises there."[2]

The inconsistencies of a character that to this day baffles a generation more skilled than his own in the science of psychology, were, in the eyes

---

[1] Dom. St. Cal., Charles II., vol. 235, No. 140. 16th February, 1668.
[2] Carte, MSS. 48, fol. 254. Duke of Ormond to Lord Ossory, Dublin, 25th February, 1667.

of the country gentlemen of England, but confirmation of their worst suspicions. Personal ambition of the most egotistical and even sordid type was in their eyes the sole and sufficient motive for this bowing down in the House of Rimmon. They therefore with one consent repudiated the "reforming of kingdoms by this sanctified Peer,"[1] and henceforward it was to foreign affairs that the Duke transferred his attention.

During the previous year Louis XIV. had invaded the Franche Comté, to which he laid claim through his wife. The campaign was a series of French triumphs. The tide of Spanish glory had definitely turned at Rocroi. France, with her young ambitious sovereign, with her galaxy of men of genius, was the predestined heir to her rival's Continental supremacy. Hitherto the sympathies of Holland had lain with France; but the threatened advance of the latter to her very portals in the Spanish Netherlands, caused a revolution in her traditional policy. As the most Catholic King appeared incapable of taking the offensive, his provinces had hitherto provided an ideal buffer State for the Dutch; while, on the other hand, Louis, though the grandson of the Huguenot Henri, was the least desirable neighbour a peace-loving Protestant community could acquire. The outcome of these alarms was the Triple Alliance, by which England, Holland and Sweden united to rectify the political balance. Yet that famous treaty, the triumph of

[1] "Litany of the Duke of Buckingham: Poems on State Affairs," vol. iii. p. 82.

Sir William Temple's diplomacy, cannot claim to have permanently advanced the interests of the Republic. In fact, when, contrary to Temple's anticipation, Spain elected to cede Franche Comté to the French, the very frontier conditions most dreaded by the States were realised. And, moreover, by their intervention the unhappy burghers had roused the undying enmity of Louis, an enmity for which the friendship of distant Sweden and the alliance of England's fickle sovereign were but paltry compensations.

Such, briefly, was the state of affairs at the Peace of Aix-la-Chapelle in May, 1668, when Buckingham seized the helm. Spain was at last recognised to have irretrievably fallen from her high estate. Holland, though bearing a bold front, was in reality dismayed and fearful, and Louis, nursing his revenge, already discounted his succession to the boundless heritage of Philip II. on which the grasp of his decrepit successor, the childless Charles II., appeared to be daily slackening.

Meanwhile England remained sullenly suspicious of the Papist King's victorious progress. But the recollection of the fatal bonfire kindled by the Dutchmen at Chatham had not yet faded from her people's memories, and her merchants were consumed with jealousy of Holland's extensive and prosperous commerce. In the recent crisis, indeed, Great Britain had held the scales between the belligerents. This position she could retain, however, only by unswerving loyalty to her national policy of coalition with other Protestant countries. Separated from these, her natural allies, she must infallibly be reduced to the rank of a second-rate Power, or sink still lower to that of a satellite of France, and be dragged into the destructive orbit of Louis the Great.

Unfortunately, Buckingham was the last man to recognise these truths. For good or ill, all his beliefs militated against it. The maritime supremacy of England was his one cardinal article of faith, and, as Holland was our only serious rival on the seas, he longed to see her crushed, or at least crippled. Nor was it, in his judgment, a slight gain to exchange the amity of a race of shop-keepers for that of the most brilliant Monarch of the day. Indeed, if George Villiers were capable of hero-worship, the Roi-Soleil shared with his Puritan father-in-law the only sentiment of this sort in his cynical nature. Such a devotion must appear passing strange to those of us who have drawn our notions of Louis XIV. from the pages of Saint Simon and the Palatine, but it was less inexplicable in the year 1668. Success is apt to dazzle saner and wiser men than the Duke of Buckingham, and it would have taxed a more critical spirit to discriminate between the King himself, and the wondrous band of wits and heroes, who made the Augustan Age of France.

Nevertheless, George Villiers' passion for Louis was not of the Platonic order. No one more than the King of France could make or mar matters for the Duke. To begin with, he had unbounded power over Madame, who dispensed her favours solely at his bidding. And Madame was not only George Villiers' particular star, but a political influence second to none with her royal brother of England. Nor was this all. There was another, and a weighty, reason, to induce him to secure Louis's protection. It was in France that Clarendon had sought refuge. He was still a fugitive and an exile; but while there were many shrewd observers, who believed that his recall was well-nigh inevitable, all recognised that it was Louis, and Louis alone, who could ensure the actual British Cabinet against so overwhelming a catastrophe. A shrewd man of business, the King of France fully appreciated the situation. He knew the ex-Chancellor's return was as much a nightmare to Arlington as to Buckingham, and, in his own words, he did not fail "to play on this phantom of their imagination."

Thus, a few brief months after the signature of the Triple Alliance, Buckingham felt constrained to despatch that worthy, Leighton, to Paris, whilst Arlington was represented there by Williamson, the future Secretary of State. Both envoys were cordially received; for, if Louis credited the Duke with greater sincerity, yet, as he remarked, "without the assistance of both the heads of his ministry, the King of England would never have the strength of mind to come to a fixed decision. The dissentient, with his following, would always be able to bring him over to his opinion."[1]

Louis never scrupled to use the tools Fate put into his hands; but the methods he judged best fitted to secure their allegiance plainly disclosed the estimate he had formed of Charles's Ministers.

[1] Mignet, "Histoire de la Succession d'Espagne," vol. iii. p. 15, 1668.

Colbert de Choisy, his representative at Whitehall, was commissioned to ascertain the proper sums he should offer to the Duke and Arlington. The King grudged no sacrifice, however heavy; but he thought it necessary to stipulate that the money for the two principals should only be paid over when the matter was finally settled.[1]

Meanwhile, Buckingham did not rely solely on Leighton's diplomacy. It was ostensibly at the Duke's request that Charles entrusted the negotiations to Madame, who, unknown to George Villiers, was already the moving spirit in mysteries the Duke was never intended to penetrate. Yet at the very outset, owing to the indiscretion of another woman, the complex scheme well-nigh miscarried. The Duchess of Richmond, then in waiting on the Queen-Mother at St Germain's, discovered something of the double-threaded intrigue. She promptly informed her brother that Charles, Madame and Louis were fooling him to the top of his bent, and that, while he fondly believed himself the mainspring of the affair, all decisions of moment were being adjusted without his knowledge or participation.[2]

When the Duchess's letter arrived, Buckingham was already beside himself with fury because Colbert hinted that he had not the power to carry out his projects. Mall's revelations set the climax to his indignation. He went storming to the Ambassador, vowing there was a plot to undo him both in politics and love; for he considered that it was nothing short of treachery to stir up against him the rivalry of the

---

[1] Mignet, "Histoire de la Succession d'Espagne," vol. iii. p. 15, 1668.
[2] *Idem*, vol. iii. p. 77. Colbert de Choisy to M. de Lionne, 18th March, 1668.

Dukes of Monmouth and Hamilton—the latter the nephew of his greatest enemy. And in this strain he ranted and raved, to the horror of the Ambassador, who declared that he dared not transcribe half the follies he uttered in that one interview concerning the Duchess of Orleans and the Duke of Monmouth. Vainly did Colbert beseech him to remember that "Madame sa Sœur" was notoriously untrustworthy. Till Henrietta's tactful assistance was invoked, he refused to be pacified, and Madame herself must eventually have become alarmed, for she spared no flattery to compass a reconciliation; in fact, she did not disdain to pander to his jealousy of Arlington, and vowed Louis's dependence on George Villiers to be so great "that he has told me he would give up the whole thing, if the Duke were to change his mind."[1] The gracious words had their desired effect. The bait was greedily swallowed, and in terms strangely passionate for a State despatch, the Duke protested his eternal devotion to the royal lady—

"You must excuse this bearer," he writes, "if he has staid here too long, because it has not been his fault.[2] I was desirous to have sent along with him a man capable of treating upon our affair, but that was impossible, and I own to you that I foresee difficulties enough in finding a person who knows the language and is versed in business, in whom I can confide: nevertheless, I will do anything in my power to accomplish it, and shall be very sorry, if not daring to send Leighton to you, and not being capable to find another, I must be reduced to the

[1] "Madame," by Julia Cartwright, p. 280. Letter from Madame to Leighton, 12th Feb. 1669.
[2] J. Dalrymple, "Mems. of Great Britain," vol. ii. p. 8, ed. 1773. Duke of Buckingham to Duchess of Orleans.

necessity of entering into the matter with the Ambassador here, as it will greatly lengthen the affair. I have been with him as you ordered, and told him that you commanded me to communicate everything to him, but that I did not dare to do it without the King my Master's leave, and for this reason desired him to ask your Pardon on my part. I have also burnt your note and beg you will believe that the strongest desire I have in this world is to obey you.

"For the love of God don't be impatient; and consider that in a place where every measure must be taken to gain the good-will of the people, one cannot act with so much despatch as might be wished."

As we have seen, Arlington was at one with Buckingham's Gallic sympathies. Yet it is doubtful whether the Ministry formed at Clarendon's downfall would have rallied to their system. The last year, however, had wrought great changes. Many of the Cabinet were odious, personally as well as politically, to Buckingham, and these he determined to cut adrift. Charles seems to have made no demur to substituting Sir James Trevor to that estimable mediocrity, Secretary Morrice, and Ormond was eventually forced to relinquish the Lord-Lieutenancy of Ireland. There remained Sir William Coventry. The soul of truth and honour, Coventry had one unpardonable defect in Buckingham's eyes — he was a firm ally of the Duke of York's, and James had lately rejected Buckingham's advances in terms so contemptuous that the breach between them was appreciably widened. Thus Coventry was doomed, but the manner of his going is sufficiently curious to deserve notice. According to the French Ambassador, it was the talk of the town that a play turning Coventry into ridicule was the work of none other than his colleague Buckingham. Not only was the absurd personage of the piece—a certain councillor —got up like Sir William, but among the stage properties a double writing-table, invented by him, with drawers labelled " Affairs of Spain," " Affairs of Holland," was intended to caricature the secretary's methodical habits. Coventry heard of this, and made a formal complaint to the King, who sent for the comedy and himself glanced through it, but as this particular scene had been omitted, he saw no reason to refuse to license it.[1]

Though the "man of the finest parts, and the best temper that belonged to the court,"[2] Coventry was no Quaker.

He now considered himself grievously insulted, and straightway despatched his nephew, Henry Savile, to demand satisfaction of the Duke. Buckingham, however, chanced to be away from home at the time of the second's visit, and a series of accidents betrayed Coventry's intention to Arlington. The Government were determined not to permit another tragedy, and took strong measures to prevent this fresh duel.

The King's bias was plainly shown by his selection of the Duke to attend on him, when he paid his evening visit to the Queen. And Colbert felt constrained on his monarch's behalf to beseech Buckingham "not to hazard his valuable life in such an affair; an action, too, singularly un-

---

[1] "Affaires Étrangères," 11th March, 1669.
[2] Burnet, vol. i. p. 478.

necessary after the proofs of courage he had so lately given."

If, however, the Duke basked in the smiles of Royalty, his opponent was undoubtedly the popular favourite. The French Ambassador could not decide whether it was from love of Coventry, or from hatred of Buckingham, but he was certain that besides the henchmen of the Dukes of York and Ormond, all the most considerable men at Court were on Sir William's side. Moreover, his adherents, not content with professing themselves his humble servants, threatened to visit the players with exemplary punishment, on the very stage itself, if they presumed to act the farce which had given rise to the quarrel. Finally, "at the council held on the matter, the King did ask the Duke of Buckingham upon his honour, whether he had received any challenge from William Coventry? which he confessed he had; and then the King asking William Coventry, he told him that he did not owne what the Duke of Buckingham had said, though it was not fit for him to give a direct contradiction."[1]

"But being by the King put upon declaring upon his honour the matter, he answered that he had understood that many hard questions had upon this business been moved to some lawyers, and that therefore he was unwilling to declare anything that might from his own mouth, render him obnoxious to his Majesty's displeasure and therefore prayed to be excused: which the King did think fit to interpret to be a confession and so gave warrant that night for his committment to the Tower."

[1] Pepys, vol. viii. p. 245.

"The truth is," wrote Charles to his sister, "Coventry has been a troublesome man . . . and I am well rid of him." But neither the King or his Grand Vizier could prevent the worthy gentleman from receiving a perfect ovation in the Tower. "Sixty coaches there yesterday and the other day," writes Pepys, "which I hear also there is a great exception taken at by the King and the Duke of Buckingham, but it cannot be helped."[1]

Such unmistakable signs of disapproval should have conveyed a warning to the Duke to walk warily, but as usual he disregarded the lesson; and one morning, three months later, it was probably less of a surprise to him than to the town, to hear that, on the previous night, as Harry Killigrew was going in a hackney coach to his house at Turnham Green, along the well-travelled highway of Hammersmith, he had been set upon by footmen and well-nigh killed, receiving no less than nine wounds in the unequal contest.

Lady Shrewsbury had never forgiven Harry Killigrew's candid criticism, and as she had openly vowed vengeance, the outrage would in any case have been laid at her door. But, with matchless effrontery, she chose to feast her eyes on her former lover's discomfiture, and actually watched the murderous assault from the six-horse chariot in which she had tracked the wretched man.

The next day, the Duke of Buckingham was cynical enough to remark that "someone" who had been present—and in the eyes of the listening Court no more exact identification was necessary—had assured him that they had but intended to cudgel

[1] Pepys, vol. viii. p. 251. 7th March, 1668.

the unhappy Killigrew, and further, stated, with delicious inconsistency, that the latter had been the aggressor in the scuffle.

Small wonder that this careless flaunting of crime, paraded as it was in the very presence not only of the King, but of the father of the wounded man, made the Duke of York "the most amazed that ever he was in his life." Nor that when Harry's wounds were at first pronounced to be mortal — his hapless attendant had been killed outright, but this was a matter of less moment — James's horror was not unmixed with satisfaction at his enemy's indiscretion. Indeed he expressed the hope that "it might cost him his life in the House of Lords"—a futile aspiration, for the divinity that hedged a king in Stuart days extended to his favourites also, however worthless or blood-stained they might be.

CHAPTER IX

INTRIGUES WITH FRANCE

THE negotiations between the Kings of England and France meanwhile proceeded apace—in 1669 receiving a fresh impetus from the conversion of the Duke of York to Romanism. Much as the more prudent Charles afterwards regretted the action of the Duke of York, now in the presence of such trusted counsellors as Clifford, Arlington, and Arundel he hysterically protested that it was an example he longed to follow. However, neither then, nor at any subsequent period, did he confide these pious aspirations to the Duke of Buckingham. Principles sat lightly on our Duke. But, lax as he was—either as a result of his experiences when he visited Papal Rome, " in as much state as a Sovereign Prince," or when, a needy refugee, he explored the highways and byeways of the Continent—it was known that he could never divest himself of an inveterate animosity against Roman Catholicism.

His unhesitating support of the Anglo-French Alliance was consequently invaluable to Charles and Louis; for it was nothing less than a pledge to the nation that no tampering with the Reformed Religion would be countenanced by so zealous a Protestant.

To keep him in ignorance of his true objects was, therefore, a chief consideration with Charles. Indeed, to accomplish it, he laid aside his strong natural indolence, and sent epistle after epistle to Madame, beseeching her to be prudent, and "to write but seldome to him (Buckingham) for feare something may slip from your penn, which may make him jealous that there is something more than he knows of."[1] For, as Charles never wearied of impressing on his correspondent, "The great secret, that which concerns Religion... he (Buckingham) must not be trusted with." Thus, while the Duke remained persuaded he was forwarding a treaty to secure for England the mastery of the seas, the Spanish-American Colonies, with Minorca, Ostend, and half a dozen Dutch ports, and for himself the command of the English contingent in Flanders, Charles was, in reality, bargaining for French troops and French gold, for the sole purpose of coercing the civil and religious liberties of his subjects.

Not the least excitement in that memorable year of 1670 was the divorce case of Lord Roos. This nobleman, a cousin of Buckingham's, had already obtained a separation of bed and board from his wife. He now wished to get a bill passed enabling him to contract a fresh union. Lady Roos's guilt was undisputed; but divorce, as distinct from the annulling of the marriage, was hitherto unknown, and the measure was strenuously opposed both by the bench of Bishops and by the Duke of York, who regarded it as a precedent the childless King would be swift to imitate. For,

[1] Dalrymple, "Mems. of Great Britain," vol. ii. p. 24.

though no word was ever breathed against the fair name of Catherine of Braganza, yet there were not wanting casuists to assert that sterility was as valid a reason for divorce as unfaithfulness.

The King's behaviour strengthened the supposition that he favoured the scheme. Lounging by the fireplace of the Upper House, he listened to the debates with eager interest, canvassing such peers as were not "stiff and sullen men," his fervent adjurations and caustic comments contributing in no small degree to the eventual passing of the measure.[1]

When Lord Roos finally attained his object, Buckingham was openly triumphant. The Queen, poor lady, wept night and day, and the fears of the Prince and the prelates proved only too well founded; for, with indecent alacrity, the King's creature, Mr Bab May, was empowered to settle a date on which to move the dissolution of the Royal marriage.

Charles never showed any of the affection for James which breathes in every line of his charming letters to his sister Henrietta. And although it is difficult to accept Burnet's statement that he "hated" his heir, he was undoubtedly never on the same terms of cordial intimacy with the morose Duke, as with the Princess of Orange or young Henry of Gloucester. It was, therefore, well-nigh unaccountable to those who knew him to be devoid of all sense of duty, that James was the one person to whom he remained faithful. Against his own interest and comfort, he steadily adhered to his unpopular brother, and though occasionally he

[1] Burnet, vol. i. p. 493.

appeared on the verge of breaking with him, in the long run, the Duke of York always carried the day. No one then, or since, has satisfactorily solved the enigma; but there were those who frankly ascribed the King's fraternal devotion to nothing else but superstition. According to them, the monarch had never forgotten the prophecy that his death would speedily follow any open breach with the Duke, and it was fear rather than love that kept him true to James.

Whatever the cause, history, on this occasion, once more repeated itself; for, as the Crown appeared to tremble on the head of the Consort, a remarkable transformation scene occurred. The King suddenly forbade May to proceed further, and in an outburst of generous wrath, declared he would hang the man who ventured to vex the Queen by indiscreet reference to her conjugal deficiencies.

Catherine's relief was intense and natural, but she might have expressed it in a more decorous fashion. Mumming and practical jokes were characteristic of the lighter moods of the Stuart Court; and now a very tarantula of masquerade bit the leaders of fashion at Whitehall. The King and Queen themselves were infected by the prevalent mania. In sedan-chairs, and in disguises so perfect as to defy detection, they frequently arrived at entertainments given by absolute strangers, where they enacted the part of Haroun al Raschid to their hearts' content. Had they at least made these midnight sallies together, they would have been less dangerous; but on one occasion, the Queen actually found herself abandoned by her chairmen, who were as ignorant as her hosts of her identity, and, very much scared and frightened, had to get home to her palace as best she could, in the first hired carriage or cart she could find. Undoubtedly, queens should eschew hackney coaches. Marie Antoinette's reputation never recovered a similar indiscretion. And the consequence of this folly might have been even more serious for Catherine; for no sooner did the Queen's escapade reach Buckingham's ears, than he attempted to utilise the incident to free Charles from his matrimonial embarrassments.[1] He "proposed to the King that if he would give him leave, he would steal her away, and send her to a plantation, where she should be well and carefully looked to, but never heard of any more; so it should be given out that she had deserted; and upon that it would fall in with some principles to carry an act for divorce, grounded upon the pretence of wilful desertion." Happily for Catherine, "the King himself rejected this with horror. He said it was a wicked thing to make a poor lady miserable, only because she was his wife, and had no children by him, which was no fault of hers."

Thus failed the wildest plot ever conceived by an English Prime Minister. Nor was Buckingham more fortunate in his next proposition "into which the King went, which was to deal with the Queen's confessor that he might persuade her to leave the world and turn religious: upon which the Parliament would easily have been prevailed upon to pass a divorce."[2] For the Duchess of York, who

[1] Burnet, vol. i. p. 473.
[2] *Idem*, vol. i. 474.

had hitherto given various specious excuses for her continued absence from the Anglican Sacrament, now resolved to take the final plunge, and then and there sent off an express to announce her conversion at Rome. Henceforward, the Pope was pledged to support the York succession, and Barbara, Duchess of Cleveland, not unnaturally, joined any alliance formed to prevent a young and beloved woman from supplanting the fat and prematurely old Catherine.

Though these junketings and jig-makings at the Court of Whitehall appeared to engross attention, the Anglo-French Alliance had by no means fallen into abeyance. But the negotiations had met with a momentary check, owing to Charles's desire, real or pretended, to preface the declaration of war by the announcement of his conversion—an arrangement which, on account of its self-evident rashness, the pious Louis as strongly deprecated; hence delays arose fraught with danger.

But Louis knew his man. After a time he hesitated no longer, but boldly played the trump card. The ablest of all his diplomatic agents, Madame herself, was sent to overcome the King's hesitations. Henrietta was delighted to revisit her native land, for though the Queen of hearts at the French Court, her home life was singularly unhappy. In all that society there was probably no more despicable character than Philippe, Duc d'Orleans. Manliness he had none, and the sole proof of energy he gave was in devising many a mortification and misery for the wife whose popularity he envied.

To escape his presence and obtain her brother's

protection had long been Henrietta's ambition—a purpose which Monsieur could not frustrate, though he guessed, and eventually made her suffer for it.

Philippe was not the only person who mistrusted Madame's expedition. In the land of her birth it excited much curiosity, and more apprehension. The reasons alleged for it were various. The gossips vowed it was occasioned by Charles's last invention, a new Court costume, "a comely dress after ye Persian mode," as Mr Evelyn describes it, meant to replace the French fashions hitherto worn at Whitehall.[1] "France did not like this small beginning of ill-humours, at least of emulation," says Lord Halifax, "and wisely, considering that it is a natural introduction first to make the world their apes, that they may be afterwards their slaves. It was thought one of the instructions Madame brought along with her was to laugh us out of these vests: which she performed so effectually, that in a moment, like so many footmen, who had quitted their master's livery, we all took it again and returned to an old service."[2]

From the moment Madame landed at Dover it was apparent how absolute was her ascendency over Buckingham. Never was man more utterly subjugated. He could refuse her nothing, and at her bidding even vouchsafed to be reconciled to Arlington, from whom he had lately seemed hopelessly estranged. Charles proved no less plastic in his sister's hands than his Prime Minister. He could not, indeed, free Henrietta from her domestic

---

[1] Evelyn's Diary, 18th Oct. 1666.
[2] "The Character of a Trimmer: Miscellanies," by the Marquis of Halifax, 1704 ed., p. 164.

toils, but she bore away his signature to a document, which merited the eternal gratitude of Louis. This paper, the celebrated Treaty of Dover, was subscribed by the King's papistical Ministers only, Arlington, Arundel, Clifford and Bellings.

In many of its clauses Buckingham would certainly have acquiesced. He would have offered no objection to Great Britain's recognition and support of Louis's pretensions in the future partition of the Spanish Monarchy. He would have welcomed the coalition against the United Provinces, entailing an English contingent of 6000 troops for operations on land, and fifty men-o'-war for operations by sea. He would have exulted in obtaining Walcheren and Cadzand as our share of the booty. But the Protestant Duke must have protested, and protested loudly, against the public profession of Romanism which, for the price of 2,000,000 French crowns, the King of England undertook to make during the course of the next six months.

Buckingham was therefore left in profound ignorance of the secret convention; and it was with the same infatuated devotion with which he had greeted her arrival, that, amidst the salvoes of artillery, he bade his Royal Delilah a last farewell.

The final echo of the Dover festivities had hardly faded into silence, when the society Madame had so lately captivated, was startled by the announcement of her tragic end. Consternation and horror were widespread. The assurance of the physicians that her death was due to natural causes met at first with scornful incredulity; and, indeed, it is only the recent discoveries of medical science, which have shaken the universal belief in

Saint Simon's circumstantial tale of the cup of chicory water, administered by the vengeful Chevalier de Lorraine.

There was no one then, least of all the English Ambassador, but was convinced she had been foully poisoned, with the connivance, or at least the knowledge, of her husband. In London, the French Embassy was surrounded by a howling mob, bent on visiting Henrietta's murder on the first Frenchman on whom they could lay hands. A squad of troopers soon disposed of the rioters, but Colbert de Choisy found the Prime Minister more difficult to deal with. In the first paroxysm of rage, "les emportements d'un furieux," to quote Colbert, nothing short of a declaration of war would satisfy him.[1] If, as Louis's representative remarked, "the King were not wiser and more prudent, and Lord Arlington more moderate, affairs would soon be entirely out of hand." It must have been a relief to the latter when the official version of the *post-mortem* arrived, as it categorically refuted the hypothesis of poison.[2] On its receipt, Charles interrupted his "lever" to send for the Duke of Buckingham, to whom he immediately communicated the report. Its precise medical details carried conviction to the majority of hearers. Buckingham was less readily persuaded, but, in time, he also was obliged to admit that England had no legitimate ground for quarrel with France. And his last suspicions were finally laid to rest by his old comrade the Comte de Grammont, who, after a series of interviews, finally

---

[1] Mignet, vol. iii. p. 204.
[2] "Affaires Étrangères," No. 48, fol. 27.

succeeded in winning him back to his former Gallic proclivities.

The crisis was over, but the strain had been severe, and Louis recognised that he had well-nigh lost all the advantages of the Treaty of Dover. Under these circumstances, he thought it politic to send the Maréchal de Bellefonds on a special mission of condolence to Henrietta's royal brother. The choice of so distinguished a personage instantly inspired Buckingham with the desire to play a similar part in France. From the most violent denunciations of the French, he now passed to the other extreme. When he visited Louis's Ambassador, to "justify himself as to his ebullitions of temper," his proposals positively astounded that worthy.[1] The Duke contemptuously dismissed the notion of "general terms," and loudly clamoured to "join with France in an offensive league against the whole world, adding, after his usual fashion, that we should abandon to them the dominion of the sea, and content ourselves with that of the land." Nor would he rest till Ashley and Lauderdale had been initiated into his programme, and their adhesion had been secured.

After such proofs of devotion, neither King nor Ambassador could offer any objection to George Villiers representing the majesty of England at St Germain's. It would have been churlish to recall his recent hard sayings. Indeed, Louis expressed himself with unwonted graciousness on the Duke's appointment as envoy extraordinary, remarking that His Grace "was almost the only English *Gentleman* he had

[1] Mignet, vol. iii. p. 244, 14th July, 1670. Colbert's Despatches.

seen."[1] De Choisy, to whom Buckingham was ever a thorn in the flesh, was less enthusiastic. But, like Arlington he rejoiced at Buckingham's absence, as it would leave them free to adjust matters, unharassed by the fear of discovery, or the weariness of rejecting the many ducal plans and propositions. Evidently the special envoy did not depart empty-handed, for the Docquet Book contains warrants to pay £2000 to R. Mason for the equipage of the Duke of Buckingham, and £3210 for his general expenses.[2]

The welcome George Villiers met with in France must have surpassed his most sanguine anticipations. Never was Ambassador more royally entertained and feasted, for the King thoroughly realised the advantages to be derived from the friendship of the Prime Minister of England.

On his arrival Louis despatched two of his principal Ministers, the illustrious Colbert and Monsieur de Lionne, his chief Secretary of State, to receive and conduct the Duke to St Germain's. Here, not only was he treated as the King's guest, but he found Madame's own apartments prepared for his reception—an attention which must have strongly appealed to his romantic nature.[3] Nor was this the extent of Louis's civility. The Parisians themselves, familiar as they were with the gorgeous festivities of the Grand Monarque, were astonished at the hospitality shown to the Englishman whom their King delighted to honour. During one long August day, the flower of the French army marched and countermarched on the plain of St Sebastien

---

[1] Echard, "History of England," vol. iii. p. 255.
[2] Docquet Book, vol. xxiv. p. 280.
[3] Dom. State Cal., Charles II., No. 5, p. 278. 23rd August, 1670.

for the edification of the Duke. On another occasion, his nautical tastes were flattered by the spectacle of a mimic sea-fight in the canal at Versailles. Masques, dances, operas, and comedies succeeded each other, and even his hostile critics were forced to admit "that his noble presence and graceful mien was very acceptable and even captivating to those who then beheld him."[1]

The Duke did not disdain other methods to enhance his popularity. There were still old men in Paris, who had witnessed the semi-Oriental profusion, which marked his father's visit there half a century earlier. The second George Villiers could not draw at will on the Treasury, nor could he borrow the Crown jewels, as his predecessor had done. We do not hear that he wore suits of cloth-of-gold, bespangled with pearls, designedly sewn so loosely that at every step the precious gems fell in a shower at the feet of the bystanders —for their acceptance. Steenie's profligate munificence was beyond the power of his son. But he was not unmindful of the paternal traditions, and if the following anecdote is correct, prudent Brian Fairfax had cause to lament that the King's favour to Buckingham, in reality, proved a fresh drain on his fortune.

At one of the balls given in his honour, and which he himself opened with a "Lady of the first rank, with wonderful gaiety and address," a diamond hatband he wore, excited the curiosity of the feminine portion of the audience. Indeed, envy and jealousy made a certain number decide that so perfect a trinket was probably counter-

[1] Echard, "History of England: Charles II., 1670," p. 255.

feit. The damning whisper reached the Duke's ears. He waited till he had led his partner back to her seat, then twisted the glittering circlet round his finger, and scattered the diamonds among the ladies, crying, "See, Mesdames, if they are true or no!"[1]

But much as Buckingham delighted in such adventures and festivities, they were chiefly valuable to cloak the real object of his mission. The King of France, writing to his English representative, plumed himself on the skill with which, "exactly in the manner that the King of Great Britain . . . thought desirable, I have managed the Ambassador.[2] That is to say, we have let him know that I have so extreme and passionate a desire to mortify the overweening pride of the Dutch, that I would even declare war against them, if the King of England could be moved to entertain these views and would conjointly come to a decision to attack them." Louis certainly did not exaggerate when he told his envoy that the Duke had from the first "entertained these proposals with ardour and pleasure," and had cordially received a draft embodying the main articles, which Lionne carried him from his Royal master. The Duke's triumph and joy were indeed unbounded, and found vent in the following letters to Arlington—letters, which must have seemed strangely humorous to one who knew that the Treaty of Dover had previously regulated most of the matters the Duke in Paris believed

---

[1] Oldmixon's "History of England, during the reigns of the Royal House of Stuart," p. 553.
[2] Mignet, vol. iii. p. 221. Louis XIV. to Colbert, St Germain's, 19th Aug. 1670.

himself to be negotiating, and negotiating for the first time :—

My Lord,—If I had had the good fortune to bring my Lord Falconbridge's secretary with me, hee would have entertained your Lordship with a whole sheete of paper full of the particulars of my reception heere; for I have had more honours given me than ever were given to any subject. You will receive within two or three days a proposition from this Court, concerning making warre upon Holland only, which you may enlarge as you please.

Monsieur de Lionne shewed me the modell of it last night and I shall see the particulars before they are sent. In the meantime having not yett your Cipher I shall only tell you in Generall that nothing but our being mealy mouthed can hinder us from finding our accounts in this matter; for you may almost aske what you please. I have written more at large in cipher to my Lord Ashley, and when you have discoursed together, if you thinke my stay heere will bee of use to His Majesty lett me know it, if not I will come away.[1]

On the 17th of August he writes again :—

My Lord,—I have nothing to add to what I wrote last but that I am every day convinced of the happy conjuncture we have at Present in our Hands of any conditions from this Court, that we can in reason demand.

The King of France is so mightily taken with the Discourses I make to him of his Greatness by Land, that he talks to me twenty times a day; all

---

[1] "Miscellaneous Works," p. 67. Duke of Buckingham to Arlington, St Germain, 15th Aug.

the Courtiers here wonder at it and I am very glad of it and am very much yours, etc.¹

Before the Duke departed, the King bestowed on him tokens of regard more substantial than the civil speeches, which caused so mighty a flutter in the Courtly circle. Already, in the early days of his visit Louis had gratified him with four of his best horses. Now, "when he took his leave of the King on Wednesday night," writes an English attaché, "the King presented him with a rich sword and belt, and putt it on his shoulders with his own hands and it is valued at 40,000 crowns and was given with all the signs of favour that could be."²

No society was outwardly more polished than that of Versailles, but the vicissitudes which befell the Royal gift throw a startling light on the thin veneer that in reality veiled its lawlessness. Such general curiosity had been aroused by the accounts of the superb workmanship of the sword, that one courtier after another came to inspect it. As the visitors were all gentlemen, it would have been highly ungracious on Buckingham's part to make any difficulty about the exhibition; yet he must have regretted his good nature when it appeared that "some of the nimble youths of the Court made a shift to pick two or three diamonds out of it, with which I believe they intend to give a lustre to their own meritt."

It was impossible, under the circumstances, for

[1] "Miscellaneous Works," *idem*.
[2] F.O. Despatches, Record Office.

the English Ambassador to draw attention to so disagreeable an incident, and Buckingham had to get the gems replaced at his own expense.

Louis's bounties did not end with the bestowal of the jewelled blade—a present which, according to the ideas of the time, the most upright Minister need not have had any scruples in accepting. Clarendon, indeed, had systematically refused presents of money from foreign potentates. But Villiers did not indulge in quixotic fancies, and when Louis informed him of his intention to settle 10,000 livres a year on Lady Shrewsbury, he received the proffered pension with grateful alacrity. Undoubtedly her good offices were valuable to Louis, for the beautiful harpy might be fully trusted to keep her lover faithful to so princely a paymaster. Yet, at that moment, the King might have held his hand, for all his donations were transcended by his promise to obtain for Buckingham the command of the British troops in the Low Countries. Martial glory had always been Buckingham's ideal. At last it appeared to be within his grasp, and whilst the glittering lure was dangled before his enraptured vision, no man in the length and breadth of France was more Louis's obedient, humble, servant, than the Prime Minister of England.

Matters being thus satisfactorily arranged, the Duke left Paris on the 15th of September. Up to the very moment of departure he was sumptuously feasted. He arranged to start for England after partaking of a farewell supper, at the house of the Comte de Saulx; but the banquet proved so agreeable, that it was three o'clock in the morning before Buckingham could summon resolution to tear himself away and to enter his coach.

The staff of the British Embassy were considerably amused at the retinue of French servants whom he had taken into his service — "some fourteen in all; a maistre d'hotel to whom he gives £100 a year, butler, cooks, barbers, tailors, in effect a very worthy tribe. God knows how long they may please him. He hath given away very liberally to the value of about £1000."[1]

"The very worthy tribe" here enumerated were not the only Parisians whom the Duke undertook to transport to England. During Madame's progress to Dover, Charles II. had made no mystery of his admiration for one of the maids of honour in her suite, Mademoiselle de Kéroualle. Had it depended on him, she would never have quitted our hospitable shores; but Henrietta, from motives either of morality or jealousy, refused to leave the damsel behind.

Louise de Kéroualle was the eldest daughter of a small Breton noble. Her father's family, who claimed descent from the Penhoëts, were one of the four great races of the bishopric of Léon, memorable in the proverb: "For Antiquity Penhoët, for valour de Chastel, for riches de Kernan, for chivalry de Kergon." At the end of the seventeenth century their fortune no longer corresponded to their lineage or pretensions, and the Seigneur Guillaume de Penancoët was thankful to obtain a post in Madame's little Court for his daughter Louise.

[1] F.O. Despatches, Mr Vernon.

Beautiful as the future Duchess of Portsmouth was, she does not seem to have excited much attention till Charles II. fell victim to her charms. The Princess's death had now deprived her of her position at St Germain's. It was natural that the King of England should not abandon one of the servants, for whom, on her death-bed, Henrietta implored his protection, and Louis, who foresaw the vast influence the lovely girl might acquire over the amorous monarch, also warmly encouraged the scheme. Yet, it is possible that all these reasons would have been insufficient to induce Louise to start on her quest, had it not been for George Villiers' persuasive tongue.

The Duke's ephemeral league with the Duchess of Cleveland had long since come to an end, and for some time past he had striven by every means to supplant her. It was through him that the two celebrated actresses, Mrs Davis and Nell Gwynn, were introduced to Charles. But after all, "poor Nelly," as Burnet quaintly, and much to Swift's indignation, remarked, "was never treated with the decencies of a mistress."[1]

"The indiscreetest and wildest creature that ever was in Court," she could not be expected to counteract the political intrigues of a Lady Castlemaine. Yet there were signs that the latter's power was waning. Clarendon had told her he was content to leave her punishment to time, and his words were being verified. It was considered significant, when the King made Will Legge sing a ballad to her, that began with these words:

[1] Swift's characteristic note runs: "Pray, what decencies are those?" Burnet, Note S. to vol. i. p. 475.

"Poor Allinda's growing old: these charms are now no more."¹

Though it did not teach her prudence, Barbara herself seems to have had no illusions as to the object of the somewhat ungallant joke; and when, by an "artifice" of Buckingham's, Charles surprised his lady-love at the instant handsome Jack Churchill was making a hurried exit through her window, her fate was sealed, though he showed his contemptuous indifference by remarking to the future hero: "I forgive you, for you do it for your bread."

All these events had occurred immediately before Buckingham's journey to Paris. He was convinced that the psychological moment had arrived when a new female adviser should be introduced at headquarters. And in Louise, the Prime Minister believed he had found that *rara avis*, an easy-going, good-tempered lady, of unusual beauty, whose gratitude would pledge her to support his interests.² Thus, when in the dawn of that September morning the Duke took leave of his Parisian friends, Mademoiselle de Kéroualle took place beside him in the ducal travelling chariot.

Buckingham, said one who knew him, "was so full of mercury that he could not fix long in any friendship or to any design."³ And certainly his conduct on this occasion strikingly exemplified the truth of the character; for when he arrived at Dieppe, he took ship by himself for England, promising to send a royal yacht to convey

¹ Lord Dartmouth's Note, *idem.*
² "Affaires Étrangères," vol. 137, fol. 499.
³ Burnet, vol. i. p. 477.

Mademoiselle de Kéroualle across the Channel. But once back in London, he seems to have thought no more of the responsibility he had so gaily undertaken, and as late as the 19th of October, the English Ambassador writes: "Mademoiselle Kéroualle hath been at Dieppe these ten days, and hears nothing of the yacht that the Duke of Buckingham, Mr Godolphin tells me, was to send for her."

Eventually Colbert de Choisy exerted himself on her behalf, and the distressed maiden found a refuge at the French Embassy. But, naturally enough, the Duchess of Portsmouth never forgave the slight; and in the years to come, George Villiers paid dearly for the dreariness and misery which, thanks to him, Louise de Kéroualle had endured, alone and forsaken, at Dieppe.

Absence did not affect Buckingham's fervid zeal for Louis XIV. On his return to England, the Duke was placed on the commission for regulating the Anglo-French convention, his colleagues being Arlington, Lauderdale, Ashley Cooper, and the Duke of York.

Charles offered no objection to the proposal that his Prime Minister should assume the duties of Commander-in-Chief during the coming campaign, and Buckingham's thoughts were so engrossed by that dazzling prospect, that he was the more easy to hoodwink. Now that success was close in view, it became more than ever desirable that Buckingham should not suspect the real objects underlying the *traité simulé* he had so energetically promoted in Paris. The millions, which were the price of Charles's conversion, were easily accounted for by being described as the French subsidy towards the Dutch War. Moreover, to stimulate the Duke's eagerness and his well-known spirit of contradiction, Colbert de Choisy and Arlington threw sham obstacles in the way of his darling project—thanks to which device he had little leisure to probe below the surface. A calmer judgment than Buckingham's might well, however, have gone astray amidst these labyrinthine intrigues; for, although some of the impediments were feigned, others were genuine, and the two soon became inextricably confounded. Charles was as ready—for a consideration—to break faith with Louis as with his subjects. Although the secret treaty had contained a clause rendering, in advance, the public agreement—Buckingham's boasted work—null and void, Charles refused to be bound to his own detriment. He saw that, come what might, the promised subsidy was his; he therefore found countless excuses for adjourning his reconciliation to Rome. Again, when his Protestant Ministers stipulated that the islands of Worne and Gorée, off the coast of Holland, should form part of the English booty, he shamelessly backed up their demands, and refused to ratify the public convention till this new demand was conceded.

In the circumstances, Colbert de Choisy was not on a bed of roses. But, much to his own astonishment, it was from George Villiers that he derived his chief consolations at this juncture.

"The Duke of Buckingham," he writes, "does wonders since his return. . . . he is continually impressing on me that he is no less interested for Your Majesty, than for the King of England, and that he will never waver in the gratitude he owes you."[1] Nor could this transformation be entirely attributed to the "compliment" which, by Louis's orders, Colbert paid about "Madame de Schrosberi's pension." For "though Buckingham received it in good part," he declared that "he knew Your Majesty's boundless munificence, and that this favour flows therefrom, and not from any misgiving as to his keeping his engagement."

Colbert's despatches are confirmed by Buckingham's own epistles. On the 13th of October he writes to Louis XIV. :—

"It is important for the welfare of this business that it should be concluded before the meeting of our Parliament. I therefore humbly supplicate Your Majesty to send your final decision on each article of the treaty, as quickly as possible, so that we may endeavour to be in a fit state to assist you in the beginning of next Spring. Since my return, Van Beuninghen has offered me a considerable sum to change sides; he has not been successful, but I apprehend that if the affair is long drawn out, he may succeed in other directions; for that reason, I shall be terribly[2] uneasy till it is completed. For the love of God, Sire, believe that never in the world has one man cherished for another so great passion, respect and gratitude as I shall ever owe Your Majesty."[3]

On the 24th of October, the Parliament so dreaded by Buckingham assembled at Westminster. The Commons, however, were more accommodating

[1] "Affaires Étrangères," No. 98, fol. 96.
[2] *Furieusement.*
[3] Buckingham to Louis XIV., 13th October, 1670.

than he had anticipated; and when the Government pleaded that, war being imminent between France and Holland, a strong fleet would be required to guard the British coasts, they readily provided a subsidy of two and a half millions. The illness, to which in the following letter, Buckingham alludes probably accounts for the small part he took in the debates at this time :—

SIRE,—I should be in despair if Your Majesty could doubt my zeal and my fidelity. I owe Your Majesty much gratitude but I feel I am even more strongly attached to your service by the personal qualities which render your Majesty so infinitely superior to, and more estimable than the rest of the ordinary world. It is those qualities, which force me to consider myself rather at your Majesty's service, than at that of any other, and will always give me courage to declare my views on all things with the utmost frankness. I protest after thus assuring Your Majesty of my devotion, I shall so place reliance upon your discernment, that Your Majesty, in return, will not misinterpret the passion that consumes me, when about Your Majesty's business.

Finally, Sire, I can no longer help saying to Your Majesty, that nothing ever so disturbed my mind as the handling of this treaty, since our return from Newmarket. There, the King was agreed on all points with Your Majesty. Nothing further was wanting but to draw up the articles we were to sign two days later, and these, I am convinced, could have been written out in less than one. My Lord of Arlington was to finish them in concert with Monsieur l'Ambassadeur, but since then we have had nothing but delays. The first stumbling block was over the islands of

Worne and Gorée, which Monsieur l'Ambassadeur has since yielded; but this should not have retarded matters, since the King my master had resolved to sign the Treaty, leaving a blank for the aforesaid islands, on the assurances I gave him of your Majesty's affection for him, and that without doubt, when you had weighed all the reasons, which could be advanced, you would reinstate them yourself. This I told Monsieur l'Ambassadeur, thinking, at first, I had worked wonders, but the next day, instead of arriving at a conclusion, we had another controversy on the preamble of the article touching the Prince of Orange. To begin with, the King my Master assented once more to all your Majesty's Envoy demanded, but that was of no profit to us, since time after time he started fresh difficulties, ultimately refusing to sign till his courier had arrived. At this moment, we are debating over one of those two millions, which were to be paid on the signature of the Treaty. During this delay, it has often been predicted to the King my Master that he would shortly have an infallible clue to the intentions of your Majesty, for, if your intentions had really changed, you would hesitate over the payment of the two millions. This prediction, agreeing so absolutely with what has taken place, confirms me in a suspicion which for some time has given me much uneasiness; and I can no longer doubt that the two gentlemen, who should have made all preparations for the conclusion of the Treaty, have plotted to break it off; and that while one suggests scruples to the King my Master, the other does as much with Your Majesty; if I am mistaken pray pardon a weakness which is part of my character. I can not be disinterested for those I revere. I look upon this matter as the only one that can add to the fame of Your

Majesty. If we consent to the dishonour that is daily recommended, and indeed thrust upon us, Your Majesty will miss the finest opportunity in the world to employ those talents with which God has endowed you, and which are capable, at the lowest estimate, of ranking you as equal to the greatest in all past history. Sire, I speak as I feel. If I am doing wrong, forgive me and let Your Majesty remember that from the instant I first knew you, my heart has been so filled with admiration for you, that I shall never more experience devotion to any other cause or know any peace till I discover some means whereby I can serve you and thus make you aware of the extent of my gratitude for the many obligations of all kinds that I have received from Your Majesty: From the depths of my heart, I am, Sire, etc., BUCKINGHAM.[1]

I venture very humbly to beseech your Majesty to forgive me the freedom of this letter.

Louis's reply to this effusion must have left Buckingham nothing to desire.

MY COUSIN,—I did not hasten to send you back your gentleman, because when he arrived, I was assured that all the difficulties, which had arisen on the other side, were already brought to an end by the orders sent by me a few days before to my Ambassador, bidding him conclude the matter, to the entire satisfaction of the King your master.[2] Yet, I can no longer regret these little obstacles, since they have furnished you with the occasion of giving me a new proof of your friendship, which I

---

[1] Mignet, "Hist. de la Succession D'Espagne," vol. iii. p. 247, London, 19th November, 1670. Duke of Buckingham to Louis XIV.
[2] *Idem*, vol. iii. p. 254. Louis to Buckingham, 15th Dec. 1670.

prize most highly, while I have an opportunity of reiterating that my friendship for you is as real as I have ever professed, or you could even desire. For the rest, I have committed to Lyonne the task of replying to several points of your letter to me and also one of yours to him; especially with reference to the suspicions you entertained, suspicions indeed, which lay me under the greatest of obligations to you, but which I can assure you are without any foundation, at least as regards my Ambassador, and I wish to think as regards the other person also. In any case, you acted with so much cordiality and energy that it would have been difficult for the business not to have been carried through to a conclusion mutually satisfactory to both of us. I could most ardently have wished that the end had been more quickly attained; but to ensure certainty and security, it has been necessary to proceed with deliberation. And on this I pray God, my cousin, to have you in His most holy keeping Louis.

Buckingham's felicity was completed by Lyonne's covering despatch to the royal missive. The astute Frenchman assured the Duke that he had "never seen the King more touched than by the important mark of friendship you gave him "[1] . . . and that "when I presented your letter, His Majesty did me the honour to say in these express terms: 'I am proud when I find the judgment I have formed of a man is correct. You see how little I erred in my estimate of the Duke of Buckingham. I am convinced that he as sincerely loves me, as any man that lives; I doubt whether you yourself have a greater zeal in my interests, for,

[1] Mignet, vol. iii. p. 253. 15th Dec. 1670.

see in what anxiety the suspicion that our affair might miscarry has plunged him.'"

Louis's honeyed words were not uttered in vain. On December the 31st, 1670, the treaty was subscribed by the whole of the Cabal: Clifford, Arlington, Buckingham, Ashley, and Lauderdale. The formal declaration of war with Holland was thereby postponed to the spring of 1672; and Louis, stickler for etiquette though he was, graciously conceded precedence over all other Lieutenant-Generals to the Commander of the English Auxiliary force.

CHAPTER X

BUCKINGHAM'S VAGARIES

THE projected treaty between the two kingdoms had lately appeared to occupy much of the Duke's attention. But it is clear that protocols did not engross all his thoughts, since, at the very same time, this strange Prime Minister could find both leisure and energy to compass nothing less than the kidnapping of the venerable Duke of Ormond.

Towards the end of 1670, the Prince of Orange came to England, on a visit to his uncle. The "Great Deliverer" was then a silent, morose young man, whose rigid decorum was a severe trial to the Merry Monarch. As his guardian, Charles felt it his bounden duty to reform such undue austerity, and deputed the welcome task to Buckingham. The tempter was only too successful; and at the close of a supper given in his honour by George Villiers, the Prince was restrained by main force alone from breaking into the wing of the palace sacred to the maids of honour.[1]

Happily, convivial as was that age, the entertainments of Buckingham and Rochester were even then regarded as abnormal; and another great feast that was given in William's honour by the

[1] Reresby, "Memoirs," p. 173.

Lord Mayor of London, was doubtless as pompous and sedate as the Duke's was riotous. But the sequel to the City Banquet was yet more disastrous, since it was on his return from the Guildhall that the Duke of Ormond's coach was stopped by Colonel Blood, acting, it was currently reported, under Buckingham's directions.

In 1663, during his Irish Viceroyalty, the Duke of Ormond had discovered a plot to surprise Dublin Castle. Most of the conspirators were executed; but Blood, the ringleader (though his property was confiscated), was more fortunate, and contrived to escape. For the loss of his estate, however, he held the former Lord Lieutenant responsible, and honoured him with an uncompromising hatred. Yet it is absurd to believe that so reckless an adventurer would for seven years have deferred taking vengeance, had it really been, as he pretended, the aim and object of his existence. Like his contemporaries, we are forced to the conclusion that in this case Blood was but a tool in the hands of George Villiers, who, thinking he could now ensure both himself and his confederates from the pursuit of justice, snatched at the opportunity to be avenged of his ancient enemy.

The moment selected by Blood for his attempt was undoubtedly well-chosen; for he waited to swoop down on his unsuspecting victim, till the Duke's heavy chariot, divided from the retinue of footmen, was lumbering up the steep and ill-paved ascent of St James's Street. Had the Colonel been satisfied with commonplace reprisals, the Duke's shrift would have been short; but nothing save the ignominy of a felon's death on Tyburn

Gallows would content Blood, or rather his patron —whose cynical ingenuity is plainly discernible in the whole affair.

Old as he was, Ormond, however, was not captured without resistance; and some minutes elapsed before he was secured, strapped, and buckled behind one of Blood's horsemen. They then started for Tyburn, but while the leader set off at a gallop to prepare a halter and gibbet, the band's progress was hindered by the Duke's persistent struggles. Indeed, when they reached Piccadilly, he succeeded in unhorsing the ruffian to whom he was attached, and captor and captive rolled in the mire together. This delay proved his salvation, for the ducal coachman, who had been forgotten, had meanwhile aroused the servants at Clarendon House—Ormond's residence—and led them in pursuit of the murderers; and such haste did they make, that they arrived to find their master still wrestling on the ground where he had fallen. At their approach, Ormond's antagonist disentangled himself, and rode off with a parting shot, which took no effect. The Duke was unhurt, but so exhausted by his valiant fight, "that his servants knew him rather by feeling his star, than by any sound of voice he could utter." [1]

After such an outrage, the King—whatever might be his suspicions—had no choice save to issue a proclamation for Blood's arrest. But neither he nor the other bandits were apprehended till the month of May, on the occasion of the failure of their daring attempt to plunder the regalia in the Tower. Then occurred the most dis-

---

[1] "Life of Duke of Ormond," by Carte, vol. iv. p. 443.

creditable incident of all. When all law-abiding citizens believed that the scoundrel was at last to meet with his deserts, Charles was induced to grant the prisoner a personal interview, which was promptly followed by a free pardon.

The fact is that Blood was a plausible and quick-witted rogue; and either "his bravadoes, or the menacing intercessions" of high officials, prevailed with Charles not only to restore him to liberty, but to grant him a substantial pension. Nor did the King's clemency end there. The ex-robber and bravo was promoted to such favour that "if anyone had a business at Court that stuck, he made his application to Blood, as the most industrious and successful solicitor; and many gentlemen courted his acquaintance, as the Indians pray to the Devil, that he may not hurt them."

Even at Whitehall, such doings created some wonder; but no one remonstrated till Ossory was driven into passionate protest.

A rumour was current—industriously circulated by Buckingham—that Clarendon and Ormond were in league to have him murdered. So circumstantial was the tale, that two men were actually designated as having been entrusted with the task, and Buckingham declared that he owed his escape solely to the assassins themselves being poisoned, and making a full confession of the plot during their last agonies. Ormond and Clarendon were too well known, and respected for the tale to command belief; it suffered also in credibility from the fact that it was by no means the first accusation of the sort that had been brought by Buckingham. It will be remembered that in 1667 the Privy Council had solemnly investigated a similar conspiracy against him. Again, in 1668, he pretended that his life was threatened by the Heir Presumptive, and went nowhere unless surrounded by an armed bodyguard. Nor would he disband his mercenaries until driven to do so by the merciless raillery of the King.

Ossory himself had no doubt as to the aim of the obvious calumny. He was convinced it was meant "to prepare the world to receive an apology for another assassination (in case the true author should be discovered), as if it were perpetrated purely in revenge for the like intended against himself, or made necessary for his own defence." And as he knew it was vain to appeal to Justice, he resolved to take the law into his own hands. He waited till one day he found George Villiers standing by the throne, and then, in the presence of the King—whom, indeed, he claimed as chief witness—he made him the following speech: " My Lord, I know well that you are at the bottom of this late attempt of Blood's upon my father; and I therefore give you fair warning; if my father comes to a violent end by sword or pistol, if he dies by the hand of a ruffian, or by the more secret way of poison, I shall not be at a loss to know the first author of it; I shall consider you as such; and wherever I meet you, I shall pistol you, though you stood behind the King's chair; and I tell it you in his presence, that you may be sure I shall keep my word."[1]

This outspoken declaration had its desired effect. Not only did the sailor lord's blunt onslaught leave even the versatile favourite

[1] Carte, vol. iv. p. 449.

speechless, but thenceforward Ormond was relieved of the dread of assassination. The petty insolence of a few time-serving courtiers continued, indeed, but this the old Cavalier treated with disdain. In fact, it was so apparent that such episodes embarrassed Charles far more than himself, that they afforded him no slight amusement. Nor did the "civil" King's confusion escape Buckingham's notice; and incapable as he was of resisting a joke, even at his own expense, he could not on one occasion forbear whispering: "I wish Your Majesty would resolve me one question, whether it be the Duke of Ormond that is out of favour with Your Majesty, or Your Majesty that is out of favour with the Duke of Ormond? For of the two you really look the more out of countenance."[1]

Some time before the events just recorded, during the months of January and February, the Court ladies were busily preparing a "grand ballet." For many a long day, nothing so sumptuous as this entertainment had been witnessed at Whitehall. Public curiosity was vastly excited by the accounts of the marvellous costumes of the dancers, who included the Queen, the Duchesses of Buckingham, Richmond, and Monmouth, and Mademoiselle de Kéroualle. When, after two months of rehearsal, the performance took place, it was so attractive that the spectators "were forced to go by four o'clock, though it did not begin till nine or ten.[2] They were very richly dressed and danced very finely and shifted their clothes three times. There

---

[1] Carte, vol. iv. p. 484.
[2] Hist. MSS., "Rutland Papers," vol. ii. p. 22. Lady M. Bertie to Lady K. Noel.

was also very fine musickes and excelent singing, some new song made purpose for it. After the ballet was over, several others danced, as the Duke of York and the King and the Duke of Buckingham. And the Duchess of Cleveland was very fine in a rich petticoate and halfe shirte, and a short man's coat very richly laced, a periwigg, cravate and a hat."

Mary Buckingham's passion for gold lace must have been gratified by this threefold shifting of gorgeous raiment. Yet under her embroideries, the "Dowager Duchess," as the wits unkindly called her, must have carried a sad heart; for Lady Shrewsbury had recently presented her faithless lord with a son, whom he had welcomed with demonstrations of delight. Indeed, on this occasion, joy must have completely turned his head, for he assumed royal prerogatives and bestowed the title of Earl of Coventry on the infant. Charles cannot have been displeased, for he stood godfather to the boy; but, amongst the general public, the irregular patent of nobility excited greater indignation than any of the Duke's previous crimes and misdemeanours. Nor did the scandal cease with the child's death, which occurred a few days after the festivities at Whitehall. Every prejudice, every canon of that punctilious age, was outraged by the pompous funeral in Westminster Abbey —a princely pageant, where kings-at-arms and pursuivants trumpeted the poor babe's fictitious titles, before consigning the little coffin to its last resting-place, amongst the ashes of our Sovereigns, in Henry VII.'s Chapel.

After so open a defiance of all conventions, the

rumour that the Duke had owned to a marriage, celebrated by his Chaplain, Dr Sprat, between him and the widow of his own making, was not incredible to his horrified contemporaries. And we may safely assume that bigamy was a less heinous offence in their eyes, than this unholy tampering with heraldic distinctions and titles of honour.[1]

Had the Earl of Coventry survived his childhood, it is doubtful whether his father would have left him aught but debts. Already, in 1668, Mr Pepys, writing of "broken sort of people," remarked that although the Duke's rent-roll averaged a total of £19,600 per annum, the £7000 he paid in interest, the £2000 of fee farm to the King, with about £6000 in wages and pensions, considerably reduced his income; and certainly £4600 was a narrow margin of expenditure for a person of the Duke's quality and tastes. The King, it is true, had been the reverse of niggardly towards him. In July, 1669, he had granted him all "that new building near Wallingford House, commonly called Pickering House, together with the tilt yard adjourning, for his better attendance at Court."[2] A little later, again, "His Majesty in lieu of the several resignations of the Duke of Buckingham, has granted him a pension of £2,500 for 21 years and one of £1,500 for life upon the Northern Excise."[3] But in spite of the royal bounty, the year 1671 saw him far advanced on the road to ruin.

---

[1] "Macpherson's Original Papers : Life of James II. by Himself," vol. i. p. 58.
[2] "Entry Book," 1669, No. 251, p. 166.
[3] Hist. MSS., Le Fleming, Rep. XII. p. 77, 21st April, 1671.

In truth, few fortunes could both have satisfied the demands of Lady Shrewsbury, and also found the bricks and mortar for the miniature Versailles now rising on the banks of the Thames. The massive silver mirrors, preserved at Osterley, are probably but an inconsiderable remnant of the treasures heaped by him on this worthless woman. And though, except the outlines of its foundations in a dry summer, nothing remains of the noble mansion he reared at Cliveden, we can trace its glories in the stupefaction it created among his contemporaries. Charles II., for instance, was unfeignedly relieved when so good a judge as Mr Evelyn assured him that, "without flattery," Cliveden did not please him "as well for the prospect and park as Windsor."[1] But, though the diarist did not think the villa could bear a comparison with the palace of our kings, he enlarges with admiration not only on the celebrated view of the "serpenting" Thames, but on "the august and stately cloisters, descents, gardens and avenue," which owed their existence to Buckingham's taste.

Neither did the Duke atone for his extravagancies by retrenching in other directions. His household was frugally managed, and he had long ago renounced both cards and dice; but these were his two sole attempts at economy, and in every other instance he was lavish. In May, 1671, he was gaily feasting sixty French noblemen of high degree, heedless of the fact that he was £40,000 in debt, and that, owing to the prorogation of Parliament, his property would no longer be protected by privilege from the demands

[1] Evelyn, vol. ii. p. 354, 23rd July, 1679.

of his creditors.¹ And, when a few days later, he was invited to stand for the Chancellorship of the University of Cambridge, we may be certain he gave scant thought to the expense thereby entailed. The satisfaction of defeating Arlington—suspected of being a candidate for the like honour—would in any case have outweighed such a consideration; and to judge from the correspondence on the matter, he flung himself into the contest with all the impulsive activity of his nature. That George Villiers, who notoriously set both the laws of God and the Church at naught, should be the elect of a large portion of the clergy, astonished even the easy moralists of that age. It was the more remarkable that he had not to contend with the scrupulous alone.

Papist though the Duke of York was, his household still contained a Protestant chaplain, and this worthy, Dr Turnour, with Mr Page, formerly secretary to the Duke of Ormond, did battle stoutly against the enemy of their respective patrons. Had they been authorised to bring Arlington's name forward, they might have been more successful; but they were "too tender of his honour" to do so without permission, and from the very outset Buckingham had lost no time. The Chancellorship "was carried as a race is won by a jockey, only by getting the start."² Express upon express passed between the University and Wallingford House. Cambridge

---

¹ A. Marvell, "Corres.," vol. ii. pp. 394-395, 9th April, 1671.
² "Domestic State Papers: Charles II.," vol. cclxxxix. No. 200. Dr Francis Turner to Williamson.

was flooded with three hundred letters of recommendation. "Letters," writes Dr Hill, "from some persons, which I could not have believed, and commendations of the Duke, which I am sure they do not believe themselves. Some are so modest as to relate his virtues with a parenthesis of 'as those that know him best say,' 'as is generally reported' or some qualification of that kind.[1] Others recalled the story that is spread about the town and made use of, that the Duke drolling on the University, on occasion of some scholars coming to see the King at Newmarket, a stander by, in their hearing, should say that his father had a kindness to the place. With his usual preface to what he is about to say, he replied, that if they would choose him Chancellor so would he too."

Undoubtedly, the Duke also scored a distinct advantage from the fact that his envoys had arrived when it happened "that the University was met together in a full body, when finding none to appear, as a competitor, they immediately visited (a custom in the University) the members in the particular College in his behalf, with that success, that a great many of them promised their voices before they well considered what they did."

Thus, owing to a series of lucky accidents, and despite the threats of the opposing faction —who declared that the business had "been suddenly huddled up"—the Duke was elected by the suffrages of 194 Regents and non-Regents

---

[1] "D.S.P.: Charles II.," vol. cclxxxix. No. 189, 11th May, 1671. Dr Hill to Lord Arlington.

*nemine contradicente.*¹ And the Christian world beheld the singular spectacle of a man whose name was a by-word in the pulpits—however unjustly, for atheism, and, however justly, for open and notorious evil living—installed as the official protector of learning and piety.

At this time the Duke used Wallingford House, which occupied the site of the present Admiralty, as his town residence, and let York House, a far larger edifice, to the French ambassador. But, on great occasions, he borrowed his own house from his tenant—a proceeding which excited infinite mockery amongst the tribe of scurrilous ballad-mongers.²

It was at York House, therefore, on the 7th of June, that George Villiers, following the example of his father, decided to have the ceremony of his installation.

The dignitaries of that Church, which Buckingham was never weary of drolling, mustered in force to do honour to their new Head. And even in those days of picturesque costume, the stately procession of doctors marching across the Strand, from Exeter Hall to York House, must have been a goodly sight. Mr Bedell led the way across the Strand, in "his Bedell's gown, velvet cap, gold hat-band and Regent's hood, holding his staff the wrong end upward." Behind him came the Regent, Masters of Art and Bachelors of Divinity, in their caps, and habits, and furred hoods, the Proctors with

---

¹ Brit. Mus. Add. MSS. 5852, f. 423.
² "Duke of Buckingham's Litany: Poems on State Affairs," vol. iii. p. 82.

their chained books, while the Doctors of Divinity and Physic, in their scarlet robes and capes, made a brave show among the sober black cassocks of the Divines of the City of London.[1] At the foot of the great staircase, the Duke, richly apparelled, advanced, with the same punctilious etiquette he would have used to his Sovereign, to welcome the five Bishops, the Vice-Chairman, and the rest of the learned cohort. He was supported by the Bishop of London and divers of the nobility. "Obeisance made," they adjourned to a sumptuous feast, on which the University Chronicler loves to dwell.

The usual profusion which marked the entertainments of that period was not lacking on this occasion; and with his French chef, the Duke had evidently imported the Parisian fashion of serving his table. All the dishes of "costly meats both hot and cold, the sweetmeats also, and the fruit," were placed simultaneously on high stands erected to receive them down the board—an arrangement we can see depicted in the sketches of French banquets still preserved at the Musée Carnavalet. At the central table, surrounded by the prelates and the principal doctors, earls and barons, sat the new Chancellor, with the orator of the University facing him. The Bishop of Durham said grace both before and after meat, and probably, like our historian, added a mental thanksgiving that so sumptuous a feast had terminated without "any disorder or miscarriage."

Nor did the unusual condescension of the Duke, who on their departure escorted his guests to the

[1] Brit. Mus. Add. MSS. 5852, f. 423.

outward Court, fail to produce a favourable impression, which he was not slow to improve; for he shortly afterwards forwarded £300 to the Vice-Chancellor to be "layd out in fair pieces of Plate," which were to bear the Duke's arms and an inscription to mark them as his donation to the Officers of the University.

In the summer of 1671, the new Chancellor went to Dunkirk to pay his respects to the Royal "Object of his veneration," and to adjust various unimportant details in connection with the Treaty. Arlington told Colbert, with a smile, that he had purposely withdrawn to the country, that Buckingham might imagine the control of foreign affairs was exclusively vested in himself. If this was true, the Secretary's abnegation did not meet with its due reward. Now that Madame was no longer there to make peace between her brother's Ministers, Buckingham's ancient hatred and jealousy of Arlington had flamed up again more fiercely than before. In fact, on his return, the Duke did his best to prevent the proposed marriage between the Duke of Grafton, the King's illegitimate son, and Arlington's daughter. He assured Charles that instead of little Isabella Bennet he "would get the rich heiress Lady Percy for young Lord Harry." But the monarch, who either distrusted Buckingham's promises, or was ashamed to retract his own word, replied it was too late, as the other match was now practically concluded.[1] Having failed to break off the matrimonial alliance, Buckingham betook himself to the French Ambassador, into whose ear he poured a hundred innuendoes and

[1] "Life of James II.," vol. i. p. 67.

complaints against Arlington. These Colbert duly reported to St Germain's, but there the matter ended, and the Duke was reduced to such consolation as he could derive from composing satirical verses on his obnoxious rival. And this can, after all, have been no slight solace, when one remembers that the "Advice to a Painter" was probably circulated from one tittering courtier to another, as the proud Minister strutted through the throng.

Indeed, our modern Cabinets must almost seem harmonious in contrast to those where one colleague could write of another:

> "First draw an arrant fop, from top to toe,
>   Whose very looks at first sight shew him so:
>   Give him a mean proud Garb, a dapper face
>   A pert dull grin, a black patch 'cross his face,
>   Two goggle eyes, so clear, though very dead,
>   That one may see through them, quite through his head.
>   Let every Nod of his, and subtile wink
>   Declare the Fool would talk, but never Think.
>   Let him all other Fools so far surpass,
>   That Fools themselves point at him for an Ass."[1]

Charles II. was so obviously under the sway of his immediate circle, that Buckingham had some reason to dread the effect of a nearer connection with Arlington. But the marriage of the little Duchess—"that lovely child," as Evelyn calls her—was less fruitful of ill to him than another alliance which at this very time was promoted by his rival. For it was at Euston, during the October of this year, that the mock-nuptials of the King and Mademoiselle de Kéroualle were solem-

---

[1] Duke of Buckingham's Works: "Advice to a Painter to draw my Lord A—ton, Grand Minister of State," vol. i. p. 211.

nised.¹ Henceforward George Villiers had to contend with a relentless enemy, whose position gave her unrivalled opportunities of influence with the Sovereign. Nor was her task less easy from the fact that Buckingham's unbridled tongue was his own worst enemy. " He would rather lose his friend (nay the King) than his jest,"² says Lord Ailesbury.

The estrangement between the two old comrades now grew apace, though it was not at first apparent to the public. In the month of October the King did the new Chancellor the honour of making a State visit to the University of Cambridge, where he was received with every circumstance of pomp. The Conduit ran with claret wine.³ The streets were thronged with students in their habits; and at the Schools, the Duke, whose ribald sermons had often charmed Charles's sabbath leisure at Newmarket, now, to the accompaniment of suitable orations, presented him with a "fair Bible."

Buckingham was not indifferent to these outward and visible signs of the royal favour, but they were rapidly effaced from his memory by the events of the next few weeks.

Already, in September, Arlington—who wished his brother-in-law, Lord Ossory, under the nominal orders of the Duke of Monmouth, to command the English troops abroad—began to put difficulties in the way of Buckingham's obtaining this coveted post.⁴ He hinted that even did the latter's minis-

---

[1] *See* Evelyn, vol. ii. pp. 266-7.
[2] " Memoirs of the Earl of Ailesbury," vol. i. p. 13.
[3] Echard, p. 281.
[4] " Affaires Étrangères," 7th Sept. 1671, No. 101, fol. 1.

terial responsibilities in this country permit him to go to Flanders, yet it was doubtful whether Lady Shrewsbury would accede to so protracted an absence of her lover. And at his instigation Charles induced Louis to reduce his demand for British auxiliaries to 2400 men, under the leadership of the Duke of Monmouth.

Thanks to this arrangement, while the King of England was enabled to gratify his son and save his money, the Secretary could likewise do a kindness to a friend and repay many a grudge he owed his rival. Yet neither had the courage to face the Duke's disappointment and anger, and it was Colbert de Choisy who was deputed to act as spokesman.

The unfortunate Frenchman does not seem to have relished the experience. Hardly had he announced the proposed change when Buckingham broke into a furious passion. He regretted he had signed the Convention—vowed his signature should not figure on the public document—declared it was sheer mockery to pretend that the state of the King of England's finances forbade his levying 6000 men—a force, too, which would not serve merely to garrison any towns which might be captured, but as a school for the training of his nobility. It was merely done, he said, in order "to dishonour him, and to give the command to Ossory," and he wound up by declaring that to the campaign he would go, if only to command 2000 troopers.[1]

Nor were his threats idle. For a whole week the Prime Minister carried out his scheme of passive

[1] "Affaires Étrangères," 2nd Nov. 1671, No. 101, fol. 76.

resistance. He would not attend the Council, and he utterly refused to transact business of any kind. At the end of that time, the dislocation of affairs was such that Charles personally intervened.

He summoned the Duke to his presence, and good-naturedly enquired the reason of his evident unhappiness, remarking "in the most obliging fashion, that he wished him well, and would gladly find means to heal his sorrow." To so pressing an invitation, it may be imagined that Buckingham did not fail to respond. Indeed, a flood of impassioned words burst from his lips. He accused both Arlington in England, and our Ambassador Montagu in Paris, of having plotted against him, merely because he was the first promoter of the happy union between Charles and Louis. He gave full vent to all the accumulated bitterness of the last few days, and he wound up by striking a patriotic attitude, and solemnly protesting against the dishonour to his country and his king, should a smaller auxiliary force be despatched than had at first been stipulated.

Charles meanwhile let him talk, but when his eloquence was exhausted, he took up the parable from another point of view. In language of studied moderation the King pointed out that a less placable monarch than himself would certainly not have condoned the ducal intrigues, which had lately cost him a parliamentary subsidy of several millions. Yet he had freely forgiven his old friend. But when it was proposed that he should burden the country with an unnecessary expense to provide the Duke of Buckingham with a military command, he must demur. In similar circumstances he would not gratify his own brother's wishes. And then suddenly changing his tone, he emphatically and angrily declared that on an occasion of the kind "he would consider the Duke of Buckingham no more than he would his dog." Nay more, that it was his express command that the signatories of the Treaty should live in peace and amity together.[1] If any one of them failed in this duty, he would promptly discover the culprit, disgrace him, and give his confidence to another.

The Royal homily worked wonders. Buckingham returned to his duties, and Ashley and Lauderdale followed his example. On the receipt of her annual "gratification," Lady Shrewsbury, after expressing her sorrow at Buckingham's disappointment, inquired whether it was Louis's pleasure that the Duke should command the remnant of the English *corps d'armée*, or remain at home.[2] She was certain, she said, that he would adopt any course she advocated. Her assurances were met in an amiable spirit; and the Duke's protestations of "veneration" were rewarded by the offer of a lieutenant-general's commission in the French army—a proposition which put him once more in good humour with the French Government.

But although Buckingham had apparently been immersed in matters political, he yet found time for other occupations; for it was on the 7th of December, 1671, that his play, *The*

---

[1] "Affaires Étrangères," No 10, fol. 93. Colbert to Louis XIV., 1st November, 1671.
[2] *Idem*, No. 101, fol. 116. 19th November, 1671.

Rehearsal, was produced at Drury Lane Theatre, by the King's servants. The Duke had long since declared war on the inflated heroics, which Dryden, D'Avenant, and others had made fashionable. He could not endure the pompous rubbish mouthed by Dryden's personages in the *Wild Gallant*, the *Indian Emperor*, or the *Conquest of Granada*. On a well-known occasion, being present at a first peformance of one of the laureate's pieces, when a lover says:

"My wound is great because it is so small,"

the Duke cried out: "Then t'would be greater were it none at all."[1] The play was damned.

Nor did he content himself with such witty raillery. He organised a band of like-minded gentlemen to hiss this "fulsome new way of writing" off the stage.[2] The undertaking was, however, attended by considerable risk, when the author was no hack from Grub Street, but a scion of an ancient and powerful race. When this was the case, as on the night of the first performance of the *United Kingdoms*, Buckingham nearly paid with his life for the wild doings of himself and his claque; for the noble author's family carried their resentment from the pit to the doors of the theatre, where they posted themselves to lie in wait for the Duke's exit. And had it not been for the general tumult and uproar in the house and passages, Buckingham would hardly have contrived his escape.

The *Rehearsal* was no hastily conceived

---

[1] Walpole's "Noble and Royal Authors," p. 304.
[2] Bibliography, "Keys to the *Rehearsal*," Arber Ed., p. 46.

farce, nor was it solely due to Buckingham. Dr Sprat, the Duke's Chaplain (afterwards Bishop of Rochester), Butler, the author of *Hudibras*, and Martin Clifford, the Master of the Chapter House, were his collaborators. The critics strove to depreciate it by pointing out that, even with such "a combination of wits," its construction had taken "as long as the siege of Troy." But the comedy of the same name, which was ready for production in 1664, was essentially different. The Great Plague and the Fire, which disorganised all theatre management, were the causes of its being taken off the boards. Then Buckingham, under the name of "Bilboa," had held Sir Robert Howard, the creator of *The Duke of Lerma*, up to ridicule. Dryden, travestied as the absurd poet-playwright "Bayes," was now substituted for Sir Robert. Seventeen dramas are parodied in the *Rehearsal*, six of which are from the pen of the poet-laureate. And noble as every lover of English must hold much of his verse, it must be confessed that his dramatic works contain even more nonsense than indecency. Such are the ironies of authorship. Dryden, like Herrick, a man of blameless life, whom his enemies could reproach with nothing worse than an occasional feast of fruit tarts in the Mulberry Gardens, with Mrs Reeve the actress, is responsible for some of the coarsest literature of that licentious age, while the debauched and profligate Duke has left a comedy sparkling with natural fun and merriment, but innocent of a single gross or suggestive word.

Buckingham did not trust merely to the

intrinsic merits of his play. He supervised every detail of its production, and himself instructed Lacy, who took the part of "Bayes," how to mimic Dryden in his rendering of the speeches. These rhodomontades must have been truly comic, since the poet was noted for his defective elocution, and "had a hesitating and tedious delivery which, skilfully imitated in lines of surpassing fury and extravagance, must have produced an irresistible effect upon the audience. And to complete the resemblance, Lacy's costume was exactly modelled on that of Dryden."[1] Thus, when on the 7th of December, "this short mock-play, A posie made of weeds instead of Flowers,"[2] was presented to the public, it was hailed with rapturous enthusiasm—a verdict confirmed by posterity, since the *Rehearsal* has held the stage till recent years, and finally inspired Sheridan to write *The Critic.*

The approbation the piece elicited was not confined to this island. Its fame spread to France, and the Royal Mæcenas, who had led the applause at the "Tartuffe," now condescended to banter the great Colbert, assuring him "he would be out of fashion" if he did not give a successful comedy to the world, like the Prime Minister of England, "who had gotten a great deal of honour by writing a farce!"[3]

For the moment, Dryden remained impassive.

---

[1] Bell's "Life of Dryden," vol. i. pp. 94-100.
[2] Prologue to the *Rehearsal*.
[3] Hist. MSS. Rep. VI. 368 : Sir H. Ingilby MSS. Sir R. Paston to his wife, 16th Dec. 1671.

But in 1681, when the ducal satirist had fallen from his high estate, he amply discharged old scores in the character of "Zimri." Buckingham would not have been human had he remained insensible to the matchless irony of that polished invective. His Commonplace Book—we are told —shows that the iron had entered into his soul.[1]

TO DRYDEN.

> As witches images of wax invent,
> To torture those theyr bid to Represent,
> And as the true live substance do's decay,
> Whilst that slight Idoll melts in flames away,
> Such, and no better witchcraft wounds my name,
> So thy ill-made resemblance wasts my fame,
> So as the charmed Brand consumed 'ith fire,
> So did Meleager's vitall heat expire.
> Poor name! what medicine for thee can I finde
> But thus with stronger charms thy charme t'unbinde.

And again, under the head of "Railing":

> When he's offended hee shoots quills like a Porcupine;
> Nothing but being let Bloud in the tongue will cure him.

Nor did Buckingham confine his indignation to his note-book. The fashionable society of the day eagerly devoured the pamphlet in which he strove to answer the poet's charges. "Some reflections on a late poem entitled Absalom and Achitophel, by a Person of Honour," sold like wildfire in 1682. But as no less a judge than Sir Walter Scott considered its "celebrity was rather to be imputed to the rank and reputation of the author than to the merit of the

---

[1] *Quarterly Review*, No. 378, Jan. 1878, p. 101. George Villiers, Second Duke of Buckingham.

performance," [1] it can readily be believed that its extreme rarity, rather than its intrinsic merit, makes it valuable nowadays.

When their pen failed them, the noblemen of the seventeenth century had, however, other and more effectual means of vengeance.

One night, at Will's Coffee House, Dryden was soundly caned; and naturally "Zimri" was credited with having put his blood-letting theories into practice. Moreover, it was said that after the drubbing, the noble Duke sent the new Juvenal a gift of £500, accompanied by a letter of polite encomium on his great poem. Both actions are characteristic. Buckingham himself, however, repudiated the charge, and there is evidence which tends to prove that the real instigators of the assault were Louise, Duchess of Portsmouth, and John Wilmot, Lord Rochester, who resented various "gross reflections" on themselves contained in a MS. "Essay on Satire" recently circulated.[2] As a matter of fact, the real author of the libel was John, Earl of Mulgrave, but they chose to attribute it to Dryden, who thus paid in his person for the impertinences of the future Duke of Buckinghamshire.

[1] Dryden's Works, vol. ix. p. 273. Sir Walter Scott, "Notes on *Absalom and Achitophel*."
[2] A. Wood, "Athenae Oxon.," vol. iv. p. 207.

CHAPTER XI

THE FALL OF BUCKINGHAM

THE Anglo-French convention had pledged Charles to war with Holland. The formal declaration of hostilities was not made, however, before the 17th of March 1672; though a fortnight earlier, in defiance of civilised usages, Sir Robert Holmes, Buckingham's friend and former second, vainly attempted to capture the Dutch merchantmen from Smyrna, which, under a strong convoy, were peacefully making their way up the Channel.

By the beginning of May, the naval preparations of the States were complete, and De Ruyter put to sea, hoping to prevent the junction of the allied fleets. On his side, the Duke of York strained every nerve to get his ships ready for action; a task in which he received more advice than assistance from Buckingham, whose countless schemes, the overworked officials complained, drove them nearly distracted.

Nor were matters improved when the King despatched the Duke and the other Ministers to visit the fleet at the Nore. The Lord High Admiral's irritation was great when he discovered that Buckingham had so infected his colleagues with his own martial ardour that the entire Cabinet volunteered,[1] as one man, for active service. Arlington was forced to admit that such a course was contrary to the Sovereign's express commands. But it taxed James's authority to drive the militant secretaries back to their desks at Whitehall, while Buckingham himself resolutely turned a deaf ear to all decrees and remonstrances. He had hired a little craft, which made him independent of the hospitality of a man-o'-war, and on board her he defiantly remained.

Yet after a time the Duke's nautical enthusiasm must have cooled, for we know that on the night of the great action at Southwold Bay he was in London actively engaged in coping with a terrible fire in the city.

The conflagration began in a Quaker's house in St Katherine's and spread with a rapidity which recalled the awful week[2] of September 1666. Buckingham promptly took command, requisitioned gunpowder and engines, and himself directed the use of both. Nor would he leave till all danger was averted, and for twenty-four hours he stayed in the scorching atmosphere encouraging the workers by word, example, and liberal gifts of money. His real helpfulness on this occasion may have caused his absence from the navy during the action to be regarded as more perhaps than a merely negative blessing.

The engagement of Southwold Bay was, for all practical purposes, a drawn battle. The Allies were victorious, but at a fearful cost of men and

---

[1] "Affaires Étrangères," 19th May 1672, No. 104, f. 224.
[2] Dom. State Cal., Charles II. vol. cccx. No. 3.

ships, while De Ruyter, though much damaged, finally escaped.

On land, however, the fortunes of the campaign were far otherwise. Louis, at the head of a splendid army of 100,000 men, marched from one triumph to another. He swept everything before him, and, by the middle of June, the French outposts were within striking distance of Amsterdam. The States-General had so long neglected their army that at this crisis they were well-nigh defenceless and could only oppose 13,000 ill-drilled recruits to the vast French host. One preparation and one only had they made which now stood them in good stead. At the outbreak of the hostilities, to propitiate the King of England, they had appointed his nephew, the Prince of Orange, Captain-General of their forces, and now, in this dark hour of terror and despair it was to the heir of William the Silent that the hearts of his countrymen instinctively turned.

Indifferent soldiers as the Dutch had hitherto shown themselves, in the arts of diplomacy they were past masters. And while the dauntless Prince strove to protect the Hague and Amsterdam from the invaders, the States despatched missions to supplicate the allied Sovereigns for peace. When the Embassy reached our shores they were not allowed to approach the King, but an interview with Buckingham encouraged them to hope for favourable terms. The truth is that the war was unpopular in England, for the British merchants dreaded the effect on trade should Spain be drawn to league with Holland; and not only Charles, but Buckingham himself, felt some misgivings at Louis' uninterrupted career of conquest. The victories of the King of France had made him almost independent of his ally, and it was conjectured that he might now be found less willing to execute the conditions for which Great Britain had previously stipulated. These considerations induced Charles to send Buckingham and Arlington as plenipotentiaries to Louis, at Utrecht, to conclude a peace with the United Provinces; and Lord Halifax, who had already been despatched thither to congratulate the King on the birth of a son, was instructed to join and to act with the Ambassadors.

On the 25th of June Buckingham arrived at the Brill in the yacht "Catherine," followed by Arlington, whose boat, the "Henrietta,"[1] ran aground in the Moes for an hour before she could be got off.

On landing, they found that a revolution had taken place in Holland, and that William of Orange had been appointed Stadtholder, to the immense relief of the terror-stricken population who regarded him "as their only cordiale."

Under the circumstances the English envoys were greeted with enthusiasm, for the inhabitants were firmly persuaded that Charles would not abandon the nephew, whose fortunes were now bound up with those of his country.

Buckingham wrote home that the enthusiasm equalled if it did not surpass the scenes he had witnessed during the Rump bonfires in 1660; and certainly his letter gives a curious picture of the Ambassadors' reception.[2]

HAGHE, 25*th June* 1672.

My Lorde,—Though our expectation to finde

[1] "Holl. Treaty Papers," 82.
[2] R.O. S.P. For: Holland. Book 189. No. 101.

disorders heere was very greate, yet what wee saw when wee arrived exceded all wee cowld imagine. Our first salutation at Maslen Sluice was, God blesse the King of England and the Prince of Orange, and the Devill take the States. The whole Towne drew up in Armes, and conducted us to the State Howse, where wee drunke the King of England and the Prince of Orange's health. If that place had beene worth keeping, wee might certainly have maintained it. Comming into the Maese, my Yaught running a grownd I was forcd to stay some time to get her off againe, and thinking my Lord Arlington had gone before to the Brill, I took a boate and went hither, where I found all things just as they were at Maeslen Sluice, in soe much that I believe I might have taken that towne my selfe.

There are noe soldiers there at all, for the Townesmen will not let them come in, who are themselves in Armes and very druncke with drinking the King of England and the Prince of Orange's health. This change began first at Rotterdam, where the people enragd against the States, sett up the Prince of Orange's coullours, and forcd the magistrates to declare him State Holder, and unsweare the oath they had formerly taken, never to admit him into that Place. From thence they sent to Dort, the Brill and Maslen Sluice, where the same thing was done, and I believe in all the Townes of Zealand, though the States heere are very nice to confesse any such thing, but by theyre lookes, and by theyre having beene compelled the very morning wee arrived heere to doe the same thing, I am apt to thinke I am not mistaken in my guesses. In short, what I have seene heere can bee compared to nothing but the burning of the Rump. The States are in the silliest consternation that ever yet was knowne, they are fearfulle and helplesse as woemen or children, and yet out of theyre strange fondnesse to governe, are capable of taking noe resolution that might preserve them, for feare of being lesse than they were before. The King of France has sent the States these enclosed Articles for a Peace in which there is not the least notice taken of the King of England. It may bee this is a paper of theyre owne making, but the circumstances of this Treaty I doe not like, for upon theyre sending Mr de Guent of Guelders, de Grotte of Holland, Ondyke of Zealand and D'Eak of Groning, the King of France refused to treate with them, except they had absolute powers to conclude; upon which De Grotte was sent back to obtaine those powers, and that cawsed a great dispute amongst the States. Zealand and Groning were positive against granting any such powers at all, Freesland refused at this present conjuncture to sende it, but yet notwithstanding the States of Holland, with those other three states which the King of France has conquered, sent back De Grotte fully impowrd without the consent of the rest, and contrary to the very constitution of theyre government. This cawsd Zealand and Groningnen to send backe for theyre deputies, soe that De Guent and Grotte only remaynd with the King of France, who upon this sent to Grotte hither with these enclosed Articles, declaring that if within five dayes they are not consented to hee will goe on with his conquest, and this is the last of those five dayes. Delfsil mentioned in the second Article is a very considerable port in Freesland. Wee are just now going to the Prince of Orange, and from thence to the French Army, both which are quarterd as my Lord Arlington has written to you. In our way hither wee came by the Dutch Fleete which wee cowld not count in all to bee seventy sayle, and those that came up to us were very poorely manned. The reason of it we learnd heere, for they have sent all the better men out of theyre ships to the Land Army. I veryly beleeve that if our Fleete should come up to them, they would not dare to fire a gun. If the Prince of Orange could be persuaded to send the Dutch Fleete to the Duke, and deliver up some townes into our hands, it would bee in my opinion not only the best way for us, but also the surest for him to finde his account in this business. Wee have thought fitt to send you now this expresse, and if His Majesty has any further commands for us, I hope hee will let us have them with all speed, for the time presses.—I am, my Lord, Your Lordship's most affectionate and most humble and most faithfull Servant, BUCKINGHAM.

At the Hague, the Duke went to pay his respects to the Princess Dowager. In the old days of exile, he must have been well acquainted with her, and enamoured as he then was of the Princess Royal, he had probably contributed to those entertainments which the rigid mother-in-law had so sternly discountenanced. On this occasion, he overflowed with affability, and presented himself and his colleagues as being "good Hollanders." [1] But the Princess was too shrewd to give credence to his honeyed words, and retorted, "That was more than they asked, which was only that they should be good Englishmen."

He assured her "that they were not only so, but good Dutchmen too; that indeed they did not use Holland as a mistress, but they loved her as a wife." To which the Princess briskly replied, "Truly, I think you love us just as you love yours!" For once the Duke was unable to think of an appropriate repartee, and remained dumb-

[1] Echard, vol. iii. p. 305.

founded till, shortly after, the envoys resumed their journey.

At Neiverbrugge they found the Prince of Orange. He did not spare reproaches for the part enacted by Great Britain, nor would he let himself be silenced by their assurances that His Majesty refused to commence operations "till he had conditioned the Prince should find his account in it." William was cast in a different mould to the egotistical politicians sent to reason with him by his royal guardian. He was not moved by the offer of the crown of Holland. "He liked better," he replied, "the condition of Stadtholder which the States had given him, and he believed himself bound in conscience and honour not to prefer his interest to his obligation."[1]

They pressed him to consult with those he could best trust, but without mentioning this secret offer of his uncle's. Accordingly, after supper, the Prince called Van Beuning and Beverling to share the audience.

Van Beuning dilated on the advantages to England of an alliance with Holland, "after his usual manner, with a multitude of arguments, drawn from morality and conscience," which, says the Secretary, "took up a great deal of time."

The arguments, however, which made the greatest impression on Buckingham were those used by William himself. The Prince drew so vivid a picture of the unhappy results for England, should Holland be "totally overunne with the

[1] "Holland Treaty Papers," 28th June 1672, 267, f. 121, quoted in Foxcroft's "Life of Lord Halifax," vol. i. p. 85.

French," that he actually made a—momentary—convert of his hearer. In fact, to the astonishment, and somewhat to the consternation, of Arlington, the Duke, with his usual oaths, then and there, swore that "the Prince was in the right, and offered to sign a Peace immediately with him." The Stadtholder was hardly less amazed at the effects of his own eloquence than the English Secretary. But he thought that Buckingham might have secret powers of which he was ignorant, and consequently ordered articles to be instantly drafted and engrossed for ratification. By the next morning, however, George Villiers' reflections, or the remonstrances of his colleague, had wrought another change in that impressionable statesman, and he was found once more to have altered his mind.

Yet he did not abandon the son of his former love without making another attempt to save him from what he believed to be certain destruction. The interview between the two men is curious and aptly illustrates the moral and mental gulf which parted them.

The Duke pressed William to put himself[1] into the King's hands, and assured him he would take care of his affairs as his own. The Prince cut him short, saying, "My Country has trusted me, and I will never deceive nor betray her for any base ends of my own." The Duke answered, "You are not to think any more of your country, for it is lost. If it should weather out the summer, by reason of the Waters that have drown'd great

[1] Oldmixon, "History of England during the Reigns of the Royal House of Stuart," p. 570.

part of it, the Winter's frost will lay them open." And he often repeated these words, "Do you not see it is lost?" The Prince's answer, as Oldmixon truly remarks, "has more of the hero in it than whatever is boasted of in Antiquity. I see it is indeed in great danger; but there is a sure way never to see it lost, and that is to dye in the last Dyke."

Thus was the tempter dismissed, and the Ambassadors proceeded to Utrecht.

Here the King of France received the Embassy, with his usual pompous graciousness. The Duke of Monmouth, who commanded the English contingent, was permitted, says the despatch, "to putt on his hatt and make his compliment with us by the King's particular approbation, though the Credentials shewed no mention of him, which being ended, His Majesty bade all the Council go out except M. de Louvois and M. de Pomponne, who staid in the room." In private the King was every whit as polite as amidst the assembled courtiers. He abounded in civil speeches, declarations of his own striking moderation, and assurances of fidelity to Charles II.'s interests. The Englishmen were convened to work the next day with his Ministers. At the hour of nine—an early hour for Buckingham—they met, and worked till twelve, to produce a suitable basis for agreement.

In the ensuing discussions the three plenipotentiaries—for Monmouth had no real powers—each took up a different attitude.

Williamson, Lord Arlington's secretary, asserts that the Duke of Buckingham "was as high as ye highest that had ever been thought of, alledging that they were bound to demand Zealand, Woorne, Cadzand, Sluys in *sovereignty* and perpetual Dominion. . . . This being, according to him, the '*something*' our nation would at least expect to have by the warre."

On the other hand, Halifax, who had now rejoined the Ministers, did not conceal[1] his strong Dutch sympathies, while Arlington seems to have struck the mean, wishing to have Zealand and the towns as *cautionary* places, till the other conditions were fulfilled.

Eventually, Arlington's arguments carried the day, and it was as hostages that the surrender of Sluys, Walche.en, Cadzand, Goree, Voorne was required. No Englishman could regret that the "honour of the Flag" for Great Britain was the first article of the Treaty. Neither was it unreasonable that our merchants should be compensated for their losses in Surinam, nor that the Indies should be thrown open to our trade. But the other terms were far more onerous for the States than Halifax desired, and it was probably thanks to Buckingham that £10,000 rent for the herring fisheries on our coasts and a million of war indemnity were included in the terms, as well as "the Sovereignty of that portion of the United Provinces, *not demanded by the belligerents*, for the Prince of Orange."

Louis' stipulations were even more outrageous. Had they been carried out, coupled as they were with a crushing war indemnity of 17,000,000 livres, they would undoubtedly have effected the partition,

---

[1] Foxcroft, " Life of Lord Halifax," vol. i. pp. 92-93.

or the ruin, of the Republic. Insult was moreover added to injury by the clause which required the sturdy Dutchmen to present the French Monarch in yearly tribute with a gold medal, bearing an inscription commemorating his signal magnanimity in not utterly taking away their place from among the nations of the earth.

The proud answer of William to these proposals is well known. Like their leader, the men of Holland showed themselves true to their traditions. They opened the dykes and saved their native land.

The Ambassadors did not await the Stadtholder's answer before they turned homewards. But urgently as Charles required the presence of the Ministers at home, Louis would not allow them to depart until they had witnessed the parade of his own regiment—a spectacle which the dazzled Englishmen admitted to be "ye regale of the season." Then, escorted by the Duke of Vendome and the Conducteur des Ambassadeurs, they travelled to the port of embarkation in two of the King's coaches.

On their arrival in England, their services, as well as that of the other members of the "Cabal," met with due reward. Clifford received a barony, Arlington and Ashley were advanced in the peerage, whilst a few months later the Great Seal was transferred from Bridgeman to the new Earl of Shaftesbury.

And here, although the fact is too well known to deserve notice, it may be well to remark that the word "Cabal," by which this administration is known in history, had for some time been used to designate that inner committee of the Privy Council, the parent of our modern "Cabinet." The expression was borrowed from the Hebrew, Kabala, and it was a pure coincidence that it was spelt with the first letter of the name of each minister—Clifford, Arlington, Buckingham, Ashley, Lauderdale.

The King of England was not the sole fountain of honour on this occasion; the gifts forwarded by the King of France, as an acknowledgment of the envoys' good intentions, were so sumptuous that both Buckingham and Arlington remarked they might have been intended for monarchs rather than subjects.

With his ally, Shaftesbury, in high office, Buckingham's influence at Court should have been doubled. That this was not the case, may be largely imputed, not only to the growing power of Louise de Kéroualle, to which allusion has already been made, but to the further alterations which took place in the Administration.

In March 1673, the celebrated Test Act was passed which made it obligatory for all soldiers and functionaries to subscribe a declaration against transubstantiation, and also to receive the Holy Communion after the rites of the Church of England.

Neither the Duke of York nor Clifford—who had long secretly been Catholic—could conscientiously remain in office under the circumstances, and the enactment of the Test Act was speedily followed by both their resignations.

Clifford had originally owed the white staff to Buckingham's friendship, and he believed he would best repay this obligation by giving the Duke timely warning of his intentions. There was no post in the Government more important than that of the Lord Treasurer, and the two men spent many an anxious hour in discussing Clifford's successor. Various names were proposed only to be rejected, till, eventually, they decided to appoint a Yorkshire gentleman, Sir Thomas Osborne.

The choice commended itself to Buckingham; for not only did he believe Osborne to be a staunch supporter of his policy, but as the estate of the future Duke of Leeds was then "much sunk"[1] he calculated, that in common gratitude to the patron who relieved him from such pressing financial embarrassments, Sir Thomas would use the vast influence his place bestowed in a fashion agreeable to himself. But the sequel proved that, since the day when the Duke invited Louise de Kéroualle to take a seat in his travelling carriage, he had never made a mistake more egregious or one more fatal to his fortunes.

With the advent of spring, Buckingham not only experienced a return of his chronic martial fever, but seems to have had good reason to hope that he might take a leading part in the approaching operations on the Continent. A plan he sketched for a descent upon Holland by the Zuyder Zee, approved itself to Charles, who went so far as to promise him the subordinate command under the Duke of York.

Transported with delight, the prospective general rushed off to Yorkshire to raise recruits for his regiment. The levies did not however respond to his appeal as they had done in 1666.

[1] Burnet, vol. ii. p. 14.

The stout northern yeomen scented Popery in every proposition of the Government; and George Villiers had publicly to receive the Sacrament at York before he could perceive the slightest chance of success in his mission. To those in whom a vestige of Christian piety and reverence had survived the sectarian controversies of the time, the spectacle cannot have been edifying. Even that age seems to have resented so barefaced an attempt to convert the temple of God into a booth for the recruiting sergeant, since a contemporary writes: "The people hearken as little to his devotion as Heaven (I believe) to his prayers, soe that had hee not prevailed with some officers[1] of his militia to pick them up (for the most parte) out of the traine bands, he had returned *re infectâ*."

Whatever his methods, Buckingham however finally mustered a set of likely young fellows, whom in detachments of seven and fifteen hundred respectively, he proudly marched to Blackheath. Here, he remained drilling them for some time, much to his own satisfaction and that of the rank and file, who adored him, though the officers were less enthusiastic, and complained that "he is too Frenchified in all he does."

Meanwhile his enemies at Court left no stone unturned to deprive him of his promised post. In consequence of the Duke of York's enforced resignation of his offices, Prince Rupert succeeded to the command of the fleet, and Marshal Schomberg, the distinguished French Huguenot, was entrusted with the English contingent for Holland. And not only was Buckingham's cherished plan of

[1] "Letters to Sir J. Williamson," vol. l. pp. 21-24.

operations reversed, but as the Marshal refused to act with him, the Duke's chances of military fame were once more forfeited.

The disappointment was bitter; and in the first flush of angry feeling he talked, not merely of surrendering his commission, but of throwing up his place as Master of the Horse. In the end wiser counsels prevailed; but it must have been balm to his wounded spirit when his regiment mutinied and refused to put to sea without their colonel.

Buckingham may not have been a military genius, but the gloomy forebodings he formed when his plans were rejected were amply realised, owing mainly to the violent personal quarrels between Prince Rupert and Schomberg. Nor was the British campaign alone to be attended with failure. William of Orange had awakened confidence not only amongst his subjects, but in the neighbouring kingdoms. In August he acquired the alliance of the Emperor and the King of Spain, and that year the States enjoyed the signal triumph of rejecting the very terms for which they had humbly and vainly sued in 1672.

The sudden check to his ambition does not seem to have had a happy effect on the Duke's temper, for the very same week that Charles signed Schomberg's appointment, Buckingham gave way to a fit of rage which created no slight sensation in London. Like most of the dubious actions of His Grace's life, this incident was not unconnected with Lady Shrewsbury. It appears that the lady's coachman—perhaps the same who had driven her on the celebrated occasion to Turnham Green to watch the dying agonies of Killigrew—had imbibed some of the high-handed methods of his imperious mistress. Happening to witness a quarrel between two troopers of the Royal Horse Guards, this valiant Jehu, instead of confining himself to remonstrance, forcibly interfered, repeatedly lashing one of the belligerents over the face with his whip.

The injured gentleman took a revenge worthy of a modern Prussian officer under similar circumstances—"with one thrust he ran the fellow through the body and broke his sword in him, with which he presently died."[1] Thus the honour of the King's uniform was vindicated, but not to the liking of the bystanders, who seized the soldier and straightway carried him off to be cross-examined by Buckingham.

No one expected—or hoped—that the Duke would show himself lenient. But when the public learnt that the Prime Minister had fallen on the man, severely beaten him, and "broken his head" general sympathy was transferred to the offender. And when the delinquent was merely found guilty of manslaughter, and, in spite of the verdict, Buckingham persisted in "promising him he should be hanged," the Duke's conduct did not escape censure.

Nor was this the only quarrel into which at this time his irascible temper betrayed him. He had long been on bad terms with Montague, the English Ambassador in France, and one day, finding that gentleman in the King's withdrawing-room, he roughly hustled him out of his path. Montague, feeling himself rudely pulled by the shoulders, re-

---

[1] H. Bull to Sir J. Williamson, Whitehall, 4th July 1673, vol. II. p. 86.

monstrated in vigorous terms. The Duke refused to apologise, and the two went no further than the ante-chamber to arrange the details of the reparation demanded by Montague. The indignant diplomat was for settling their differences then and there, "and soe make only a rencounter of it, and not a sett duel." But this was a proposition the Duke would not entertain, though he agreed on, an assignation for the morrow. A scuffle between two such high and mighty personages, in the very presence of the Sovereign, could not however escape notice. The combat was forbidden, and Montague was committed to the Tower, while to the disappointment of the majority of the courtiers Buckingham went scot-free.[1]

The withdrawal of his command and the rejection of his plan of campaign were not the only reverses which befell Buckingham in 1673.

The long series of personal defeats, which his policy encountered during that year, had begun in March, when, to calm the popular excitement, Charles finally cancelled the Declaration of Indulgence to the Nonconformists. It had been a measure entirely in harmony with the Duke's views. Indeed, to support it, Buckingham[2] was supposed to be willing to invoke the military, and with their assistance to remove any recalcitrant Members of Parliament from Westminster. This rebuff was closely followed by another, on the subject of the Duke of York's marriage. Buckingham was too staunch a Protestant not to regard the betrothal of the heir-presumptive to a Popish princess as a serious menace to the national faith. He had therefore

[1] Williamson, vol. ii. pp. 89, 90. [2] Burnet, vol. ii. p. 7.

strongly advocated a match with the Countess of Northumberland; and when, in spite of his remonstrances, James wedded the Roman Catholic Mary of Modena he more than shared the universal resentment the union provoked in England. These causes made him desert Whitehall for the country, where he remained during the autumn, brooding over his troubles, financial and political, while the King and his fellow Ministers were "holding a 'junto' to put the Duke of Buckingham into the strait path, or to take from him the power of doing ill."[1]

Yet it must not be imagined that the Duke was unaware of the intrigues directed against him. He told Louis' representative he was convinced that when Parliament met he would be made the "scapegoat" for the sin of the Government[2] in concluding the French Treaty. Nor did he remain passive, though the steps he took to divert impending fate may be open to criticism. It was to Louis XIV. that he turned, and, under the seal of secrecy, he appealed to that monarch to give him the wherewithal of converting the country members to the French interests. He dared not, he said, confide in Colbert de Choisy, who repeated everything to Arlington, but he suggested the King should send over the Marquis de Ruvigny or the Maréchal de Bellefonds, the friends he had made during his long sojourn in France, to either of whom he would gladly unburden his mind. The request was graciously received and, under the pretext of bearing

---

[1] "Affaires Étrangères," No. 108, f. 30, 25th Oct. 1673, French Amb. to Louis XIV.
[2] 30th Oct., *idem*.

Louis' congratulations to the Duke of York on his marriage, Ruvigny was accordingly despatched to England. Had George Villiers, however, only known it, the Marquis was less trustworthy than Colbert de Choisy, for though he was told [1] to offer every pledge of secrecy the Duke demanded, he received at the same time instructions from Louis to keep Charles II. informed of every detail of Buckingham's proposed scheme.

Parliament met in January 1674, and the "great baiting," as Andrew Marvell calls it, began in good earnest. The country gentlemen were in a stern mood, and were not disarmed by the King's evident anxiety to propitiate them.

They opened proceedings by demanding who were the counsellors responsible for the most obnoxious measures of the last few years. The chief points they singled out for indictment being the French Treaty, the Declaration of Indulgence, the levying of an army without constitutional sanction, and last, but not least, the marriage of Mary of Modena to the Duke of York.

Lauderdale, whose tyranny had made life intolerable to thousands of his fellow-countrymen in Scotland, was the first Minister to be attacked. The Commons voted that the King should be entreated to remove him from "all his employments, and from the Royal Presence and Councils for ever." Warned by this decision, Buckingham thought to conciliate the Parliamentary critics by an act of deference. He determined to waive his rights as a peer, and to plead his cause in person

[1] "Affaires Étrangères, Mem. pour servir d'Instruction à Monsieur de Ruvigny."

before the Commons. In an age when jealousy of their lordships often interrupted the most useful measures of the Lower House, he was no doubt justified in counting on the effect of this notable condescension. Had Lauderdale stooped to similar methods, his ungainly figure, his thick and stuttering utterance, would probably have made him ridiculous as well as hateful to his judges. Buckingham might reasonably count on the favourable effect his silvery tongue and graceful deportment were bound to produce in an assembly of gentlemen. Nor perhaps at an ordinary season would he have been found to have miscalculated his chances.

At this juncture, however, the House was possessed with an agony of apprehension for the future civil and religious rights of the country, and was in no vein for bandying witticisms. When the Duke begged permission to "inform them in Person of some Truths relating to the Publick,"[1] he was instantly and "with great ceremony"[2] admitted to their presence, but the exposition did not meet with their approval, and they even detected "something loose and uncertain" about his discourse. And on Buckingham's saying "he was weary of the company he was joined with, and knew how to kill a hare with hounds, but could not hunt with lobsters"[3]—meaning Charles and his brother—the House, far from being amused, immediately adjourned the further hearing of the case till the following day. The ducal jester cannot have felt reassured, when the Commons gravely informed

---

[1] Add MSS. 33,051.   [2] Echard, vol. iii. p. 346.
[3] Williamson, vol. ii. p. 115.

him that at the next audience they would require him to render full and precise answers to a formidable category of questions, which they immediately drafted, and thanks to which they hoped thoroughly to sift his reminiscences.

But whatever misgivings the Duke experienced when on that winter's morning—January the 14th—he presented himself once more at Westminster, neither his manner nor his language appeared at first to betray anxiety. To the onlookers, in fact, both must have seemed in keeping with the festive raiment which he had assumed — garments well calculated to enhance his handsome person. Indeed, no detail, however trifling, by which he might propitiate the arbiters of his destiny had, apparently at this crisis,[1] been forgotten by Buckingham. Before the House met, according to an ill-natured contemporary, as he strove to make friends with the more debauched portion of the assembly by drinking and revelry, so he courted the curious sympathy of the graver sort by receiving the Sacrament in their company.

It may therefore be imagined that the Duke had devoted no little attention to the speech which was to justify his conduct. Not that his language became more ornate than was his wont. He realised that florid eloquence was not his strong point, and carefully eschewed the periods and classic allusions common to the oratory of that time. But in a style conversational to the verge of bluntness, he employed no mean address to insinuate that the very actions for which he now

[1] Williamson to Sir G. Talbot, vol. ii. p. 205, 2nd Jan. 1673-74.

stood arraigned were those which he had constantly, though vainly, combated.

"I hope," he began, "you will consider the condition I am in, in danger of passing for a vicious person and a betrayer of my country. I have ever had the misfortune of bearing other men's faults." If amongst these measures there were some which he did not disavow, it was, he declared, that it was the execution—and for this he was not responsible—rather than the matter which was at fault. For instance, both he and Shaftesbury had strenuously "advised not to begin a war without the advice of Parliament and the affections of the people, but this was not my Lord Arlington's opinion." Had his policy rather than that statesman's prevailed, it was conceivable that the French Alliance itself—now so unpopular—would have commended itself to an assembly of patriotic Englishmen. For the Duke would have bargained that the contribution made by our French allies to the joint campaign should take the form of money instead of ships. Or, again, he would have insisted "that some towns of their conquest in Holland should be delivered into our keeping." But strive as he would, his meritorious efforts were frustrated at every turn by Arlington, the real and ubiquitous evil genius of the Administration and the State. And thus having exhausted every weapon of his arsenal against his colleague, the Duke concluded with a pathetic appeal to his judges, "not to look on me as a Peer, but an honest English gentleman, who has suffered much for the love of my country. . . . I am sure I have lost as much estate as some there have gotten, and that is a big word. I am honest, and when I appear otherwise I wish to dye. I am not the man who has gotten by this, and yet after all this I am a Grievance. I am the cheapest Grievance this House ever had."[1]

The pathos of Buckingham's peroration did not deter the House from instructing the Speaker to proceed with his cross-examination. The inquisition promised to be formidable, since the Duke was expected to explain himself fully in answer to eleven searching questions. He must have known that it would tax his skill to come unscathed through the ordeal, but at first his replies lost nothing of his characteristic jaunty assurance, and it is only towards the end that a certain uneasiness becomes perceptible in his answers.

The Speaker's first query was "whether anyone had declared ill-advices or purposes against the liberties of this House, or to alter this Government; who they were and what they advised." Buckingham gaily retorted, "There is an old proverb, Mr Speaker, over shoes, over boots;" which cryptic saying, he followed up with the equally ambiguous remark, "that since the person that declared such ill-advices was dead, he feared to give what might be thought a malicious invention." Guarded as was this speech, it yet unmistakably conveyed the impression that it was Lord Clifford who had been guilty of such unconstitutional counsel. Nor was this the only occasion on which he thus covertly referred to his dead friend and colleague. At a later point in the proceedings, and in the same veiled fashion, he insinuated that the suggestion "of bringing up the army to awe the debates and

[1] Echard, vol. iii. p. 346.

resolutions of the House of Commons" had originated with the late Lord Treasurer.

He vehemently repudiated any responsibility for the closing of the Exchequer in 1672, saying ruefully that the transaction had personally cost him £3000.

He also declared that he had nothing to do with Sir Robert Holmes' attack on the Smyrna Fleet. That indefensible action was, he vowed, due to Lord Arlington, and he had even incurred displeasure in high places by opposing it.

He could truthfully assert that he had no hand or part in Schomberg's appointment as Commander-in-Chief, but he frankly admitted that he had supported the Declaration of Indulgence to the Nonconformists, and that the French Alliance was his handiwork. He gave a vivid account of his embassy to Utrecht and of "the people in the same breath crying 'God bless the King of England, and cursing the States,' and, he vowed, had we then landed in Holland we might have conquered the country. The Prince of Orange would have had the same share with the Peace with France that we had, but, though the King's nephew, I thought he must be kind to his own country. . . . I never could consent that France must have all and we nothing." [1]

He once more affirmed that he and Lord Shaftesbury—whom throughout he shielded—"were for advising with the Parliament and averse to the prorogation," and he wound up by volunteering the patriotic sentiment that in his belief "Parliament will never be against a War for the good of England."

[1] Echard, vol. iii. p. 274.

Under the circumstances, Buckingham could probably not have devised a better apology for his policy. It was a matter of notoriety that of all the unscrupulous statesmen of the Cabal, none was a more thorough-going partisan of the prerogative than Clifford. As he was now beyond the reach of Parliamentary reprisals, the Duke might reasonably admit what was already generally suspected.

As we know, both at Utrecht and elsewhere Buckingham had made repeated attempts to secure terms rather more profitable for England than those advocated by Arlington. And distasteful as it must ever be to see one man seeking to justify himself at the expense of another, we should remember that collective ministerial responsibility was not then part of the political code. Yet it would be a great mistake to infer that the nature of the average Englishman has undergone a radical change in the last two hundred years. Individuality is less trenchant, the angles of character have been rubbed off. The most pessimistic must own that although our progress has been rather material than moral, the present occupants of the parliamentary benches are undoubtedly more humane and probably less prejudiced than their predecessors in the seventeenth century.

But when all this is admitted, the fundamental instincts, the bedrock of national character, were much the same under the second Charles as they are under the seventh Edward. Buckingham's contemporaries were less concerned to mete out to each Minister respectively the due proportion of blame than to arrive at a sound general conclusion. They knew George Villiers; his character did not inspire them with confidence and his protestations were extravagant. That he should claim for himself all the successes, whilst he charged Arlington with all the failures of the Administration, jarred on their rough and ready sense of fair play. Indeed, loyalty, however misplaced, would have appealed more to that gathering of sturdy country gentlemen than the Duke's evident design to whitewash himself at the expense of his colleague. It might not be just, it was certainly not logical, but they evidently experienced something of that repugnance for Buckingham which the most law-abiding of us cannot stifle for the zealous King's evidence. And we can only gather that it was under the influence of such sentiments, that they finally voted an address to His Majesty begging him to " remove the said Duke of Buckingham from all his employments that are held during His Majesty's pleasure and from the Councils for ever."

Thus fell George Villiers, never again to hold office. But within an incredibly short time we find him once more a foremost figure of the political stage, and in truth exerting far greater influence in his new character as Leader of the Opposition than he had ever achieved as Prime Minister. Undoubtedly the conditions of this new position were more favourable to his peculiar temperament. The non-constructive eloquence of the popular orator, the weblike intrigues of the plotter were as congenial to him as the steady labour, the prosaic detail of administration had been distasteful.

Hitherto also, in dealing with the worthy country members or even with the politicians of the Cabal, he had committed an initial blunder. He had so profoundly assimilated the maxims and methods of gallantry that unconsciously he brought something of the atmosphere of the boudoir with him to the Council Board. It was an error. His posturing, his sensationalism, merely alienated the matter-of-fact British legislator. In dealing with the mob, however, it was far otherwise. The feminine element, which underlies its fierce and varying moods, wrought them instantly to a high pitch of sympathy and mutual understanding. All the passion he had brought to the worship of his perverse mistress he now lavished on the wooing of the multitude, till at last he reaped the signal glory of seeing London ablaze with bonfires in his honour, and every street and alley resounding to the cry of " A Buckingham! a Buckingham!"

Yet it must be owned that, for the moment, Buckingham's present outlook could not well be more gloomy. The Duke's revelations had been insufficient to make his peace with the Commons, but they had proved profoundly irritating to the King.

In fact the easy-going monarch was unusually aroused, and denounced his late favourite to Ruvigny in unmeasured terms. George Villiers, he declared, was a worthless fellow who had not only betrayed State secrets but, merely in order to injure his personal enemies, had also seriously misrepresented and distorted matters which had been discussed at the Council Board.[1]

It was peculiarly unfortunate for Buckingham that at this juncture the Sovereign should take so uncompromising a view of his behaviour, for seldom had he stood in greater need of support.

[1] "Affaires Étrangères," 25th January 1674, Ruvigny to Pomponne.

Indeed, just then the Duke, as a devout believer in astrology, must have been tempted to think that the stars in their courses were fighting against him. Never was there a more striking instance of a man's sins coming home to roost, for in the same week that saw his fall from power, and his proscription at Court, his foes mustered courage to summon him before his Peers to answer for his immoral conduct in the past.

The storm had been already brewing for some considerable time. On the Earl of Shrewsbury's death, he had, as will be remembered, provided himself with a plenary pardon, and when disgrace overtook him even the ingenuity of Crown lawyers proved unequal to picking holes in it. But though his person and estate were insured against the depredations of Mr Bayliff Bennett he had yet to reckon with the half-canonical laws, which, though dormant, could still be invoked in the highest tribunal in the land.

Now it happened that none of George Villiers' crimes had so aroused public opinion as the folly of giving a princely funeral in Westminster Abbey to that poor baby, "Lord Coventry." The aristocratic world found it easier to condone the Duke's domestic outrage on his wife than this flagrant disregard of their most cherished traditions. The trustees and relatives of the Earl of Shrewsbury's son and heir now saw their opportunity in the Duke's unhappy situation, and therefore promptly presented a petition to the House of Lords. It was introduced by a brother-in-law of the Countess, the "idiotic" Earl of Westmoreland, as Ruvigny obligingly calls him.

Lady Shrewsbury as Minerva.

In this bulky[1] document the petitioners alleged that "had the unhappy lady and her complice imploy'd the usual care of such offenders to cover actions of Guilt and Shame," they would have held their peace. But, as their ward grew to manhood, they realised the danger incurred by the continuance of the "wicked and scandalous life" of his mother and her lover, "multiplying day by day new provocations to two noble families by the insolent and shameless manner of their" common existence.

Nor was it only scandal the guardians dreaded on behalf of the orphan. They invoke the protection of Parliament from "such unjustifiable ways of resentment as have already plunged that noble house into so sad and bloody a misfortune." There is nothing to prove that the petitioners had any grounds for making so terrible an accusation, insinuating conduct even more unnatural than that already ascribed to Lady Shrewsbury. But the Peers may well have thought it would be unwise to disregard these sinister hints; though judging from the references in the ensuing debate, it was—as has been already said—rather the indignation caused by Lord Coventry's burial than any fears for the young Earl, which roused them to take action.

Under the existing Church statutes, the prospect was not reassuring for the Duke. Since the meeting at Barn Elms, much of the wild passion, which had wrecked two homes, had probably burnt itself out. The lady, having well-nigh ruined her profligate adorer, felt the need of compounding with the money-bags of the Talbot

[1] Harl. MSS., 1579, pp. 146-47

family. The gallant, disgraced at Court, his name struck off the list of the Privy Council, was constrained to come to terms with his prosecutors. From the first their loves had been of the earth, earthy, and in the day of reckoning it was with small dignity that they faced their common danger.

The Duke's speech, or rather his act of submission, when cited by his Peers to answer for the bygone years of dalliance, has been preserved. Even a man of his rare ingenuity must have found it difficult to strike the proper note on such an occasion. Before the Commons he had, at least, been able to pose as a patriot. Now he was forced to plead guilty, and the humility of his style must grate on the taste of a modern audience. Yet it is only fair to admit that the "honour which rooted in dishonour stands" was a quality almost unknown and wholly repugnant to his generation; and few of his contemporaries would have dared to defy the verdict of the House.

Buckingham began by admitting "that his life has not been so regular nor so free from blame as that he should be willing that the House should be troubled with a revelation of all his faults against temperance and the strict rules of morality.[1] On the other hand, he thanks God he is not delivered up to so profane a temper of mind as to justify the least misdemeanour, and he hopes no resolution he may have taken to look more strictly over his behaviour in future, will be thought inconsistent with his endeavours to take off those horrid and black representations which are made of him." He

[1] Hist. MSS., Rep. IX., House of Lords, Cal., 1673-74, p. 36.

declares he would not rely for his defence on any "nicety or evasion of law," but that he intends to deal frankly and openly with their lordships, knowing them to be "not only the supreme Court of Judicature, but an assembly of the highest honour and conscience." And he prays them consequently to believe "that many arguments and excuses, which he might in strict justice have alleged, he has purposely omitted."

After this preamble, he indignantly repudiated the charge of having brought about the fatal duel by scandalous and provocative behaviour—"there was no such thing, and he believes that if the Earl had been left to the goodness of his natural disposition, and had not been exasperated by others, he had not resented a thing so much for which there was so little ground." The Countess of Shrewsbury had indeed left her husband and had taken refuge in a Paris monastery; and "the Earl, upon the groundless jealousy of the Duke's being the cause of her going away, was much incensed against him." But in truth the lady's flight was due not to his influence, but "because she thought her honour was not vindicated upon one who had done her a public and barbarous affront." After the Earl's death, for which George Villiers professes "he had as sensible a grief as any of the gentlemen that subscribed the petition," the Countess returned to England. She was disowned by her friends and relations, and the greatest part of her jointure injuriously kept from her. Under the circumstances, when she sent to the Duke to desire his assistance, he put it to his judges what "man of honour could deny a lady in her condition."

Thereafter, though some things were grossly exaggerated and others falsely alleged against his behaviour, "yet he forbears to use any extenuations, because he knows their lordships will better suggest all arguments of favour and charity than he can do for himself. . . . But omitting all further justification of himself, he humbly asks God's forgiveness and their lordships' for anything in this, or in his whole life, which may have given occasion of scandal, and seriously promises he will take care to avoid any reproach of the same nature for the future."

When he had finished, Ormond rose, and with all the bitterness of personal rancour vehemently supported the petition, being seconded by the Earl of Bristol. On the other hand, Lords Anglesea and Berkshire blamed the proceedings, the discussion grew heated, and a division was demanded. For a man in utter disfavour with both King and Parliament, Buckingham was, however, not as destitute of supporters as might have been expected. There was an impression abroad that he was only under a momentary cloud, that the Commons[1] would tire of their severity, and address the King in his favour so that he would speedily regain more than all his previous influence.

Such a supposition was undoubtedly helpful to the Duke in the present crisis, and assisted his friends to pass a resolution giving him eight days' grace wherein to prepare his defence.

No one rejoiced more unfeignedly at this sign of leniency in his judges than the Duke's

---

[1] Ruvigny to Louis XIV., Mignet, vol. iii. p. 79

ill-used wife. Her conduct is indeed the sole redeeming feature of the sordid business. Conway told Essex with—very natural—astonishment that he had seen her in the extremity of her distress "crying and tearing herself." And she "solicited with the greatest passion in the world"[1] not only for her faithless spouse, but also for her rival.

Perhaps the Duchess's touching self-abnegation had a softening effect on others, for when, on the 30th of January, the House met to reconsider the petition, the Earl of Cardigan came forward to plead his daughter's case.

He had received a "letter of submission," he said, from the Countess of Shrewsbury, and "begged she might not be made desperate."[2] The father's advocacy undoubtedly carried weight, and he was ably supported by Lord Shaftesbury, who now amply repaid Buckingham's recent good offices.

After much discussion, a committee of bishops was appointed to draw up a deed, binding the guilty pair to an absolute separation under forfeiture of £10,000 each to the King.

George Villiers offered no objection to the Prelates' conditions, but at first the ingenuity of the lawyers was sorely taxed to find a property on either side, which, not being vested in trustees, could be charged for this purpose. Finally the Duke arranged to engage a pension of £2500 per annum secured on the Irish revenue, whilst the Countess made a conveyance on her jointure.

[1] Essex Papers, vol. i. p. 160, Lord Conway to Earl of Essex, Jan. 10, 1673-74.
[2] Rep. II. Hist. MSS. House of Lords, Cal., 1673-74, p. 36.

Thus amid legal quibbles and ridicule, the curtain was rung down on the most notorious amour of that dissolute epoch.

Lady Shrewsbury wisely withdrew, though only for a short time, to a convent at Dunkirk. Two years later she bestowed her hand on Mr George Rodney Bridges, for whom she purchased a small Court appointment, and after this concession to public opinion, Charles II. persuaded those virtuous matrons, the Queen and the Duchess of York, to receive her once more at Whitehall.

The Duke of Buckingham had to make another very lowly recantation to the Houses of Parliament "acknowledging the lewd and miserable life he had led; and though it was a very heavy burthen to lye under the displeasure of the House and the sense of his transgressions, yett he had reason to give God thanks for it, since it had opened his eyes and discovered to him the foulness of his past life, which he was resolved for the future to amend; and having added severall patheticke expressions of his repentance, the House at last absolved him."[1] Nor was this act of contrition the sole sign of grace exhibited by the Duke, for the following Sunday the congregation of St Martin's-in-the-Fields was edified by the spectacle of the reformed sinner attending divine service in company of "his owne lady."[2]

[1] Essex Papers, Lord Angier to Lord Essex, vol. i. p. 174.
[2] *Ibid.*, vol. i. p. 167.

CHAPTER XII

BUCKINGHAM IN ADVERSITY

RETRIBUTION steadily dogged the Duke of Buckingham's footsteps in the year 1674. The Peers had granted him absolution for his offences against the Decalogue; but Charles remained furious with his former Minister, and showed no inclination to forgive the mingled indiscretion and impertinence which, in his opinion, characterised the Duke's recent utterances in the House of Commons.

Buckingham's friends believed that he might escape actual prosecution if he would only retire to one of his country houses.[1] But it was difficult to persuade him that this was the best course to pursue. Thoroughly affrighted by the accusation of having betrayed State secrets, and still more by the unwonted sternness of the Royal mood, he even meditated seeking refuge in France. Not only did he employ Ruvigny to ascertain what reception he might expect from Louis, but he actually despatched Leighton abroad on the same errand.

The Ambassador's eloquence was sorely taxed to persuade him that Cliveden or Burley would be more suitable residences than some obscure provincial town of the Grand Monarque's dominions. And before he would relinquish the idea Ruvigny

[1] "Affaires Étrangères," 12th March, Ruvigny, 1674, 112, p. 29.

was reduced to hint—in no obscure language—that George Villiers "might not meet in France with the respect he required."

Undoubtedly, Buckingham had some reason for alarm. After the fashion of that period he had sunk large sums in the purchase of Court appointments. Custom had invested such arrangements with proprietary rights, and the world was startled when the King proposed to dispossess the Master of the Horse without allowing him to come to terms with his successor. Had it not been for the unusual wording of the patent, George Villiers' unfortunate speech would have cost him no less a sum than £20,000.

This peculiarity appears, however, to have baffled the Crown lawyers, and the Duke took advantage of the delay to address the following dignified remonstrance to his Royal master.

MAY IT PLEASE YOUR MAJESTY,[1]—I desired my Lord Treasurer to beg leave of Your Majesty that I might have the honour to speak with you, which Your Majesty refused. Afterwards he promised to lay before Your Majesty the hardness of my present case, which he tells me he hath done, though I confess I should hardly believe it, if I had not great experience of his honour and truth in general to all men, as well as of his kindness to me in particular. I am not the least surprised at my having enemies about Your Majesty; but I wonder very much, after the many observations I have made of Your Majesty's good nature to all

---

[1] "Correspondence," vol. iv. p. 249. I am aware that in the "Fairfax Memorials" this letter is supposed to have been written in 1666. But Buckingham did not then fill the office of Master of the Horse, nor had he so extensively mortgaged his estates.

the world, that you can find it in your heart to use me with so much cruelty, who have ever loved you better than myself, and preferred the following you abroad in the worst of your misfortunes, before the staying at home to enjoy a plentiful estate.

Pray, sir, what have I done that should make you thus angry with me? Was it my fault that other men did really prejudice Your Majesty's affairs upon the hopes of doing me a mischief. Did I say anything in my defence which could possibly be wrested to a reflection upon Your Majesty? Or if I was forced to reflect upon others, was it anything more than what you yourself gave me leave to do? In case I should be first accused, I beseech Your Majesty examine your own heart well upon this subject, and if those that heard me speak do not clear me from having behaved myself disrespectfully to Your Majesty, I desire no favour from you. I am told the House of Commons have addressed to Your Majesty that I may be deprived of all places which I hold of Your Majesty's pleasure, the severity of which censure I shall not take upon myself now to dispute. But Your Majesty may please to remember that by your gracious permission I bought the place of Master of the Horse, which I hold by patent under the Great Seal during my life, with power of nominating my deputy. It is therefore my most humble request to Your Majesty I may be allowed to name such a deputy as Your Majesty shall approve; that so I may not wholly lose my right to a favour which I purchased by Your Majesty's favour, and which the House of Commons were so far from desiring should be taken from me, that upon the mention of it in the House it was universally agreed to that no man's freehold ought to be invaded, and for that reason the address to Your Majesty was worded accordingly.

Your Majesty knows I have often told you that I would depend on no man's favour in the Court but yours, and that nothing could make me desire to stay there but your kindness. These have been always my thoughts and are so still.

If it be upon the score of the House of Commons' address to Your Majesty that you are resolved to remove me from my place, I hope at least you will not be harder to me than the House of Commons were. And if it be only because Your Majesty has a mind the Duke of Monmouth should have it, even in that case I shall not complain of Your Majesty, neither I do not think it strange that you should love him better than me; but I cannot believe Your Majesty would for his sake do any man an injustice.

Consider, I beseech you, that I had the honour to be bred up with Your Majesty from a child; that I lost my estate for running from Cambridge, where I was a student, to serve Your Majesty and your Father, at Oxford, when I was not thought of age sufficient to bear arms, and for that reason was sent away from thence to travel. That after the end of the wars, returning into England and having my whole estate restored to me by the Parliament, without composition, a few weeks after my return, there happening to be a design laid to take up arms for Your Majesty, my brother and I engaged in it, and in the engagement he was killed.

That after this the Parliament voted my pardon in case I would return within forty days; that I then being concealed in London, chose rather, with the hazard of my life, to wait upon Your Majesty in the Fleet, where I found you, than to stay, possessed of my estates upon condition of having nothing more to do with Your Majesty's fortunes: That afterwards, when Your Majesty went out of Holland into Scotland, I was offered my composition for £20,000, a sum not considerable to me at that time, my estate being then worth £30,000 a year: That even as to Your Majesty's return into England I may justly pretend to some share, since without my Lord Fairfax, by engaging in Yorkshire, Lambert's army had never quitted him, nor the Duke of Albemarle marched out of Scotland; and without me it is sufficiently known to many persons yet alive that my Lord Fairfax had never engaged.

That in all the employments I have had under Your Majesty I have been so far from getting, that I have wasted the best part of my estate in following and waiting upon Your Majesty. All these things being considered, I conceive it will appear but just, that if Your Majesty have a desire to make me quit my place I may be allowed to receive for it the full of what it is worth. Were I now as well in my affairs as when I first came into Your Majesty's service, I should never have thought of making this request. Nay, would the condition of my fortune give me leave to yield, I should not dispute with Your Majesty anything you could have a mind to take from me. But my whole estate being mortgaged, and I having lived to this age without being acquainted with any way of getting money, I hope Your Majesty will not be offended if, being forced to part with my freehold, I desire at least to sell it for the payment of my debts.

I humbly ask Your Majesty's pardon for this trouble I have given you, and beg of you to believe that nothing shall ever separate me from my duty and allegiance to Your Majesty; as I cannot despair but that one day Your Majesty will find the difference between those that truly love you and those that serve you only for private ends of their own. —I am, may it please Your Majesty, Your Majesty's most dutiful and most obedient Subject and Servant,
BUCKINGHAM.

Either the Duke's letter or some other cause—most probably the legal impediment of which mention has already been made—had the desired effect on the Sovereign's course of action.

Buckingham did eventually forfeit his appointment, but he received considerable compensation for the loss thus incurred. His place as Gentleman of the Bedchamber, worth £1000[1] a year, brought him £6000, and he received £6000 for the Mastership of the Horse, with £1500 per annum charged—as usual—on the Irish Establishment.

The King, like a good parent, designated Charles Lennox, Duke of Richmond, his son by Louise de Kéroualle, for the latter post, and at the same time appointed three commissioners to hold it in trust during the boy's minority. Nor did Charles forget his firstborn. The University of Cambridge were instructed to depose their present Chancellor, and to elect James Duke of Monmouth in his stead—an injunction to which they dutifully gave instant effect.

Thus disgraced and impoverished, Buckingham had no choice but to retire into private life, and for the next year his interests appear to have centred in the ordinary pursuits of a country gentleman. Much of his time was devoted to beautifying Cliveden, much also to foxhunting, for he had lost nothing of his early passion for sport. At Empingham, a little hamlet near his splendid mansion of Burley, a humble tavern, the White Horse Inn, was long pointed out as a resort of His Grace's when thus employed. Here he delighted to waive

[1] "Essex Papers," vol. i. p. 181.

the punctilious formality which then encompassed those of his station. Indeed, the freedom which characterised his relations with the landlord of the White Horse was hardly a cause of edification to the neighbouring squires, the least of whom would have felt outraged had his inferiors adopted a similar tone. The man was not slow to avail himself of the Duke's indulgence, and the village gossips remembered that on one occasion, when Buckingham was calling[1] with some vehemence for a pot of ale, the innkeeper actually emancipated himself so far as to mutter, "Your Grace is in a plaguey hurry; I'll come as soon as I've served my hogs," which so amused His Grace that he improvised the following quartrain :—

> "Some ale, some ale!" the impetuous Villiers cried,
> To whom the surly landlord thus replied,—
> "Plague on Your Grace, you treat me as your dog,
> I'll serve Your Lordship when I've served my hog!"

Buckingham had however more agreeable companions than the boorish host of the White Horse. None was more constant than John Wilmot, Earl of Rochester, who from the following letter, conceived in a strain of solemn banter, seems to have been as much in sympathy with the Duke's sporting proclivities as with the less reputable amusements chronicled by Grammont. Buckingham writes to his friend,—

MY LORD,[2]—As persons inclined to corroborate the intentions of other men are ever more incumbent to a voluminous ubiquity than any way

---
[1] Nichol's "Leicestershire," vol. ii. p. 213.
[2] MSS. Brit. Mus., 7003, f. 272.

condescending to the notions of a just medium, soe all true lovers of art doe naturally prefer the cimetery of resolutions before the convocation of any concatinations whatever, and the reason of this is plaine, because else all vocall determinations would be frustrated, and then (as Aristotell observes very well) no man could propperly say "Consummatum est." The meaning of this simile is that, if Your Lordship will give me leave, I shall imediatly wayte upon you with the best pack of hounds that ever ran upon English ground. I had done it sooner, but I stayed for my Lord Dorset and Mr Shepherd's company, but they having both failed me, and not knowing how long your occasions will give you leave to stay in the country, I thought fitt to know of Your Lordship by this bearer whether it would not be inconvenient at this time to receive a visit from my Lord, your etc.

During his visits to the Court of France, Buckingham may possibly have been inspired with the ambition to rear monster carp similar to those which to this day the tourist sees in the reservoir of Fontainebleau. His passionate absorption in the caprice of the hour is illustrated by a letter also addressed from Cliveden to John Wilmot.

CLIFDEN, *Sunday, 19th August.*

My Lord,[1]—Your kinde letter has given mee more satisfaction than I am able to expresse, for I doe assure your Lordship that I hartily love you, and shall doe so till the last minute of my life; and nothing is truer than what is elegantly expressed in a French song: "Le plaisir est extrême d'aymer et d'etre aymé quand on ayme." I am sorry I did not aske Mr Povey's opinion upon this song, who came

[1] Harley MSS., 7003, f. 272.

hither the other day to see my building and give mee instructions about the breeding of carpes which I shall acquaint your Lordship with when I have the honour to see you. The circumstances of the matter are something long, but this in short is the summe of it. That you must be sure to cleanse your pond very well and lett no fish be in it whatsoever, only two carpes, a male and a female; and then that the next yeare you must take them out of that pond and put them into another for feare of theyre being eaten by Pykes; this, he says, will make them breed infinitely and grow very fatt, though he has not yet bene pleased to tell me what they are to be fed with. I wish with all my hart that hee and our Grand Politicians were always to goe together in couples; for it is a very great pitty that persons of such extraordinary parts should ever be parted—hee is as angry against Lampoons as they, and as much affrayed of them tho' he does not deserve them soe well, for he is a foole that only makes one laugh, the others make one cry too, which that it may be theyre turns to doe in God's propper time is the harty wishes of My Lord, your Lordship's most humble and most obedient servant,
BUCKINGHAM.

If the master of Requests, Mr Povey, described by Evelyn as "a nice contriver of all elegancies," was a fool, his recipe for the breeding of carps evidently proved successful, for at a later date Buckingham writes once more to his correspondent:—

MY LORDE,[1]—I am now very busy drinking your Lordship's healthe, and shall very shortly have the honour to receive your and Mrs Nelly's

[1] Harley MSS., 7003, f. 282.

commands. In the mean time I have sent you two of the civillest carpes that ever I had to doe with, and if they could speak they would infallibly (according to Mr Boyle's way of moral reflections) assure your Lordship that I am more than any man living your Lordship's.

While Buckingham appeared engrossed in the rearing of the "civillest carpes," the world had not stood still.

Both Lauderdale and Arlington weathered the Parliamentary tempest which had proved fatal to Buckingham. But the Earl's ascendency was already yielding to that of Osborne, Lord Danby. Arlington was now forced to part with his place as Secretary to Williamson, and was relegated to the office of Lord Chamberlain—a position of far less influence.

Meanwhile the fortunes of war were shifting to the side of Holland. The King of Spain and the Emperor had openly espoused the cause of the Protestant Republic, and backed by these allies, William of Orange forced the French to beat a precipitate retreat. The States then made separate overtures to Charles. The terms they offered were accepted, and in spite of all Louis' endeavours to prevent it, peace was formally proclaimed between England and Holland in February 1674.

In April 1675 the Duke returned to Parliament to oppose a new Test Act introduced by Lord Danby's administration.

The measure considerably increased the disabilities under which the Protestant Dissenters already laboured. Indeed as the formula prescribed passive obedience not only to the King but also to his Ministers, and contained a pledge to abstain from any attempt to alter the existing government of Church and State, it aimed at a state of affairs little short of despotism.

In the strenuous opposition he offered, Buckingham did not want for allies. Shaftesbury abandoned the cherished work of plantation at St Giles, his young lime trees, his new filbert groves, and fought the good fight at Westminster. Halifax, long estranged from George Villiers, as well by differences in foreign policy, as by his relationship to the unfortunate Lord Shrewsbury, forgot these feuds in the cause of liberty. The bishops, the natural champions of coercive conformity, fared badly at their hands. Halifax, with perverse wit, inquired how these latter-day successors of the Apostles reconciled the Test with the Divine precept "Swear not at all." Few could surpass the great tractarian in the ingenious art of raillery. But, during the long hours of the unending debates, it was Buckingham who, with the tireless zest and happy instinct of the born debater, kept the episcopal bench under a perpetual fire of ridicule, invective and mordant criticism.

The Duke's tactics found a warm admirer in Andrew Marvell, who writes: "Holy Church goes to wrack on all sides.[1] Never were poor men exposed and abused all the Session as the bishops were by the Duke of Buckingham upon the Test: never the like, nor so infinitely pleasant: and no men were ever grown so odiously ridiculous."

The prelates had at least the consolation fo not

[1] A. Marvell's Works, vol. ii. p. 465, 24th July 1675.

suffering in vain for righteousness' sake. Not all the piety and wit of the opposition could counteract the restrictive sentiments of the House. Sixteen or seventeen days and nights were devoted to define the clause "those that are commissioned by the King," till at last Buckingham, finding argument unprofitable, tried the effect of what we should term obstruction. "As general of the party [1] and last in the field," says a contemporary, "he made a famous speech of eloquent, regular, and well-placed nonsense, hoping that might prevail when nothing else would, and so brought confusion into the House."

This victory was, however, only momentary. But the Opposition contrived to "enervate" the Bill by inserting the amendment that no peer should, by refusing to take the oath, subject himself to the penalty of losing his place or vote in Parliament or his liberty or debate therein. This was all pure gain, and Buckingham effectually laughed away the next proposal to impose a Præmunire on any recalcitrant lord. "He desired their lordships[2] to consider what a Præmunire was, which they were to be under if they did not take the oaths, though they were to keep their seats in Parliament. By a Præmunire we are to be stripped of all we have, and as we go along the streets anybody may take our clothes from us, saying, 'You are in a Præmunire.' If anyone in compassion should give a lord a new coat to cover his nakedness, the next man he meets may take it away again, saying, 'You are in a Præmunire and have right to nothing.' However, the stripped peer has his seat in Parliament still, and may sit here

---

[1] Echard, vol. iii. p. 383.   [2] Oldmixon's "History," pp. 87-88, 1675.

without waistcoat or breeches." The burlesque apocalypse thus evoked by Villiers' Rabelaisian fancy proved too much for the gravity of his noble audience. They burst into a Homeric shout of laughter, and no more was heard of the proposed Præmunire.

Yet in spite of the individual successes he achieved, the Duke could not prevent the Act from receiving the assent of the House of Peers, though whether a measure so fatal to freedom would ever have become part of the statute book must remain uncertain. Indeed it was currently reported that Buckingham and Shaftesbury had taken good care it should never reach the Commons. One of the perpetual disputes on privilege between the two Houses, which took place at this juncture, was generally ascribed to their fostering solicitude. It rapidly assumed such threatening proportions that Charles had no choice but to prorogue Parliament. The obnoxious Test was consequently never introduced into the Lower House, and thus had no chance of becoming part of the law of the land.

In October, when Parliament met again, Buckingham once more entered the lists on behalf of the Protestant Nonconformists. The speech he made on this occasion has been preserved. To the modern reader it abounds in truisms, but the notion that interference by the State with religion was "positively against the express doctrine and example of Jesus Christ" must have then seemed rank heresy to the majority of his hearers. From that point of view the subjoined discourse may be of interest to those who would estimate the progress our poor humanity has achieved towards " Christian charity . . . and good-nature in the niceties of religion" since the days when Buckingham made his unwelcome confession of faith in the following words :—

"My Lords,"[1] he said, "there is a thing called liberty, which (whatever some men may think) is that the people of England are fondest of; it is that they will never part with, and is that His Majesty in his speech has promised us to take a particular care of. This, my Lords, can never be done without giving an indulgence to all Protestant Dissenters. It is certainly a very uneasy kind of life to any man, that has either Christian charity, humanity or good nature, to see his fellow-subjects daily abused, divested of their liberties and birth-rights and miserably thrown out of their possessions and freeholds, only because they cannot agree with others in some opinions and niceties of religion which their consciences will not give them leave to consent to, and which even by the confession of those who would impose upon them are in no ways necessary to salvation. But, my Lords, besides this and all that may be said upon it, in order to the improvement of our trade and increase of the wealth, strength and greatness of this nation (which with your leave I shall presume to discourse of some other time), there is, methinks, in this notion of persecution, a very gross mistake, both as to the point of government and to the point of religion. This is so as to the point of government, because it makes every man's safety depend on the wrong place; not upon governors or man's living well towards the civil government established by law, but upon his

[1] Proceedings of the House of Lords, Ed. 1742, vol. i. pp. 164-5.

being transported with zeal for every opinion that is held by those that have power in the Church that is in fashion. And I conceive it a mistake in religion because it is positively against the express doctrine and example of Jesus Christ. Nay, my Lords, as to our Protestant religion, there is something in it yet worse; for we Protestants maintain that none of those opinions which Christians differ about are infallible; and therefore it is in us somewhat an inexcusable conception that men ought to be deprived of their inheritance, and of all the certain conveniences and advantages of life, because they will not agree with us in our uncertain opinions of religion. My humble motion to your Lordships is that you would give me leave to bring in a Bill of Indulgence to all Protestant Dissenters. I know very well that every peer of this realm hath a right to bring into Parliament any Bill he conceives to be useful to this nation. But I thought it more respectful to your Lordships to ask your leave before; but I cannot think the doing of it will be any prejudice to the Bill, because I am confident the reason, the prudence, and the charitableness of it, will be able to justify it to this House and the whole world."

If Buckingham's judicial reasoning did not convert their Lordships they yet gave him leave to introduce his Bill. A revival, however, of the late dissensions between the two Houses put an abrupt end to this and all other business. The Government were much alarmed by the situation. Nor was their perplexity lessened when Lord Mohun brought forward a motion—warmly supported by Buckingham—for a dissolution.

Charles saw no alternative but a prorogation, and on November the 22nd suddenly went down to Westminster with that object. The secret of his intention, however, had not escaped Buckingham. Rising at an unusually early hour, the Duke reached the House in time to register a remonstrance, largely signed by the Opposition, against the continuance of the present House of Commons, and demanding dissolution.

The protest was vain, for the Government dreaded nothing so much as a general election, but the Duke's action did not tend to reconcile him with Charles. In fact, George Villiers considered that he was consulting his safety as well as his convenience by withdrawing shortly after to a mansion he had acquired in Dowgate. Here "Alderman George," as the King sarcastically called him, was in constant touch with the popular leaders, while he enjoyed all the ancient protective privileges of the city. Shaftesbury followed his example, and for the moderate sum of £160 a year rented Thanet House, in Aldersgate Street; and during the next few years, most of the schemes and plots of that restless period were supposed to originate in one or the other residence.

Louis was quick witted enough to grasp the possibilities of George Villiers' situation. On the 17th of February 1676 the King of France concluded a secret agreement with Charles II., by which, in return for the latter's bond to abstain from alliances with foreign powers, he promised to grant him an annual subsidy and help at home should his unruly subjects prove troublesome.

But ally as he was of his royal brother of England,[1] Louis was too prudent to neglect the leader of the Opposition.

In a minute drawn up for the guidance of Courtin, he emphatically warns his new envoy to remember that not only had the Duke a multitude of friends, but that he would always be able to do much in any Parliament. Also " tho', now living in retirement away from the Court, and to all appearance holding himself aloof from public affairs, yet he will always have to be reckoned with, since whenever he chooses to give himself the trouble to pay his court to the King, he will be able to regain his position with him."

Courtin seems to have obeyed the Royal commands readily enough, for, unlike Colbert de Choisy, he was evidently on excellent terms with "Alderman George." But naturally enough after Versailles, where the distinctions of rank were as the Law and the Prophets to its inhabitants, George Villiers' democratic propensities were no small trial to the worthy Frenchman; and he perpetually laments that His Grace should be surrounded merely by common people,[2] and estranged from all intercourse with the well-born and respectable. "I have done all I can," he continues, "to induce him to retreat to the country till the meeting of Parliament . . . or I fear the Court will make it an excuse for ill-treating him."

Had the Ministers succeeded in penetrating the conspiracies hatching in the recesses of

---

[1] "Affaires Étrangères," No. 125, pp. 84-88, Mem. pour servir d'instruction a Courtin, 17th April 1676.
[2] "Affaires Étrangères," vol. cxix. f. 54.

Dowgate, it is probable that Courtin's gloomy forebodings would have been realised. That Danby did not do so is the more remarkable as Buckingham was generally credited with an absolute incapacity for holding his tongue. Already, in the year 1676, Shaftesbury was preparing the way to place James Monmouth on the throne of England. It was a design which provided incomparable opportunity for the tortuous intrigues so dear to the heart of Buckingham. Yet it must be confessed that it never commended itself to him, and that for once George Villiers infinitely preferred the constitutional remedy offered by a general election. Nevertheless, it would be folly to ascribe the Duke's attitude wholly and solely to a distaste for revolutionary methods. Personal prejudice had no small share in Buckingham's sentiments. The dislike he entertained for the young man probably dated far back to the day when Charles' paternal weakness had given his first-born precedence over all other English dukes. Later, Madame's marked partiality for her handsome nephew had added fuel to the fire, and quite recently Monmouth's appointment to the Chancellorship of Cambridge had not tended to reconcile the two men. Moreover, Buckingham held that his own descent from the Plantagenets gave him a better claim to the throne of Great Britain, than could be alleged by the son of Mrs Barlow. It is true he did not openly preach this doctrine. But the prophecy which promised him a crown was of long standing, and the suggestion was already germinating in his busy brain.

On the 15th of February 1677, after the longest

prorogation known, Parliament reassembled. The gossips declared that the Duke would not be able to take his place in the House of Lords, as he "had been suffering from a generous attack of gout."[1] But when the King's and the Chancellor's speeches came to an end, Buckingham rose "in great bravery, in liveries of blue, but all diversified," ready and eager for the fray. It was clear that the Government had no intention of going to the country, and the Duke was equally determined to force a general election.

The fact that an Act of Edward III. enjoined that a Parliament should be held once every year proved to his satisfaction that since the present assembly had not been called together within the twelvemonth, it was consequently dissolved, and that fresh writs were needed before it could have a legal status. "Statutes of the realm," he exclaimed "are not like women, for they are not a jot worse for being old."[2]

The words of this "just statute are as plain as a pike-staff, and no man that is not a scholar," he feelingly remarked, "could mistake them." He deprecated being considered "an unquiet or pragmatical man; for in this age every man that cannot bear everything is called unquiet." But the fear of being false to his own convictions touched him yet more nearly, for "though it does not always follow that he is pragmatical whom others take to be so, yet this never fails to be true that he is most certainly a knave who takes himself to be so." He did not depend on legal technicalities alone to

---

[1] Hist. MSS. Rutland, vol. ii. p. 38.
[2] Echard, p. 413, 15th Feb. 1676.

support his case. With some astuteness he pointed out that the perpetual conflicts between the two Houses might well be due to the nature of the House of Commons having suffered a complete alteration. "They do not think now that they are an assembly that are to return to their houses and become private men again; they look upon themselves as a standing Senate and as a number of men picked out to be legislators for the rest of their lives; and if that be the case they have reason to believe themselves to be our equals." Next to the distrust the Peers harboured against the Commons, was their dread of encroachments from the royal prerogative, and Buckingham did not fail to play on this responsive chord. Either Magna Charta bound the Kings of England, "or else the government of England by parliaments and law is absolutely at an end; for if the Kings of England have power by an order of theirs to invalidate an Act made for the maintenance of Magna Charta, they have also power by an order of theirs to invalidate Magna Charta." For these and many other reasons, he therefore wound up with a motion "that we humbly address ourselves to His Majesty, and beg of him for his own sake as well as for the people's sake *to give us a new Parliament;* that so we may unanimously, before it be too late, use our utmost endeavours for the safety, the welfare and the glory of His Majesty's service."

In so condensed a version of this lengthy speech it is difficult to give an adequate notion of the consummate art with which Buckingham handled his subject. He carefully abstained from anything that could justly irritate his audience. The jokes with which the discourse is besprinkled are strictly decorous. He appealed alike to the Englishman's passion for freedom and to his ingrained reverence for precedent. He pleaded for the rights of the people, while he deprecated the inordinate pretensions of the Commons. Nor can his tactics have been much at fault, since Shaftesbury, the most accomplished wire-puller of his generation, backed the Duke's arguments with all the resources of his rare eloquence.

Yet it soon appeared that if the Peers regarded the ascendency of the Commons with impatience, they resented infinitely more the action of one of their own number in calling their very existence in question.

When the Duke ceased speaking, Lord Rosherville sprang to his feet and demanded that the bold speaker should instantly be summoned to the Bar to answer for the "insult" he had offered the House. Buckingham's supporters were fewer than on previous occasions, but Lords Shaftesbury, Wharton and Salisbury valiantly defended him. Finch, the Chancellor, strove to prove that the passing of the Triennial Act of 1694, Charles I. overruled the Duke's contention. But their Lordships were less anxious to deliver an equitable decision on a disputed point of law than to avenge the fancied slight perpetrated by Buckingham. For five long hours the turmoil raged. Finally, George Villiers rose once more, and, turning to the judges and the bishops, asked them whether a new proposition he had just drawn up "was not a true syllogism?" This "maxim" asserted that "since any order or direction of the Kings of England is only binding if made *pro bono publico*," it follows that the last prorogation being "contrary to an Act of Edward III.'s for the greatest common good, was consequently null and void in law."

This was the last touch needed to goad the Lords to frenzy. The debate "rose to that height that all the four lords—Buckingham, Shaftesbury, Wharton and Salisbury—were ordered to be sent to the Tower for contempt of the authority and being of the present Parliament, and the House of Peers."

The Duke had thus only succeeded in rallying three Peers to his "syllogism"; but Lord Anglesey, in happier times a trusted adviser of Cromwell's, though he did not endorse all Buckingham's arguments, yet mustered courage to remind their Lordships that their vindictive action bade fair to endanger the most precious of their privileges—Free Speech.

Reason and common sense were however impotent to stem the tide of passion; and Charles must have rejoiced to see the House, generally so stubborn, fighting the battle of his dispensing power.

The four lords were ordered to retire, and in their absence it was voted that they should be called and make an acknowledgment at the Bar in these words, "I doe acknowledge that my endeavouring that this Parliament is dissolved was an unadvised thing, for which I humbly beg pardon of His Majesty and this honourable House."[1]

Black Rod was then sent to summon the culprits, but returned to say that Buckingham was not about

[1] Hist. MSS. Le Fleming, Rep. XII., Dr Thom. Smith to D. F., 15th Feb., 15, 17.

the House,[1] and further that a gentleman had seen the Duke, with his head bent and muffling up his order, go forth to embark in a small boat.

The boatmen were then cited, and in their turn reported that Buckingham had caused himself to be first taken to the Savoy, next to Somerset House, and finally to the Temple, where, having landed, they saw him get into a hack coach. Thereupon, Black Rod was despatched to seek him in his own house, but neither there could he be found. A recollection of the successful game of hide-and-seek which the Duke had played some ten years previously, must have occurred to the Peers, for they were now transported into "such a rage," that they designed a proclamation for stopping the ports, apprehending him wherever he should be discovered and bringing him to the Tower, there to remain prisoner till he should be delivered in due course of law.

[1] Affaires Étrangères, No. 122, f. 173, Courtin au Roi, 1st March 1677.

CHAPTER XIII

BUCKINGHAM IN THE TOWER

IF Buckingham had meditated escape, reflection soon caused him to abandon the scheme. On the following day, he walked into the House of Lords and quietly resumed his accustomed seat. The assembly, though still seething with excitement, had so far settled down to its ordinary routine that the "Frauds and Perjuries and the Unnecessary Suits Bill" had just passed the first reading. But all calm and decorum vanished with the reappearance of the Duke. The vociferations[1] of the Court Lords crying out, "To the Bar! to the Bar!" converted the Upper Chamber into a pandemonium, till His Grace, who could easily turn anything into a jest and extricate himself out of any difficulties, rose up and said that he begged their Lordships' pardon for retiring the night before; that they very well knew the exact economy he kept in his family, and perceiving their Lordships intended he should be some time in another place, he only went home to set his house in order, and was now come to submit himself to their Lordships' pleasure."

The House, however, was not to be disarmed by Buckingham's pleasant wit. "He was ordered to[2]

[1] Echard, vol. iii., p. 415.
[2] Hist. MSS., Com. le Fleming, Rep. XII., Feb. 15-17, 1677.

be withdrawne and the usher commanded to bring him to the Bar, when being come and kneeling and then standing up againe was tould what apprehensions the House had of his facts, and the words of submission being given into his hands, he tould them that if he offended His Majesty and this House in anything he alleged, he begged their pardons, but could not ask pardon for thinking and speaking his thoughts, and soe refused to make submission as directed and being withdrawne, he was ordered to be committed to the Tower during His Majesty's pleasure."

Thither the other members of the devoted little band had already preceded him. Shaftesbury created a sensation by petitioning for the ministrations of his own cook, a request which unmistakably pointed to a fear of foul play. Charles did not readily forgive the insinuation, though at the moment, without any sign of disquiet, he merely remarked, "You see, my Lords, what a good opinion he has of me!" and gave instructions that the petition should be granted. Buckingham followed Shaftesbury's[1] example, asking for his cook and another servant, but declined any other attendants. He explained that having had two ague fits the previous day, he feared to present himself while still shivering with fever before their Lordships, lest they should attribute his condition to nervousness. Moreover, as the river passage would probably make him worse, he begged to be removed to the Tower by land. The House acceded to these requests, but gave order that the prisoners should not be allowed to communicate

[1] Affaires Étrangères, 1st Mar. 1677, Courtin au Roy, No. 122, f. 173.

with each other, "nor were they to be visited without leave of the King or the House, and particular observations[1] were made of those that asked leave." So rigorous a detention was unusual, and excited comment, and later, when Lord Danby received the same treatment at the hands of his opponents, it was considered "a just retaliation." Both King and Parliament had, however, forgotten to guard against the opportunities afforded for intercourse by divine worship. The first Sunday the conspirators were in the Tower, a relative writes, " the four lords mett at divine service, and made use of that time to talke all the service while, but care will be taken to prevent that hereafter."[2] Some of their womenfolk were evidently much scared by this show of severity. Lady Chaworth writes, " My sister (Lady Shaftesbury) takes on furiously and terrifies herselfe (her husband) will be put to death, but I thinke it impossible he not being criminall, only mislead, yet heare the King is very angry att him, saying hee that first would insinuate the King designed poysonning him by demanding his own cooke, he hath reason to suspect intended poysonning his Royal person!"

Meanwhile, outside the Tower events followed one another rapidly. The loss of their leaders disorganised the Opposition, and the various measures conceived by the militant Protestantism of both Houses practically came to naught.

Charles spent his French pension to such good purpose among the Commons, that they proved unexpectedly compliant about money matters,

---

[1] Burnet, vol ii. p. 118.
[2] Hist. MSS., Rutland Papers, vol. ii. p. 39, 20th Feb. 1676-77.

and he actually obtained an extension of the excise for three years. A somewhat unexpected result of their liberality was that when Louis' conquests in Flanders occasioned something like a panic in England, and in May Parliament made a subsidy of £600,000 conditional on war with France, Charles' excellent financial position enabled him to take up an independent position, and adjourn Parliament first until July, again until December, and finally until April 1678.

Hitherto the captive noblemen had been sustained by the knowledge that their confinement must necessarily terminate with the close of the Session. Thanks to these repeated adjournments, however, it was now impossible to foresee when that event would take place, and their imprisonment threatened to become indefinite. Apart from personal convenience, it would have been, on tactical grounds alone, an error to remain under lock and key for the benefit of Danby and his policy, and they took strenuous measures to recover their liberty.

One and all, therefore, they invoked the assistance of influential friends and kinsfolk. Lord Oxford interceded for Lord Salisbury, Mr Henry Coventry for Lord Shaftesbury, Lord Middlesex, a connection of the Villiers family, was "the most earnest man alive" for the Duke.

At the outset,[1] however, only Lord Oxford's efforts appeared destined to meet with success. It was not unusual during the hot summer months, when the pestilential miasmas from the

[1] Savile Corres., p. 50, Henry Savile to his brother, Whitehall, May 1677.

river well-nigh poisoned the luckless beings cooped up in the Tower, to release State prisoners on parole. Yet when the burning days of June began, Lord Salisbury alone was granted a "month's leave." Undoubtedly things looked black for the other two. Danby and his master would gladly have kept Shaftesbury for ever safely caged, and so far as his companion was concerned, it was remembered that when some weeks before Lord Middlesex had presented Buckingham's petition to the Monarch, Charles had made the grim comment on the document? "that though there was great humility used to himself there was no reparation to the Lords." Shaftesbury, ever a partisan of bold measures and impatient of the futile courtly methods he had hitherto essayed, adopted the drastic course of applying for a writ of *habeas corpus* in the King's Bench. But though he pleaded his case with conspicuous ability he did not gain his freedom. The judges held that they had no jurisdiction in the matter. Shaftesbury found he had only made his original position worse, and returned to the Tower to console himself as best he might by reading and studying the war maps of Europe.

For once Buckingham was better inspired than the wise Achitophel. Middlesex's decorous, well-meant efforts having signally failed, he now addressed himself—according to Andrew Marvell—to "Nelly, Rochester, and all the merry gang." It is only fair to say that these worthies did not abandon their old comrade; and from the moment Mrs Gwynn undertook the management of his affairs they sensibly improved. Indeed, if the following note formed her credentials—as it is not unlikely it did—

evidently not content with befriending her first patron in adversity, the sombre purlieus of the Tower itself had no terrors for Nelly. We do not possess the Duke's answer, but it is safe to conclude that he can never have hailed her cheerful presence with greater delight than on this occasion.

The note is as follows :—

The best woman[1] in the world brings you this paper and at this time, the discreetest ; pray my Lord resign your understanding and your interest wholly to her conduct ; mankinde's is to be redeemed by Eve ; with as much honour as the thing will admit of, separate your concerne from your fellow-prisoner, then an expedient handsome enough and secret enough to disengage yourself ; obey and you are happy.

Needless to say, the Duke was not insensible to the persuasion of the " best woman in the world " ; and a harder disposition than the Merry Monarch's might well have been touched by the fervour of the following appeal entrusted to the new Eve for his perusal :—

I am soe surprised with what Mrs Nelly has toulde mee, that I know not in the world what to say. The more sensible greefe I had in being putt away from Your Majesty was not the losing my place, butt the being shutt out of Your Majesty's kindness ; and if the aspiring to that bee a fault, it is at least a more pardonable one than the aspiring to wealth, the making one's owne fortune. What has made this inclination more violent in mee than perhaps it is in other people is the honour

[1] Brit. Mus. Add. MSS., 27872, f. 18.

I had of being bred up with Your Majesty from a childe, for I hope affections are ever strongest in men which begin in their youngest yeares, and therefore I beseech Your Majesty to believe me when I say that I have ever loved you more than all the rest of mankind, and that I have not only once chosen to follow you in misfortune rather than bee in never soe greate plenty any other way, but that I would willingly doe soe agayne to-morrow if Your Majesty could take it kindly of mee. What should I say? I am not one that pretend to a preciseness in Devotion, but yet I am sure Your Majesty never found mee to be a knave, and I wish that all the curses imaginable may fall upon mee if I tell you a lye or if I would tell you a lye to save my life. I have lived long enough in the world not to care much about it, and have mett with soe much ungratefulness from almost all mankind that the pleasure of conversing with man is even quite taken from mee, and yett I beseech Your Majesty to soe believe that greefe which in my whole life did ever sitt nearest to my heart was the losse of Your Majesty's kindness. You, that have been a Lover yourselfe, know what it is to thinke oneselfe ill-used by a mistress that one loves extreamely, and it is that only I can truly compare my great misfortune to. Yett there was besides my owne misfortune in it a greate deale of art used to make mee believe that Your Majesty hated mee, and I can hardly forgive them that did it, since it was done with as much undutifulness to Your Majesty as ingratitude to mee.[1]

Estranged, as the best observers now held Charles to be, from his old schoolmate, either this letter or, more probably, Mrs Nelly's influence had a remarkably softening effect on him. Indeed,

[1] Add. MSS., 27872, f. 20, Duke of Buckingham to Charles II.

the merry gang soon began to conceive hopes not merely of the Duke's release, but of his complete restoration to favour. That which Nell Gwynn's pleadings had begun could best be completed by the personal magnetism of Buckingham, and consequently all their efforts were now directed to secure an audience for him with the King. It was, however, no easy task, for their opponents had learnt by repeated and bitter experience the strange power the Duke possessed over the debonair monarch, and, had the subject been openly broached, a hundred unanswerable reasons would have been alleged against an act of grace so strongly savouring of caprice. The gloomy atmosphere of prison, however, had not affected Buckingham's innate resourcefulness, and it is with genuine satisfaction in a new-found stratagem that he expounds to Charles the method by which, without arousing the jealous alarms of his adversaries, he can attain his object.

MAY IT PLEASE YOUR MAJESTY,[1]—I cannot but tell Your Majesty I am soe perfectly overjoyed at the kindness you have beene pleased to expresse of mee to my Lord Middlesex, that I shall bee sottisfied in mine owne mind whether I come out to-day or noe: but there is a necessity of speaking to you immediately in order to your owne service, and it is necessary also that it bee done with all kinde of privacy, and therefore, you Sir, pray let this dull man doe it in his owne dull way. I doe not thinke him very good at invention, and yett in my opinion he has litt upon noe very ill expedient at this time. For it is most certaine that a little mistake in my builders at Clifden may cost me above £10,000,

[1] Add. MSS., 27872, f. 34, Duke of Buckingham to Charles II.

because I shall certainly pull it downe againe if it be not to my owne mind; we say that there is a very just pretence for Your Majesty's giving me leave to goe out dayes and yett going out upon the condition he proposes, which is to have him ["Sir John"[1] scratched out] always with mee. I shall be in as ill company as I was before (which will give great satisfaction to some well-natured people about Your Majesty), and I may easily then have the happiness of speaking to Your Majesty without its being noticed. I beseech Your Majesty to believe that I would rather be hanged than bee thus earnest in this business if I did not know I should please you when I speake with you, and I am not such a beast as to make you have mee as long as you like by telling you a flim-flam story in order to the getting a thing for which I shall not be one jot the better. My designe is to let you see (I) love you, and I am sure I shall convince you of it, and that I ever shall be, etc. etc.

Whatever the cause, whether due to the renewed blandishments of Buckingham's fair ally or to uncontrollable curiosity on the monarch's part, it seems tolerably clear that the Duke eventually gained his point.

Henry Savile tells us "that it was so ordered" that when the warrant for the noble lord's leave to view the building operations reached the Tower the day was already too far spent to get further than his residence in the city.[2] Here from six o'clock in the evening to the following morning he was a nominal prisoner only, and heaven knows what visitors may have come and gone unmarked from

---

[1] Sir J. Robinson, Lieut. of the Tower.
[2] H. Savile, p. 61, 29th June 77.

that house in Dowgate, which had been specially chosen as a suitable centre for mysterious plots. The next day, with Sir John Robinson at his side, he posted fifty-two miles to and from his riverside villa. Bearing in mind the lamentable state of British highways in the seventeenth century, the travellers made good speed, for the same night saw the gates of the Tower close upon them once more. Yet Buckingham had well employed the interval, since three days later he was set free for a month. Lord Salisbury was even more fortunate as he obtained his complete liberty; while Lord Wharton was treated with special graciousness. The King jested[1] with him, and said he would teach him a text of scripture. "It will be very acceptable from Your Majesty." "Sin no more." "Your Majesty has that from my quotation of it to my Lord Arlington when he had been before the House of Commons." "Well, my lord, you and I are both old men and should love quietness." "Ay, my lord, but you have an aching tooth still." "No, indeed, mine are all falling out!"

Thus Shaftesbury was the only one of the recalcitrant peers left in the Tower, and with small chance of enlargement. To his restless spirit the prospect must have been particularly galling. Already indeed the close confinement must have told on his nerves, for in a moment of uncontrollable irritation he had descanted somewhat freely on his chief associate. In the Tower as elsewhere Ashley's were winged and barbed words which did not fail to

---

[1] "Welbeck Papers," vol. iii., Hist. MSS., p. 355. A. Marvell. Sir E. Harley.

reach their victim, and it was with deep resentment that Buckingham heard himself described "as a man *inconstant* and *giddy*." The speech rankled, and when the hour of release struck he welcomed the opportunity to retort the gibe. As His Grace was taking coach, the Earl looked out of a window and cried, "What, my lord, are you going to leave us?" "Ay, my lord," said he,[1] "such *giddy*-headed fellows as I can never stay long in a place."

By one of those abrupt transitions habitual to his career, Buckingham passed directly from the State prison to Whitehall. Here he remained quietly in Lord Rochester's lodgings for the next few days and was privately introduced into the Royal presence.[2]

Under the Stuarts the Government of England was scarcely less at the mercy of a palace intrigue than that of Turkey in the present century. The report that Buckingham bid fair not only to regain Charles' favour but to be appointed Lord Steward, unluckily for our hero's fortunes, leaked out prematurely. It was only to be expected that the Duke of York and Lord Danby would oppose such a suggestion to the uttermost. But when we remember that Buckingham was shortly to be identified with the most vehement of Monmouth's supporters, it is curious to find the Protestant Duke amongst his bitterest enemies. Andrew Marvell, in a letter to that worthy country gentleman, Sir Edward Harley, gives a vivid sketch of the uneasiness which pervaded ministerial circles. The Treasurer and Monmouth were said "to have re-

---

[1] Echard, "History," vol. iii. p 415.
[2] Carte MSS., 79, f. 112; 1st August 1677.

monstrated to the King that this was to leap over all the rules of decency and to suffer his authority to be trampled on, but if he had a favour to him he might do it in the regular way. Nevertheless,[1] it was for some days a moot point betwixt the Ministers of State and Ministers of Pleasure who should carry it. At last Buckingham was advertised that he should retire out of Whitehall. He obeyed . . . People were full of their imaginations. What changes he would make at Court, but he loves pleasure better than revenge, and yet that is not the meanest luxury."

The Ministers of State must indeed have been sorely exercised and puzzled how to oust the gayest of the Ministers of Pleasure, since, to judge from the following letter of Buckingham to Rochester, they were reduced to crediting him with imaginary crimes over and above his actual ones.

My deare Lord,[2] — After the obligations I have to you I should not bee so unmannerly as to desire Your Lordship to neglect any of your owne occasions for my sake, but my noble friends at Court have now resolved as the most politick notions they can goe upon to ly most abominably of Your Lordship and mee, in order to which they have brought in a new treasonable lampoone of which Your Lordship is to be the author. For this and for severall other reasons there will be a necessity of Your Lordship being here when the King comes to towne, but Mr Shepheard and I will entertaine you more upon this subject before it bee long, for we are resolved to wayte upon you at

[1] A. Marvell, " Hist. MSS. Welbeck Papers," vol. iii. p. 415.
[2] Brit. Mus. Add. MSS., 11th August 1677, 7003, 282.

Woodstock, where I shall be Your Lordship's unalterably, My Lord, etc.

This sudden downfall of all his hopes must have been peculiarly bitter to Buckingham, as he had evidently counted on re-enacting the triumphs of 1667 when, to a superficial observer, the situation had been well-nigh identical.

The Duke forgot, however, that the ten years which had elapsed had not strengthened Charles' moral fibre. "Sauntering," as Sheffield said, was now more than ever "the King's favourite Sultana." At all times arguments and recriminations from his immediate domestic circle had been eminently distasteful, now they had become intolerable. Then, Barbara Villiers had joined forces with the Duke. Now, he had no more formidable antagonist than Louise de Kéroualle. And it must be remembered that Charles had never known with the Duchess of Cleveland the serene existence which he enjoyed under the auspices of the shrewd Frenchwoman. In her society he found the advantages of domesticity without the tedium inseparably connected to a man of his temper with the marriage tie. Of old, Buckingham had but to contend with Clarendon, the very embodiment of those virtues most irksome to the Sovereign, whereas he himself possessed the envied secret of giving freshness and variety to Charles' well-worn round of self-indulgence. In 1677, on the contrary, instead of the prolix exhortations of an aged statesman, he had to compete with the wiles of a beautiful woman. In fact his adversary was the crafty diplomatist who had made herself the pivot of

Charles' life, and who, as mother and mistress, great lady and harpy, held the amorous monarch enthralled till his dying day.

Under the circumstances, the forged lampoons were a work of supererogation. The victory of the Ministers was a foregone conclusion. At intervals Buckingham was again visited with the dream of repossessing himself of his old schoolfellow's affection, but in the main he bowed to the inevitable and turned his ambitions elsewhere. Henceforward he aimed rather at being the tribune of the people than the mayor of the palace.

During the twenty-four hours' leave the Duke had obtained for visiting his constructions at Cliveden, an event took place which marked the end of an epoch in his career. Anna Maria, Countess of Shrewsbury, the "widow of his making," "owned her match" with a Somersetshire gentleman, George Rodney Bridges. Her parents were so dissatisfied with this new freak of their wayward daughter that she was obliged to leave Cardigan House. Nevertheless, though Mr Bridges was but the second son of Sir Thomas Bridges of Keynsham, and had to be dowered by his bride with a Court appointment worth £4500, the marriage benefited her, for, as we have seen, Charles II. made it an excuse for desiring his wife and sister-in-law to receive her back into their intimacy.[1]

Buckingham, unlike Lords Salisbury and

[1] Mr Bridges survived her, inheriting her estate when she died in 1702. Their only son long represented Salisbury in Parliament. At his death, having no children, he left much of his property to the Admiral Lord Rodney, so that it may be said that only one life separates the Dutch incursion in the Thames from our glorious West Indian victories of the late eighteenth century.

Wharton, had hitherto "not acknowledged unadvised discourse concerning the prorogation . . . with obligation to make the same submission to the House of Lords when sitting." His petition[1] was grounded on "having contracted several indispositions." But, about the same time he wrote to Rochester, he seems to have judged a further struggle hopeless, and subscribed a humbly-worded declaration of penitence which promptly obtained his full release.

In February 1678 Parliament was called together. It was impossible to retain Shaftesbury any longer in prison, since he now fully recanted his errors, and begged pardon of the House on his knees. He was therefore, says a contemporary, "let loose, like the dragon[2] in Revelations full of wrath." He had indeed a good many wrongs to avenge, for since the unsuccessful issue of his law-suit his confinement had been made doubly rigorous, and his literary and geographical studies cannot entirely have consoled him in his enforced retirement.

Thus Danby had apparently worsted his enemies, and the marriage he negotiated between William

---

[1] MS. Carte 228, folio 106.
To the Right Honourable the Lords, etc.
The humble Petition of George, Duke of Buckingham.
Sheweth,—That your Lo'pps having comited your Petioner to the Tower of London because he did not obey your Lo'pps order, and he hath suffered much by reason thereof.
In obedience therefore to your Lo'pps he doth acknowledge that his endevorin to maintain that the Parliament is dissolved was an ill-advised action, for which he humbly begs the Pardon of the King's Maty and of this most Honourable hous, and prays that your Lo'pps would be pleased to discharge him from the said comitment, and restore him to your Lo'pps favor, and your Petioner shall pray.
(Endorsed)—Copye of ye Duke of Buckingham's Petition.
28th January 1677.

[2] Ralph, "Hist. of England," vol. i. p. 331.

of Orange and Princess Mary, the eldest daughter of the Duke of York, was deservedly popular in England.

The Government unquestionably improved its position by the Dutch matrimonial alliance, and by the proposal to conclude a treaty defensive and offensive with Holland; yet the situation still offered ample opportunities for the aggressive tactics of the Opposition. These opportunities their leaders, Buckingham and Shaftesbury in the Upper and Lord Russell in the Lower House, were not slow to perceive or to act on. Great as was the sympathy the Commons felt for the Stadtholder in his struggle with Louis, they equally dreaded the power a standing army and large subsidies would confer on their own unprincipled monarch. In fact, had they perused those secret clauses of the Treaty of Dover, by which such a contingency was to be utilised for the wholesale conversion of England, they could hardly have exhibited greater uneasiness. Louis, who was bent on detaching Charles from his nephew, did not fail to play upon these fears. Barillon, the French Ambassador, was enjoined to leave no stone unturned to secure their adhesion. Nor was he left unassisted. The Marquis of Ruvigny was also despatched to London to second his efforts with his numerous friends, and especially with his relatives the Russells. Money undoubtedly played a large part in these transactions. But where there is so much to blame it is satisfactory to be able to state that no French gold found its way into the Duke's empty pockets. Barillon indeed bears emphatic testimony to the disinterestedness of the noble spendthrift. If occasionally he requested[1] a loan it was to cement the strange connections he diligently fostered in the City or at Wapping amongst old Cromwellians, religious fanatics, discharged and penniless seamen—confederates whom he gravely assured the Ambassador were of untold service to the Grand Monarque.

On the Continent, statesmen and nations alike desired a conclusion of the war, but William of Orange refused to accept terms which would leave him practically at the mercy of Louis XIV. whenever it pleased the most Christian King to resume hostilities. Tournai was the fortified town which, in spite of Charles' repeated efforts to bring about a compromise, neither of the belligerents would surrender at any price. The manœuvres of the English Opposition naturally stiffened the King of France's attitude; and while the Commons were wrangling and debating, the important city of Ghent surrendered to Louis.

So great a disaster caused an immediate reaction in England. Supplies were voted, though on conditions purposely made onerous for the King, and Buckingham and Shaftesbury plainly told the French Ambassador that they no longer dared to stem the current of popular sympathy for Holland.

Buckingham was the more lukewarm in the matter, that in the beginning of the month of March he evidently had hopes of a reconciliation with the Court. He was anxious to obtain a pardon under the Great Seal, and with that object would even, it is said, have signed the following Declaration:—

The Right Honourable George Duke of

[1] Affaires Étrangères, No. 127, f. 245.

Buckingham doth hereby declare that he believes himself bound in honour and conscience to God and His Majesty to reveal to His Majesty all that any way comes to his knowledge of any plot or conspiracy against his sacred Person and the present Government; or any of His Majesty's Ministers of State. And he doth hereby engage upon his honour to do so.[1]

The wording of the above has undoubtedly an ugly ring, and it was perhaps fortunate for Buckingham's reputation that he did not finally endorse this somewhat comprehensive pledge.

Meanwhile, in spite of the money grant and the efforts made in England to recruit troops for the campaign in Flanders, negotiations still proceeded between the two Sovereigns.

In his eagerness to win Charles, Louis did not neglect the Opposition. Ruvigny was keenly alive to the advantages to be derived from their co-operation, and never wearied of impressing their views on his Sovereign. He considered himself authorised to pledge Louis to abstention from any interference with their personal interests.[2] And, moreover, as in spite of previous declarations, it was possible they might accede to Tournai, as well as Valenciennes, and Condé remaining French, he pleaded that the Whigs should not be "scandalised" by the additional retention of Ypres.

Louis, however, intoxicated with success, was less fearful of giving offence to the English lords than his representative. Indeed the arrogance of

---

[1] Hist. MSS. Rep. xiv. App. part ix.; Lindsay MSS., 9th March 1678, Draft of the Pardon desired by the Duke of Buckingham.

[2] Affaires Étrangères, No. 28, f. 162, 13th March 1678.

the royal bearing stung Charles to action. The King of England flung compromise to the winds, and formally invited Spain, Holland and the Empire to join with him in bringing pressure to bear on France.

That the Protestant Opposition, who should have been foremost in resisting the most Christian King's aggressions, were in reality his secret counsellors is not the least curious feature of a complicated situation. Yet unnatural as such conduct may appear, Buckingham and Shaftesbury, Russell and Holles were not altogether without excuse.[1]

According to the French Ambassador, who immediately sought their advice, they were persuaded that, under the pretence of a foreign campaign, Charles was levying a force to enable him to deal with his own refractory subjects at home. They argued that they themselves would be the first to suffer, and that deprived of its natural leaders the nation would be at the mercy of a despotic Government. France, too, would be the loser by such a catastrophe, since if Charles was freed from his domestic embarrassments he would be enabled to despatch men and arms on a larger scale to Flanders. The English lords therefore held that Louis would be consulting his own—as well as their—interests if he put an end to the baleful uncertainty of the present position, and forced Charles' hand by presenting an ultimatum. They did not add, but the astute Barillon divined, that such a course would relieve his friends of a two-fold anxiety, as they could not shake off the

[1] Affaires Étrangères, 11th April 1678, No. 128.

suspicion that, despite appearances, Charles and Louis might all the time be hand in glove, secretly plotting the ruin of England's faith and freedom.

Beyond this, however, with the exception of Buckingham, now "the boldest of them all," the lords of Cabal would not commit themselves or make any definite proposals to the King of France.

Nevertheless, when Parliament met, their understanding with the French minister produced important results.

Charles had expected that his warlike schemes would find favour with the militant Protestantism of the country members. But the Opposition so handled matters that the House of Commons insisted on devoting its energies exclusively to the administration of the anti-Popery laws and to passing a vote of censure on the Duke of Lauderdale—the King's trusted Minister. Supplies for fleet and army they stubbornly refused.

On their side the Dutch showed no enthusiasm for Charles' quadruple alliance. Holland was thoroughly exhausted, and even William of Orange could not galvanise his countrymen to the further endeavours his uncle's new league would have entailed.

In the circumstances Charles' new-born ardour was effectually checked. He made conciliatory overtures to the King of France, and as Louis, overbearing as he was, began to realise that the French Treasury would be hard pressed to meet the demands of a new European war, he no longer showed himself unaccommodating.

Some month selapsed, however, before a definite end was put to hostilities—months spent in bickerings between King and Parliament, and haggling between Louis and his antagonists. There were moments when the most optimistic must have despaired, but ultimately terms were signed by the delegates of Louis and the States at Nimeguen on July 31st. Yet it was considerably after peace was concluded " between the sun and the frogs," to quote the Electress Sophia, that all the belligerents laid down their arms. The month of August, however, saw Charles and Louis reconciled.[1]

The British troops in Flanders were then re-shipped for England, and Ruvigny, faithful to his engagements with the opposition, offered Charles a large sum if they were immediately paid off. But, impecunious as was the British Government, the army was not disbanded by the time specified. Under the pretext that there was no money available for the purpose, the troops were kept —a standing menace for the next Session—within striking distance of London. Small wonder that the Opposition judged this to be the first step towards the fulfilment of their darkest prophecies, and Burnet expressed but the common opinion when he declared "they gave all for lost."

[1] Corres. de la Duchesse Sophie de Hanovre, avec le Palatin du Rhin, 22 et 30 Juin 1678, quot in le Marechal de Luxembourg et le Prince d'Orange, 475.

The Duke of Buckingham.

CHAPTER XIV

BUCKINGHAM AND THE POPISH PLOT

GLOOMY as the prospect undoubtedly was for the Opposition, Buckingham's ingenuity and resource were as unflagging now as in many a previous crisis. Unfortunately his schemes suffered from one radical defect. They hinged on the disposal of considerable sums of money, and the Duke's credit was exhausted. So conscious, indeed, was he of his own penury, that he was morbidly anxious to impress on Louis that he was not seeking assistance for himself under a political pretext. To prevent any misconception he therefore suggested that £1000 should be paid over to the City Treasurer, to be refunded later if not spent meanwhile in winning over the principal men in the City for the King of France.[1] Should this grant be withheld, the Duke said he feared he might lose his influence for France with his friends, as they would consider his promises had been merely general.

Never, indeed, had he shown himself more eager in forwarding any of his manifold projects. He was prepared not only to cross secretly to Paris to obtain Louis' adhesion, but even—he declared—to swallow his pride and allow his travelling expenses to be defrayed by the King

[1] Affaires Étrangères.

of France should his own slender resources not suffice for the purpose.¹

Barillon did not disapprove of the journey in itself, but he implored the Duke to make it openly, since he was too prominent a personage for his absence to pass unperceived. Buckingham turned a deaf ear to the advice, but Barillon's sagacity was promptly vindicated, for it was the King of England himself who announced the Duke's arrival in Paris to the mortified diplomatist, and he was fain to hope from the Sovereign's manner that Charles did not attach much importance to the affair.

But if the King paid slight heed to Buckingham's doings in the French capital, the Duke's advent did not escape notice. During the months of August, when the Court had taken up its summer quarters at Fontainebleau, Paris, the gay city, that Mecca of the libertine, was a desert, in which so brilliant an apparition as the Duke of Buckingham was doubly conspicuous. It is true that His Grace industriously spread the report that "he was shutt off with some kind females"; but had a love affair been his true object, the world in general, and our Ambassador in particular, shrewdly opined he would not have encumbered himself³ with a disguise or an assumed French name, nor have restricted himself to the sole company of Sir Ellis Leighton. Lord Sunderland, in some perturbation of spirit, charged his friends in England "to discover the Duke's business if they could." The professional news-

---

¹ Affaires Étrangères, 1st September 1678, No. 130, p. 25.
² Letters of H. Savile, Paris, 27th August 1678, p. 69.
³ Carte, f. 225, 103, and f. 226, News letter for Hon. Mr Wharton, September 1678.

writers were the next to scent an intrigue, till at last, when an unexpected[1] alteration took place in the treaty between France and the Netherlands, it was universally referred to Buckingham's masquerade. Louis XIV. was better informed, but accustomed as he was to be served by diplomatists equally remarkable for discretion and efficiency the clumsy mystery cannot have been to his mind. In mid-September, therefore, without having achieved anything notable, Buckingham returned to Cliveden, there to seek such consolation as could be derived from feasting the Duchess of Portsmouth.

Undoubtedly the entertainment of the King's mistress was a matter of no slight importance. Yet the fêtes at Cliveden were scarcely concluded when an event occurred which reduced all else to insignificance. On Michaelmas Eve, Titus Oates solemnly denounced the Popish Plot to the Privy Council.

For some time past the political atmosphere had been in a highly inflammable condition, so charged with dread and suspicion that the merest spark was liable to produce an explosion. Neither the truth concerning the Treaty of Dover nor the King's religion had become known, but the conviction that the national faith and liberties were threatened by positive, if ill-defined, dangers was widespread. Had it been otherwise, Buckingham and Shaftesbury would not have dared to oppose the war with France during the recent Session, and now that an army was encamped at Blackheath the outlook was yet more threatening.

From the point of view of the Opposition it

---

[1] Carte MSS., f. 225, 103, and f. 226, News letter for Hon. Mr Wharton, September 1678.

must be owned that Oates' revelations were suspiciously opportune. So much so, indeed, that others besides Charles II. believed that the whole monstrous fabric of lies originated in Shaftesbury's subtle brain. Had Ashley Cooper, however, fathered the scheme, it would undoubtedly have lacked the glaring, ludicrous inconsistencies which betray its base origin. It can never, in truth, for a moment have imposed on that acute intellect, but Shaftesbury welcomed the ghastly delusion—he did more, he fostered it—because he saw that his best chance of defeating the real plot lay in combating the imaginary conspiracy.

As for Buckingham, every conviction, every prejudice, naturally led him to identify himself with Shaftesbury's manœuvres. Even had it not been so, "to weave the spider's web and to hatch the cockatrice" was a task too congenial to him not to silence any misgivings the Duke might feel as to the Doctor's veracity.

Already in the summer one Kirkby had tried to start a Papist scare. He had solemnly warned the King that his life would be attempted if he allowed himself to be separated from his suite during the walks which were part of the daily routine at Court. The alarmist was not successful, for Charles was too shrewd either to credit the tale or to slacken the pace which made attendance something of a trial to his less energetic Gentlemen of the Bedchamber. Unlike Kirkby, however, Titus Oates was destined neither to be ignored nor sneered out of notice. Yet the fellow's sinister countenance should alone have awakened doubts in the minds of his hearers. "A low man of an ill-cut, very short neck," says Roger

North; "and his visage and features were most particular. His mouth was the centre of his face, and a compass there would sweep his nose, forehead and chin within the perimeter," or, as Dryden describes him,

> "Sunk were his eyes; his voice was harsh and loud:
> Sure signs he neither choleric was, nor proud:
> His long chin proved his wit; his saint-like grace,
> A church vermilion, and a Moses face."[1]

Oates' past was as repulsive as his face. Some of its incidents do not bear repetition. Nor does it argue well for the perspicacity of the Jesuits that they should have employed the prying scoundrel even at the low daily wage of ninepence.

The Salamanca Doctor's romance belongs to history, but to understand Buckingham's line of conduct it may be well to recall the main lines of the tragic episode.

Sensational as was Titus Oates' earliest version of the plot, it was tame in comparison to the later editions he issued. At first he contented himself with denouncing a gigantic scheme, the conception of the Jesuits, assisted by the faithful at home and abroad, to restore the province of England to the Roman obedience. The design was, however, fairly comprehensive, since it included the assassination of the King, the landing of a great army from the Continent, and the firing of City and fleet.

Amongst the individuals specially singled out for attack by Oates was the Jesuit, Coleman, who had filled the post of secretary to the Duchess of York. It was part of the Duke of York's

[1] "Absalom and Achitophel," vol. ix. p. 236.

characteristic unwisdom that he should have encouraged the brainless bigot in his immediate circle. This priest—an intriguing fellow by all accounts—entertained a close correspondence with Louis XIV.'s celebrated confessor, the Père la Chaise, and copies of these letters were now seized and examined. At all times they would have created a dangerous scandal, for Coleman wrote of his plans, religious and political, in language recklessly offensive to Englishmen and Protestants. But now, read in the light of Oates' revelations, they assumed a truly sinister aspect.

Nevertheless, Charles II. might yet have succeeded in laughing the informer and his tale off the scene but for the untimely death of Sir Edmundbury Godfrey.

That worthy gentleman—"the best justice of the peace in London"[1]—was the magistrate who had received Oates' deposition. He had always lived on remarkably happy terms with the Roman Catholics, but thereafter he was observed to be depressed, and was heard to say that if there were any danger in the plot "he believed he himself would be knocked on the head."

Thus, when, a fortnight later, his corpse was found in a ditch near Primrose Hill, pierced with his own sword, and bearing marks of strangulation, the vast majority of citizens instantly concluded that he must have fallen a victim to Papist assassins. They argued that neither robbery nor personal enmity could have been the motives of the crime as his pockets were not rifled, and it was well known that the good man had not a foe in the

[1] Burnet, vol. ii. p. 162.

world. But the fact that Godfrey's clothes were covered with wax, which might conceivably have guttered from Church tapers, was proof positive to these lucid intellects that he had met his death in the company of some Mass priest. A proper medical examination might have cleared up many obscure points. But this Sir Edmundbury Godfrey's brothers would not permit. They were only too well aware of the taint of melancholia in their family, and feared that a verdict of suicide would deprive them of the coveted heritage.

Buckingham instantly saw the party capital to be realised out of the melancholy occurrence. The coroner's judgment had not been pronounced, says Barillon, and already the Duke had sought him out with a full blown scheme for which he desired his assistance. The Duke told him "it was absolutely necessary instantly to hand over 5000[1] pièces partly to encourage well-meaning folk in London and partly to make a stand against the artifices employed to subvert the people about this conspiracy. I told him that as I had imagined I should need no money till the meeting of Parliament, I had not pressed for the despatch of any considerable sum, and so had no funds to draw on before that time. I thought this the best excuse to make. For the moment he had to content himself with it. But yesterday he came again and brought with him the miniature case, which I gave him by Your Majesty's orders. On its security he wished me to raise 5000 pièces from some goldsmith or banker. I told him I could not do what he proposed since I could not pledge

[1] "Affaires Étrangères," No. 131, f. 77, 20th October 1678.

diamonds belonging to him. He sought, he said, for money, because he would not miss the present occasion. His plan was to get a petition presented to the Lord Mayor of London, which, under the pretext of assuring the safety of the town, would compel him to call all citizens to arms. This proposal would greatly embarrass the Court, especially if the petition was granted and the City armed, for the civic forces would not identify themselves with the Ministry but would demand many unforeseen things." Two weeks later, "without any grant of money," as the Ambassador had prophesied, "the burgesses were armed . . ."[1] and Monsieur de Buckingham was boasting of the fashion in which he would utilise them against the Court." Panic indeed proved a more effectual means of arousing the townsfolk than bribery, however profuse. Previous to Sir Edmundbury Godfrey's interment, his corpse lay in state visited by a vast concourse of people. It was then borne to the grave by seventy-two ministers besides a multitude of mourners of all ranks, who needed not the passionate adjurations of the orator, Dr Lloyd, of St Martin's-in-the-Fields, to be wrought to a frenzy of revengeful fury. Already in ordinary winters, if we are to believe Lord Shaftesbury, men and women hardly slept at night for "fear of fire[2] and massacring by Catholics." How much more now did it seem impossible to avert the threatened St Bartholomew, without elaborate street barricades, the arming of every householder, and the constant patrolling of the Trained bands.

[1] 3rd November 1678.
[2] "First Whig," p. 39, by Sir G. Sitwell.

Hundreds of citizens hastily furnished themselves with quilted silk armour or flails hung with leaden weights, inventions of the artisan College, whose ingenious fanaticism earned him the title of the "Protestant joiner." In the upper classes the alarm was no less acute, and it became the fashion for timorous ladies to go equipped with tiny pocket pistols concealed in their muffs ready loaded [1] for an emergency.

The day following the demonstration at St Martin's, Parliament met and summoned Titus Oates before them. That villain's evidence, says Dr Burnet, "was now so well believed that it was not safe for any man to seem to doubt any part of it. He thought he had the nation in his hands, and was swelled up to a high pitch of vanity and insolence." [2] Nor were new editions of his discovery wanting to whet the morbid curiosity of the hour. In particular, Titus loved to expatiate on the patents drawn up by the general of the Jesuits—documents he repeatedly swore to having both seen and examined—for the appointment of various Papist gentlemen to positions of trust in Army and State.

Yet surely never was there a stranger selection of leaders for a vast revolutionary undertaking. Lord Stafford, one of the most prominent, says a contemporary, "would have trembled [3] at the sight of a drawn sword." Lord Belasyse, the Guise of this latter-day League, was "a perfect martyr to gout; Lord Petre, a weak man who had never held

---

[1] "Lord Ailesbury Mems.," vol. i. p. 28.
[2] Burnet, vol. ii. p. 165.
[3] "Lord Ailesbury Mems.," vol. i. p. 28.

any military command, was to be Lieutenant-General . . .; Lord Arundel, who was seventy-two years of age and timid and feeble, was to be Commissary-General; Thomas Howard, third[1] husband of the Duchess of Richmond, who had long been dying, was to be a colonel." Had Lambert, after eighteen years of rigorous captivity, yet retained his wits he must have marvelled to find himself associated with such a helpless, dotard crew.

According to Oates, the ingenuity of the conspirators in disposing of the Merry Monarch was nothing short of prodigious. If, during his rambles at Newmarket, Charles did not receive his quietus from a silver bullet, at Windsor Irish desperadoes were in waiting to despatch him, or again at Whitehall, for the trifle of £15,000, Wakeman, the Queen's physician, had orders to poison him.

Oates had not forgotten that the Great Fire was still fresh in men's memories, so with fiendish cunning he announced a general conflagration as the fit accompaniment to a butchery of one hundred thousand souls. Nor amidst the general confusion could the humblest Protestant pamphleteer hope to escape. Dr Tonge—Oates' accomplice—provided a much-needed advertisement for his leaflet, "The Jesuit's Morals," by announcing that his own name figured prominently in the black list of the society. Dr Burnet was singularly "complimented"; nor were Buckingham and Shaftesbury forgotten, Buckingham himself being allotted to the dagger of a certain Pritchard.

The great men in both Houses were not a whit less ridiculous and crazed with suspicion than the

[1] Burnet, vol. ii., p. 166.

general public. One noble lord could unreproved assert "that he would not have so much as a Popish man or a Popish woman to remain here, not so much as a Popish dog ... nor so much as a Popish cat to pur or mew about the King." The fact that Oates was the solitary witness to the plot, for Tonge's knowledge was second-hand, derived from the Doctor, had at first formed a bar to prosecutions. But the treatment accorded to Titus, so lately starving in the streets of London, was a direct incitement to the cultivation of the imaginative faculties, and Bedloe, who had "long made a shift to live on his wits, or rather on his cheats," with the true instinct of the bird of prey, was the next to grasp the possibilities of the situation. Sent to London by a credulous Bristol magistrate to unravel the momentous mystery, he swore to having seen Godfrey's body at Somerset House and indeed to have been offered £4000 to dispose of it. Here then was the second witness, and things began to look truly alarming for the incriminated noblemen, Lords Powis, Stafford, Petre, Arundel and Belasyse, who were already lodged in the Tower. As soon as the legislators had made themselves acquainted with Oates' lurid tale they appointed a Committee to investigate the plot, and in their turn this body delegated its powers to a smaller sub-committee, consisting of the Duke of Buckingham, Marquis of Winchester, Lord Shaftesbury and Viscount Halifax, while everywhere Catholics were removed from positions of trust.[1]

The heir to the Crown was less easy to deal

[1] Hist. MSS , House of Lords, 28th October 1678.

with than the unfortunate Roman Catholic gentlemen. Nevertheless, Shaftesbury in the Upper and Lord Russell in the Lower House moved an address to exclude him from the councils and presence of the Sovereign; and, urged by his more politic brother, the Duke bowed to the storm and announced the resignation of his seat on the Privy Council. In this onslaught on their future Monarch, Buckingham had not been less forward than Shaftesbury. "When the Heir-apparent announced that he [1] took this step to content those who consider his presence harmful to the State, my Lord Shaftesbury and the Duke of Buckingham insisted that the Duke's promise should be made by proclamation, that the public might know that the motive of his resolution was no mere pandering to the suspicions of a few individuals, but sprang from acquiescence in the wishes of the nation. The House, however, declared itself satisfied with the Duke's statement."

Naturally, when so vehemently assailed, the Court party cast about for means of defence, and Barillon believed they intended to impeach Buckingham. The Duke's readiness to head a rebellion had leaked out, and failing other proofs of high treason, the imprudent expedition to France might well be brought up against him. Nor was the Ambassador reassured when he learnt that Leighton, Buckingham's trusted confidant, had scarcely touched English soil before he was thrown into prison. Sir Ellis was not cast in heroic mould, and Barillon feared he would show no greater stoicism under examination than Coleman,

---

[1] "Affaires Étrangères," No. 131, f. 192, 14th November 1678.

who had promptly confessed to having distributed French[1] bribes amongst Members of Parliament.

Possibly the Duke shared the envoys' gloomy forebodings. Otherwise it is hard to account for his attempt to renew intimate relations with the eldest son of the Church, at the very moment when he himself was leading a Protestant Crusade. The only other hypothesis is that the plot obsession had slightly affected his brain, and that he genuinely believed the cock-and-bull story he now charged one Mr Scott to unfold to Louis. The following letter represents the credentials of his messenger :—

I should be in despair if you doubted my gratitude for all the benefits, particularly the last, I have received at your hands.[2] But as it is my dearest ambition—more to me than anything else in the world—to be of some use to His Majesty, I hope he will pardon me if I venture a small complaint on the hindrances my zeal in his service encounters here.

If without his personal assistance I could give evidence of my devotion I would assuredly sooner die than importune him; but as I am not so fortunate as to compass this, I beseech His Majesty not to take it ill that I once more implore it may be promptly sent me. That Time presses more than he can readily conceive is shown by a new incident of which the bearer (Mr Scott) is charged to inform you. And I beseech him most humbly to give faith to all that he will say from me. As also to believe that no power on earth could have overcome the aversion that I have for this sort of

---

[1] "Affaires Étrangères," 17th November 1678, No. 131, f. 203.
[2] Buckingham to Louis XIV., "Affaires Étrangères," vol. cxxxi. f, 183, November 1678.

impudence, had it not been for the fear of giving (His Majesty) the impression of being an impostor and a man who has undertaken more than he can perform. Do me justice on this score for the love of God, and rest convinced that I am with my whole heart and soul, your very humble, very obedient and much obliged servant,

BUCKINGHAM.
Saturday.

Mr Scott was likewise a bearer of a note to Monsieur de Pomponne, which was to secure his admission to the Royal presence.[1]

There are many things which it is necessary you should be acquainted with, but which would be too wearisome to send you by letter. The bearer will inform you of them in detail, therefore I beg you to conduct the gentleman bearing this note to the person in the world whom I honour and love the most, and to believe me ever your very humble and obedient servant.

Neither of these epistles differs greatly from those which Buckingham had addressed to the same personages in the course of the last ten years. The original of the following letter is, however, so curiously illiterate and ungrammatical that though apparently the determining cause of Mr Scott's expedition, it could hardly have been revised by the Duke, who as a rule expressed himself far more correctly in French than in his native language. It is possible that Scott was not

[1] Monsieur de Buquinham au Marquis de Pomponne. "Affaires Étrangères," vol. cxxxi. f. 187, November 1678.

granted an audience, and was told to put his news in writing, but at anyrate, though ill-spelt and badly expressed, the story he tells is startling.

"A person of quality and one of the best accredited and most intimate friends of the Duke of York and the Treasurer told the Duke of Buckingham that the Duke of York and the Treasurer had resolved to shift the Government of France into other hands. And that several persons had taken the Sacrament on it to assassinate Your Majesty. The Duke of Buckingham considered that it was his duty to communicate the matter to Your most Christian Majesty and he begs Your Majesty to beware of strangers, and in particular of Irishmen."[1]

Duly filed, carefully treasured, these strange documents still repose amongst the official papers of the Grand Monarque at the Quai d'Orsay, but not the slightest marginal note survives to tell what were Louis' impressions as he perused the incredible tale.

In England, meanwhile, every fresh absurdity of Oates and Bedloe only served to foster the madness which possessed the nation. In the first instance Oates had fully exonerated the Duke of York from any participation in the Plot. But after Bedloe's intervention, it was possible to retrieve this tactical error; and, in this fresh development, Shaftesbury, who "hated the Duke much more than he did Popery," was the prime agent. The intimacy of the Heir-presumptive with Mr Pepys made him vulnerable to attacks directed against the latter. The Committee, of which Buckingham and

[1] *Idem*, folio 186.

Shaftesbury were the moving spirits, therefore eagerly embraced an opportunity which soon arose of putting pressure on the worthy Secretary of the Admiralty.

Bedloe swore that a clerk in Mr Pepys' employment, Samuel Atkins by name, had been an accomplice in the murder of Godfrey. If the accused could be induced to clear himself at his master's expense, there was always the chance that Mr Pepys might adopt the same course with regard to the Duke of York. Undoubtedly the plan was a shrewd one, for if his contemporaries did not enjoy the same insight as we do into the workings of the incomparable diarist's mind, yet it could not escape them that Mr Pepys, "an elderly gentleman who had known softness and the pleasures of life," might not prove of adamant. The Committee consequently welcomed Bedloe's tale with enthusiasm. The unlucky scribe was immediately haled before them, and was subjected to a severe cross-examination. He proved however unexpectedly stubborn. The united efforts of their lordships failed to make him admit that after the discovery of the plot he had remarked in conversation with a cousin "that there was a want of friendship" between his patron and Sir Edmundbury Godfrey. Vainly did Buckingham, who—according to North—"had an advanced post in these matters," try the manner theatrical when the judicial proved useless, and, "laying his finger on Atkins' forehead, exclaim, 'I see the great workings of thy brain: come for thy'n own sake, declare what thou know'st!'"[1] Neither to blandishments nor to threats did the honest clerk succumb.

[1] North "Examen," p. 243.

Stoutly and persistently he refused to testify against Pepys, and finally, more fortunate than many another innocent man, escaped with a severe spell of imprisonment.

A vulgar charlatan at a rustic fair could hardly have struck an attitude more sensational than Buckingham in his dealings with Samuel Atkins. But the next glimpse we obtain of the Duke in his magisterial functions tends even less to edification. Yet it must be admitted that during the subsequent reaction, when the following deposition probably appeared, the Tories were not slow to retort their own methods on the much harried Whigs, and that Caryll's statement may have been grossly exaggerated.

The case in question was that of Francis Caryll, a hackney coach driver whose insignificance should have preserved him from being involved in affairs of State. But at that unhappy time, when the lavish rewards offered for unsifted, uncorroborated denunciation were a direct encouragement to private enmities, no one, in however humble a station, could hold himself secure. All Francis Caryll's woes — if we are to credit his tale — sprang from nothing else than the venomous malice of a certain Master Fowler, keeper of the Half Moon Tavern at Cheapside. The murder of Godfrey gave this man the opportunity to gratify his spite, and accordingly he charged Caryll with participation in the mysterious crime. The poor coachman was instantly arrested, and, despite all his protestations, dragged before the Committee at Wallingford House. Here the oath was administered to him by Lord Halifax, but Shaftesbury and Buckingham conducted his examination. The language addressed by Shaftesbury to the recalcitrant witness—for Caryll stoutly maintained he knew nothing of Godfrey's death "except what was common report"—would hardly have been disowned by Scroggs or Jeffreys. Shaftesbury called him "bloody-minded[1] rogue, and threatened him with a cruel death by being rolled down a hill in a barrel of nails." Buckingham, however, transcended even this wild rhetoric. He assured Caryll "he should not be long a-dying, for he would run him through presently, and so striking him and calling him bloody rogue and dog, he then drew his sword and ran it several times at this deponent's breast, but seemed to be prevailed with by the Earl of Shaftesbury not to kill him presently, but to preserve him alive for some more cruel death. Then the Earl of Shaftesbury, saying it was time to go to Parliament, whispered Richardson in the ear, and sent him back, having first menaced this deponent with the certainty of death." . . . Caryll was then removed to Newgate, where, in the interval before another interrogation, he endured positive tortures. On the next occasion, at Wallingford House, he was confronted with a gentleman who accused him of "being the man who took up the body of Sir Edmundbury Godfrey in Somerset House." The Committee told him that if he would confess that certain persons had hired him to take up the body there he should have his pardon and £500, showing him a bag of gold; and if he was afraid of the parties he was to accuse, he should be lodged there safe, and have his wife there

---

[1] Fairfax, "Correspondence," vol. iv. pp. 300-305.

with him and a guard to secure him. To all which, when the deponent declared he knew nothing of the business, nor would accuse anybody of a thing so false, they then with new threats and reproaches thought to affright this deponent, as he verily believes; for the Earl of Shaftesbury bid him consider what a sad hearing it would be when the judge should say, "Take him, away and hang him," to which this deponent replied it would be a sadder to hear God say, "Take him, devil, he has foresworn himself." The poor wretch was then returned to Newgate, loaded with chains, kept without food or drink for four days, denied the ministrations of his wife, and proclaimed a lunatic, "that nobody that passed by might believe his lamentable complaint." After six weeks of such treatment he was again cross-questioned by their lordships. Nor was the ordeal this time less strenuous than before, as not only did they repeat he should be hanged, and once more addressed him as a hardened Papist, a dog, and a bloody villain, but the Duke of Buckingham "*hove* him by the hair, and buffeted and pricked him in the breast with his sword." With admirable constancy, however, Caryll stuck to his former declarations, and had to endure a further imprisonment of several weeks before he was permitted to give bail.

Few of the many accusations levelled against Buckingham display him in a more unpleasing light. Yet, as has been said, even setting aside the suspicious date of Francis Caryll's petition, one may fairly question whether the Duke would have ventured on such brutal intimidation in the presence of the humane Halifax.

By the end of 1678 the Popish Terror was in full swing. On the 3rd December Coleman suffered, " dying much better than he had lived."[1] The Queen was marked down as the next victim, and Oates "recollected" that he had heard Catherine of Braganza give her consent to the murder of her unfaithful spouse. Frequently as Buckingham had plotted the undoing of the poor lady, he was said not to favour this new iniquity, and even to have exclaimed, " This rascal will spoil our business. He can't govern himself; it is not yet time to bring the Queen forward."[2] Though the leaders were not unanimous, it would, however, have gone hard with Catherine had it not been for the King's determined attitude. Fortunately, though Charles believed "that God would not damn a man for a little irregular pleasure," he also looked "on falsehood and cruelty as the greatest of crimes in the sight of God, and considering his faultiness to her in other things, thought it a horrid thing to abandon a weak woman[3] who was only guilty of some disagreeable humours."

The King could still shield his wife, but he was not permitted to extend his ægis to the Lord Treasurer. Danby had hoped to protect himself by joining in the persecution of the Roman Catholics, but he counted without Shaftesbury, who said, "Let the Treasurer cry as loud as he pleases against Popery,[4] and think to put himself at the head of the plot, I will cry a note lowder' and soone take his

[1] Burnet, vol. ii., p. 178.
[2] Hist. MSS., House of Lords, 1678-88, p. 97, quot. from French Pamphlet.
[3] Burnet, vol. ii. p. 180.
[4] James II. Mems., vol. i. p. 546.

place." Nor was it Shaftesbury alone who had sworn to compass Danby's downfall. The fatal blow was ultimately struck against him by Montague, the English Ambassador in Paris. A short time before Montague had vehemently protested "how real he was in all my Lord Treasurer's concerns," but, like all alliances founded on interested motives, the friendship of Danby and Montague was not remarkable for its stability; while the cause of their estrangement aptly illustrates the singular code of honour then prevalent.

During the days of exile in Paris it appears that Charles II. had come across an astrologer who not only foretold the Restoration, but also declared that the King would make his entry[1] into London on May the 29th, 1660. Not unnaturally Charles conceived a high opinion of his talents, and ordered Montague to consult the seer again on his behalf. The Ambassador obeyed, but could not resist the temptation to work the oracle for his own ends. The sage did not prove incorruptible, and the answers Charles eventually received to his questions were those which Montague had prompted. Had it not been for the tender relations then subsisting between the Ambassador and the Duchess of Cleveland it is possible that the trick would have succeeded, but Montague, who was as much besotted by Barbara as ever his royal master had been, could not refrain from imparting the whole story to her. Shortly after came the inevitable rupture and quarrel. The Duchess, who burnt for Montague with much the same passion she had once experienced for Jacob Hall, the rope-

[1] Burnet, vol. ii. pp. 151-52.

walker, now in a paroxysm of jealous fury poured the tale of treachery into Charles' ear. The King was indignant, and Montague was either recalled or returned in disgrace, to England, vowing vengeance against his false friend, Lord Danby, who had not prevented his downfall. Thanks to a couple of documents which the Ambassador had retained this proved no difficult task. All through the autumn Montague was in close communication with Barillon and the Opposition, and as soon as his election to the House of Commons had insured him against the reprisals of the Court he produced these papers. They were indeed of a startling nature, for one was no other than the letter written, at Charles' express dictation, by Danby to Montague on the 25th of March 1678.

In this celebrated despatch Danby instructed the envoy, should he succeed in negotiating a peace, to solicit a pension of £300,000 per annum for three years from Louis XIV., as "it would not[1] be convenient for the King of England to meet a Parliament in all that time."

The excitement produced by these revelations was intense, and promised to rival the ferment created by the Popish Plot. Vainly did Danby strive to appease the infuriated Commons by showing proof in Montague's own hand that the French politicians regarded him as their bitterest foe. They were not to be pacified. The charge of constructive treason which had brought Strafford to the scaffold was an obvious precedent, and six articles of impeachment were instantly presented against the Treasurer. Buckingham, who had

[1] Burnet, vol. ii. p. 183.

transferred to Danby the hatred with which he had once honoured Clarendon, was naturally deeply engaged in the Minister's prosecution, and much astonishment was felt when he did not lead the attack in the Upper House. It soon, however, became known that Danby had threatened him, should he attempt to re-enact the scenes of 1667, with a counter charge of a personal nature. The notorious profligacy of Buckingham's past life now brought its punishment, for even to gratify his vengeance he did not venture to face a trial rich in opportunities of perjury, and consequently abstained from taking a conspicuous part in the debates, while his solitary attempt to make another his mouthpiece could hardly be called successful.

The person he selected with this view was Robert Dormer, Earl of Carnarvon, son of the handsome cavalier, whom Clarendon considered the best cavalry officer in Charles I.'s army, and who found a soldier's death with Falkland at Newbury. The second earl, however, a complete contrast to his brilliant father, was the recognised laughing-stock, of the dissipated society which he frequented. He had never yet spoken in the House of Lords, but Buckingham plied him so vigorously with wine and flattery, that he was at last incited to "display his abilities," and with some pomp delivered himself of the following oration :—

"My lords, I understand but little of Latin, but a good deal of English and not a little of English history; from which I have learnt the mischiefs of such kinds of prosecutions as these, and the very ill fate of the prosecutors. I could bring many instances about very ancient; but, my lords,

I will go no further back than the latter end of Queen Elizabeth's reign, at which time the Earl of Essex was run down by Sir Walter Raleigh, and your lordships know what became of Sir Walter Raleigh. My Lord Bacon he ran down Sir Walter Raleigh, and your lordships know what became of Lord Bacon. The Duke of Buckingham he ran down my Lord Bacon, and your lordships know what became of the Duke of Buckingham. Sir Thomas Wentworth, afterwards Earl of Strafford, ran down the Duke of Buckingham, and your lordships know what became of him. Sir Harry Vane he ran down the Earl of Strafford, and your lordships know what became of him. Chancellor Hyde ran down Sir Harry Vane, and your lordships know what became of the Chancellor. Sir Thomas Osborn, now Earl of Danby, ran down Chancellor Hyde, but what will become of the Earl of Danby your lordships[1] best can tell. But let me see that man that dare run the Earl of Danby down and we shall soon see what will become of him." This being pronounced with a remarkable tone and humour, the Duke of Buckingham, both surprised and disappointed, after his way, cried out, "The man is inspir'd! And claret has done the business!"

The Peers were so far attentive to Lord Carnarvon's eloquence that they refused to commit Lord Danby to the Tower. Charles, however, recognised that the Commons would give no quarter, and a month later dissolved Parliament.

Buckingham seems to have taken no small part in deciding the choice of members for the

[1] Echard's "Hist. of England," vol. iii. p. 497.

new Parliament. In 1672 he had been made Lord High Steward of Oxford, and had ever since remained on excellent terms with that city. It was no uncommon thing for him to entertain members of the corporation "at his new house of Clifden in Buckinghamshire," and the gold cup made of sovereigns which he presented to that body, is still preserved amongst the municipal treasures at Oxford.

On their side the burgesses were eager to assure him of the high value they set upon "his noble favours" and of their anxiety to return the member whom, in the following letter, he did them the honour to recommend :—

LONDON, 25*th January* 1678.

GENTLEMEN,—The extraordinary markes I have lately received of your kindness make mee presume soe farre as to desire this new one from you, that you will give Mr Broome Whorwood and mee leave to discourse with you before you conclude upon your choyce of members for this next Parliament. Hee has deserved soe well that I cannot beleeve you will thinke of putting anybody into his place, and I confesse I have also the vanity to thinke that my earnest concerne for the good of the whole nation, and my perticular respect to your Corporation, will put mee out of the hasard of your denying this favour to your most affectionat and humble servant, BUCKINGHAM.

Within a few dayes I shall bee at Woodstock, where I shall desire to speake with some of your Corporation.[1]

[1] City Archives of Oxford. Addressed :—To the Mayor and Alderman of the Citty of Oxford.

In company with a certain Alderman William Wright, Mr Broome Whorwood was accordingly chosen to represent Oxford at Westminster. He had, however, a stiffer fight than was anticipated, as one Mr George Pudsey, thanks to his "extraordinary expense upon ye comon sorte of people had gott a greate multitude of ye comons" on his side. The city fathers grudged no trouble to carry out their patron's orders; but their enthusiasm was slightly damped when at the last moment that great man saw fit to recall his recommendation of Mr Whorwood and to suggest they should select one of their own order instead. Under such a strain even the obedience of the docile citizens broke down; and in language of studied humility they protested their inability to substitute another candidate for the Duke's first nominee, so that Mr Whorwood was duly elected.

In other places besides Oxford the polling was adverse to the Royal policy, and, while the electoral campaign still rioted through county and borough, the King took measures to safeguard his brother and Minister.

In the hopes of allaying popular irritation, Charles ordered the Duke of York to withdraw with his family to Brussels. But at the same time, and by the latter's request, he made a solemn declaration before the Privy Council that "he had never entered into any contract of marriage save with his wife Queen Catherine now living." Such a statement was urgently needed, as it was reported that the Duke of Monmouth would produce evidence of the King's marriage with Lucy Walters.

Left to his own devices—as the sequel proved—Monmouth was not a very formidable opponent, but, at this stage, his shortcomings and deficiencies were amply compensated by the counsel of the wise Achitophel, whose subtle guidance was discernible in every move of the pretender's. Buckingham, on the other hand, though he hated the Duke of York to the full as much as did Shaftesbury, was never favourable to Monmouth's claims. Such an attitude in so confirmed an opportunist as Buckingham would be inexplicable but for the reason assigned by Barillon, who in this matter appears to have possessed the Duke's confidence.

"He glories," says the Ambassador, "in having . . . openly set his face against the pretensions of the Duke of Monmouth He has always been the Duke of York's enemy. But notwithstanding, he declares he will never consent to his exclusion in favour of bastards who have no rights, and some times, after he has supped, Buckingham lets drop that through his mother, who descended from Edward IV., he inherits the claims of the House of Plantagenet." Barillon remarks that the "notion closely resembles a chimera."[1] But, with the true Gallic distrust of all things English, he adds, "however, in this country chimera are not so absurd as elsewhere."

When the new Parliament assembled it soon appeared that their chief concern was the prosecution of Danby. Charles, however, fearful of the disclosures his ex-Minister might in self-defence be driven to make, showed unexpected resolution in defending him. The Treasurer, he told them, had

[1] "Affaires Étrangères," No. 135, f. 40, 13th July 1679.

done nothing but by his order, and therefore he had pardoned him, and if there was any defect in the pardon, would pass it over and over again until it should be legal. This announcement filled the measure of the Commons' wrath. Nothing but an attainder would satisfy them, and, after a long struggle, the Upper House committed Danby to the Tower.

Charles was now deprived of the assistance of a responsible Minister. The situation was anomalous, and by Sir William Temple's advice he embarked on a constitutional experiment. He dissolved the existing and created a fresh Privy Council, by whose advice he announced he would henceforward be guided. This new body was to be composed in equal halves of Crown officers and members of the Opposition, chief amongst whom were Shaftesbury and Halifax, though Buckingham was markedly excluded from a part in their deliberations.

The Duke appears to have felt the slight keenly, and was not sparing in criticism of his ally, Lord Shaftesbury. The prosecution threatened by Danby remained meanwhile suspended over him, so that he took little or no part in the stormy debates of the Exclusion Bill. He affixed his name indeed to the minority protest against peers spiritual sitting and voting in capital cases in the House of Lords, but this seems to have been his only notable action.

When, at the end of May [1] Charles prorogued Parliament, the Duke's fears were quickened, and he betook himself to one of his hiding-places till

[1] "Affaires Étrangères," 13th July 1679, No. 135, f. 40.

July, when he reappeared and succeeded in convincing the monarch of his innocence.

During Buckingham's voluntary exile the Jesuit hunt had not slackened. Indeed some of the trials which most deeply sully the annals of English justice took place in that summer of 1679. Shaftesbury had given vent to ungovernable fury at the prorogation: "He would have the heads of those who were its advisers," he cried. But these advisers, Essex, Halifax and Temple, now counselled a dissolution, and on the 10th of July Charles gave effect to their advice, "amidst the dissatisfaction of the whole Board."

Apparently the Duke bestirred himself greatly during this election. We find him consulting with Mr Hampden in Buckinghamshire, and generally strengthening the hands of the Opposition. Nor was he unsuccessful, since the new members were reported to be as devoted to a thorough-going Exclusion Bill as their predecessors. In August, however, Charles was taken ill with intermittent fever. Till the doctors could be induced to administer Jesuit's powder, as quinine was then called, his condition excited great alarm, and Buckingham was not the only person who believed that the King was poisoned,[1] and would not recover.

Charles himself thought it imperative to recall the Duke of York, but, by the time that James reached Windsor, the danger was over. The sudden crisis enabled the Prince, however, to stipulate that if he agreed to leave England, and to reside for a time in Scotland, Monmouth, on his part, should be

[1] "Affaires Étrangères," vol. xiii. f. 177, 14th September 1679.

made to resign his military command and to retire from Court. Buckingham did not conceal his satisfaction at Monmouth's disgrace. "Neither of the two Dukes' factions were destined to succeed," he said, "but the party of the people of which he himself would be the leader." As a rule Charles would have been the first to laugh at this piece of braggadocio. But some echo of George Villiers' electioneering doings had reached his ears, and tended to increase his alienation from his former favourite. "The Duke of Buckingham,"[1] writes a contemporary, "coming last Thursday to see ye King, he refused to see him and said 'twas because he had stood up for som men for Buckinghamshire who would cutt his throat. My Lord Rochester being there, askt him why he thought so, to which he made no answer by, but pouted and nodded his head att him." The King did not long confine himself to such platonic manifestations of displeasure as pouting and nodding. A month later it was currently reported that a warrant was actually issued against the Duke of Buckingham. The prosecution was grounded on an incident which had occurred during the last Circuit.[2] It appears that after the Lord Chief Justice had charged the grand jury diligently and strictly to execute the laws against the Papists, Buckingham, who was in court, stood up and said "that it was well indeed that were done, but that my Lord Chief Justice when he gave that charge did not mean that it should be observed, that he was a favourer of the Papists, and

---

[1] MSS. Carte 228, f. 121, G. Wharton to T. Wharton, 25th August 1679.
[2] Hist. Le Fleming, MSS., Rep. xii. p. 162, 23rd September 1679.

he, Buckingham, knew that he had private orders to assist and favour the Papists all he could." Not unnaturally the Lord Chief-Justice was indignant at being thus openly flouted. Grounding himself on the statute which made it treasonable to say that the King was a Papist,[1] he appealed to the Sovereign to allow the machinery of the law to be set in motion against the insolent nobleman. This he received permission to do, and, more remarkable still, obtained the signature of Sunderland to the document. Such a step was indeed significant, for that astute Minister would never have attacked Buckingham had he not believed he could do so with impunity.

Apparently, however, Sunderland gathered courage from the fact that in the recent contest for the office of sheriff Buckingham's nominee and fanatical adherent, a certain Jinks, had been ignominiously defeated by the Court candidate.[2] As the city was regarded almost as the Duke's close borough, the event might be held to show that even there his influence was waning and that a writ might safely be launched against him.

Buckingham himself took fright, and sought refuge in one of his numerous retreats; but meanwhile Sunderland must have reconsidered his decision, for when the Duke finally emerged from hiding he was not molested.

Of all the statesmen of that age of plot and stratagem, Sunderland was probably the least governed by impulse or caprice. It would therefore be interesting to learn the motive of his sud-

---

[1] "Affaires Étrangères," vol. cxxxvi., f. 20, 2nd October 1679.
[2] *Idem.*

den and unaccountable forbearance. Unluckily on this occasion, Barillon, who often supplies the missing link, is silent, and we are reduced to speculation based on the sifting of contemporary transactions.

The mystery is not lessened by the fact that circumstances seemed at that moment to deliver Buckingham into Sunderland's hands. It is clear that the Minister was not hampered by any lingering tenderness on Charles' part for his old friend. Nor can Sunderland have been restrained by fear of Shaftesbury, as the King now felt himself strong enough to dismiss Ashley—"that snake he had nourished in his bosom"—from the post of Lord President of the Council. Moreover, in October, Parliament was prorogued for a year, so that Buckingham could count neither on influential allies in the ministry nor on a hearing at Westminster. Altogether the hour appeared eminently propitious for the destruction of a seditious peer, and that Sunderland held his hand can only be explained by the appearance on the scene of Dangerfield. Sunderland may well have argued that by imprisoning the Duke for a patriotic speech he ran the risk of converting him into a popular martyr, while, if Dangerfield's charges could be proved, Buckingham's restless spirit might find its quietus on Tower Hill.

A protean scoundrel, Dangerfield certainly devised his plot with greater attention to probabilities than his forerunner, Dr Oates. Perhaps he owed something to his accomplice, Mrs Cellier, a Popish midwife of more wit than virtue. This woman had found him starving in prison, had instantly judged the voluble and insinuating rogue to be the fit instrument of a Tory reaction, had rescued him from his sorry straits, and presented him to her patroness, the Countess of Powis. "A zealous and managing person," of masculine intelligence, the Countess, whose husband was still imprisoned in the Tower, was eager to retort their own methods on the persecutors, and exerted herself to procure an interview for the plausible Dangerfield with the Heir-presumptive.[1]

Mankind is ever ready to credit that which it desires, and James heard with positive delight that Dangerfield might enable him to convict his bitter Whig and Presbyterian enemies of rebellion. Dangerfield showed the Prince commissions issued by Monmouth, Buckingham and Lord Grey in an army they proposed to raise to compass James' banishment and the King's dethronement. Even Charles' scepticism was not proof against the agreeable intelligence. He did violence to his habitual carefulness, and actually bestowed forty guineas on the adventurer. Mr Secretary Coventry was, however, more difficult to convince. The only proofs Dangerfield could adduce of his intimacy with the Opposition were two letters, addressed indeed to Lord Shaftesbury, but turning on wholly indifferent matters. Much as the two Princes would have rejoiced to trace the conspiracy to their opponents, they knew an English jury would never convict men so popular on such flimsy evidence. Dangerfield, however, was equal to the occasion. To a man, who had successfully counterfeited coin of the realm, it was but child's play to forge a packet of letters referring to the imaginary

[1] Burnet, vol. ii. p. 244.

league. On the pretence of hiring a chamber he obtained admittance to the house of a certain Colonel Roderick Mansell, a trusted retainer of Buckingham's, and contrived to pin the compromising papers, addressed to Mansell, behind the bedhead. He then betook[1] himself to the Custom House and informed the officials that the Colonel was a receiver of smuggled goods, and that they would find £2000 worth of lace concealed in his rooms. Such a haul was not to be despised, and guided by him, the officers instantly proceeded to Mansell's lodgings in Axe-Yard, Westminster.

But although they conscientiously ransacked every hole and corner in the old soldier's apartments their exertions were not rewarded by any discovery, and they were about to give up the search when Dangerfield insisted on their hunting behind the bed curtains, where he himself brought his own documents to light, crying out, "Here is treason!" Next, he sought to have the papers carried to the Secretary of State, but the excisemen, jealous for their department, would not hear of this, and, much to his disappointment, insisted on laying the writings before their masters, the Commissioners of Custom. This delay gave Mansell, who was a man of resolution, time to act. He was determined not to allow his own or his master's throat to be slit without protest; and strong in his own innocence and the knowledge he had acquired of Dangerfield's character, he did not fear to evoke the case before the Privy Council.

His courage and promptitude were rewarded.

---

[1] Oldmixon's "Hist. of Eng. during the Reigns of the Royal House of Stuart," p. 642.

When the matter was sifted at the Council Board the truth was revealed, and two days later, on searching Mrs Cellier's dwelling, the original draft of the design, "a paper book ty'd with ribbons," was found concealed at the bottom of the meal-tub, a circumstance to which the plot owes its appellation in history. Mrs Cellier did penance in the pillory. Dangerfield turned King's evidence. Yet, even to hang a Catholic lord, he was not considered a credible witness.

Thus were the fowlers fallen into the pit they had made and digged for others, and the only result of the episode was an immense recrudescence of the persecuted Duke's popularity. Indeed by December he had so far recovered his normal assurance as to venture on a new pilgrimage to Paris. According to Charles, who told it as a good joke to the Ambassador, he had no less an object than the conclusion of an alliance between Louis XIV. and the British nation. "As the Prince did not appear to treat the matter very seriously, I answered," says Barillon, "that if the Duke had been in Paris the fair sex had more to do with his voyage than politics. Upon which His British Majesty added that a man who had passed through Calais three days ago assured him that Monsieur de Buckingham was staying in a house with Leyton and some ladies."[1] Whereupon the envoy was forced to conclude that though Buckingham "had all the talents fitted to seduce the people, yet his plans were now assuming so wild a character as to render him rather an object of ridicule than of alarm to the Government."

[1] "Affaires Étrangères," 14th December, No. 136, f. 160.

Charles could well afford to laugh at Buckingham's pompous schemes for reconciling the irreconcilable Louis, the incarnation of Despotism, with the inchoate British Democracy. Nevertheless, George Villiers did not go scot-free, for soon after his return from Paris, Charles struck the volatile Duke's name off the list of justices in every county of England.

CHAPTER XV

THE END

THE exposure of the Meal-tub Plot revived popular animosity against the luckless Papists; and the year 1680 witnessed not only a fresh banishment of the Duke of York, but a series of tragedies culminating in the judicial murder of Lord Stafford.

Through its representatives, the nation was set upon the passing of the Exclusion Bill, and it puzzled others besides Buckingham that Charles so steadfastly continued to oppose the measure.

The Duke had never assisted at one of the Royal drinking bouts, he said, without being struck anew by the singular bitterness,[1] akin to hatred, which characterised all the King's references to his brother. "In vino veritas." It was therefore inexplicable that when England was within an ace of exchanging the Monarchy for a Republic, Charles should imperil the crown itself for the sake of James of York.[2]

The chief supporters of the Exclusion Bill were Lord Russell in the Lower, and Lords Shaftesbury and Essex in the Upper House. The discrepancies between Ashley's and Buckingham's policy, due to the Duke's dislike of Monmouth, grew more marked as the popularity of the handsome

---
[1] "Affaires Étrangères," 31st October 1680, No. 140, f. 119.
[2] "Affaires Étrangères," No. 139, f. 407, 30th September 1680.

Pretender waxed daily greater. When the Bill reached the Lords, Buckingham had a convenient illness, and took no part in the debates, and, indeed, was even reported to meditate a reconciliation with the Duke of York. This was probably an exaggeration, for Buckingham must have known only too well that James "was not born under a pardoning planet."[1] The rumour doubtless originated in the abuse which at this juncture Buckingham unsparingly lavished on Shaftesbury and his tactics. In the bitterness of his heart the Duke told the French Ambassador "that Ashley had not the prudence to direct so mighty an affair, and that he knew that lord was certain to make mistakes when he assumed the leadership of the Opposition."[2]

But if the Duke abstained from interference at Westminster, in other spheres he displayed a morbid activity. According to Barillon he was now engrossed in promoting with Charles II. the fortunes of Miss Lawson, the niece of Colonel Howard, his brother-in-law.

Herein, dreadful to relate, he found a stout ally in his sister. The Duchess of Richmond so hated Louise de Kéroualle that she would have gladly offered up her kinswoman to bring about the Frenchwoman's disgrace. Even that notorious rake, Rochester, felt his gorge rise at the hideous scheme, and in a poem—"The Royal Angler" — paints the maid's sad fate, and bids her pause.

Judging from the poor girl's portrait in the Beauty Room at Hampton Court, the Duchess of

---

[1] Burnet.   [2] "Affaires Étrangères," No. 111, 1680.

Vandyck, Pinx. Walker & Cockerell, Ph. Sc.

The Duchess of Richmond.

Portsmouth had good cause to fear Miss Lawson's rivalry. In the end, however, either Rochester's advice or the damsel's virtuous instincts prevailed. She chose the better part, and to the wages of sin preferred the austerities of the cloister.

During the elaboration of these unsavoury intrigues, and in spite of Shaftesbury's efforts, the Exclusion Bill was thrown out by the Peers.

Halifax, who more than anyone had combated the measure, then came forward with a compromise — a project for limiting James' powers on his accession to the throne. A proposal so full of common sense was, however, unpalatable to both sides, and was instantly rejected.

Next, Buckingham, who had now recovered, suggested a new alternative—the appointment of a committee of both Houses to concert the series of precautions best adapted for the welfare of the Protestant religion and the preservation of the national liberties. The matter was eagerly canvassed and debated. But as limitations of the regal power were distasteful alike to the secret partisans of Monmouth and of the Princess of Orange, Buckingham's scheme met with no better fate than that of Halifax's.

Although he had apparently drifted far from his nominal allies Buckingham yet maintained a show of friendship with the Opposition. The riverside quarters of London had always been his favourite haunts, and a few days before Christmas,[1] in the company of Monmouth and other notable persons, he went to dine at a seamen's tavern at Wapping. Toasts were freely drunk to the con-

[1] "Affaires Étrangères," 26th December, 1680, No. 140 f. 438.

fusion of Popery and the triumph of the Protestant religion. Buckingham was the presiding genius of the orgy, the last to leave the convivial board. Nor when the company broke up did the excitement subside, and it was amidst continuous cheering that the populace escorted Monmouth home to his palace at Soho. The King smiled sardonically when he heard the tale. And Buckingham justified his own share in the proceedings by remarking that he merely did it for popularity's sake.

It is but fair, in recording such levity, also to say that before the close of the Session Buckingham joined Shaftesbury in earnestly advocating one eminently desirable reform. This was a proposal that a peer when put on his trial should have the right to challenge any one of his judges. So evident an act of justice had, however, scant chance of becoming law in the assembly which sent the innocent Lord Stafford to the scaffold, and the project was at once rejected by their lordships.

With Lord Stafford's execution the high-water line of persecution was reached, and the unhappy old man's death practically, though not entirely, closed the long list of proscriptions.

Nevertheless, the reaction did not immediately set in, and when Charles, alarmed by the seditious spirit of the capital, summoned Parliament to meet at Oxford, in March, Shaftesbury made an almost Royal entry into the "loyal city." The great tribune's day of power was, however, well-nigh ended. Thanks to the new financial arrangements, which Charles had now secretly concluded with Louis XIV., the King was once more independent of the Commons; and was consequently enabled to take up a surprisingly firm attitude, both with regard to the Exclusion Bill and to the latest sensation of the hour—the FitzHarris and Everard conspiracy.

These two worthies, the former of whom commanded no inconsiderable amount of backstairs influence at Court, had concocted a treasonable pamphlet accusing the King of aiding and abetting the Duke of York in his sinister designs on the liberties of England. Each probably intended to earn the informer's reward by denouncing the other's authorship. But Everard, with greater foresight than his associate, had witnesses concealed in his room to testify to FitzHarris' disloyal conversation, and the latter was arrested and sent to Newgate.

A bold reliance on popular credulity was the best means that offered itself to FitzHarris to escape from so dangerous a predicament. And accordingly he volunteered to give evidence on a new Popish Plot, directed against the King's sacred person and kingdom. Hackneyed as was this device, the scoundrel had evidently not miscalculated the effect it would produce, since both the public and the Opposition leaders eagerly swallowed the bait.

On the other hand Charles was equally determined not to permit a revival of the Romish Terror. He transferred FitzHarris from Newgate to the Tower, and absolutely refused to defer the man's examination and trial to Parliament. The House of Commons was transported with indignation. On successive days, rejecting the compromise offered by the King, they once more re-enacted the principle of the Exclusion Bill and formally demanded the surrender of FitzHarris to their jurisdiction. The second of these stormy scenes took place on Saturday, March 27. On the following Monday, at an early hour, the King surprised them by his sudden appearance in crown and robes, and then and there dissolved Parliament.

When the King previously had recourse to the same expedient it proved singularly ineffectual, but now, though the Londoners and their leaders showed no sign of satiety, it seemed evident that the nation had drunk its fill of horrors.

The sober portion of the community were beginning to fear that the excesses of the exclusionists would lead to a fresh revolution, and they felt that even a Romish sovereign was less to be dreaded than civil war. The Royal intervention gave the needed stimulus, and when Charles caused a vindication of his policy to be read from the pulpits he was overwhelmed with loyal addresses.

In fact the tide was on the turn, and before long London was left the last citadel of freedom, rising solitary above the invading flood of Tory reaction.

From the moment of the Dissolution, Shaftesbury knew himself to be a marked man. Nor were the subsequent executions of FitzHarris and College, the renowned "Protestant joiner," calculated to reassure him. In July Ashley was committed to the Tower. The Government, it is true, could produce no more credible witnesses against him than the infamous turncoats Dugdale and Turberville, whom he himself had employed against Lord Stafford. Yet such were his apprehensions that he was ready to purchase pardon by voluntary self-banishment to Carolina.

In the circumstances Buckingham must have congratulated himself on having abstained from taking an active share in the Exclusion Bill and from sharing in the protest against FitzHarris' trial. Nevertheless his position was not exempt from anxiety.

Haynes, the chief evidence against Shaftesbury, a man who had once enjoyed a large share of the latter's confidence, deposed to the Earl having said "that the Duke of Buckingham had as much right to the crown as any Stuart in England."[1] In those days the developments of a charge of high treason were as far reaching as they were deadly. And it was to be feared that should the Earl's remark be traced home to such a rhodomontade of Buckingham's as had once scandalised the French Ambassador, it might go hard with the descendant of the Plantagenets.

Prudence as well as loyalty therefore enjoined that Buckingham should watch the proceedings when Shaftesbury's case was brought before the grand jury. Nor on this memorable occasion was he the sole representative of "his Cabal"—as Barillon calls the Whig lords.[2] Salisbury and Essex, Russell and Grey were also there with a large muster of retainers. Sympathy with the accused ran so high that the mob nearly killed the witnesses for the prosecution. On their side, the Government lawyers neglected no mean trick or contemptible quibble to win their suit. But lie and threaten as

[1] Kennet's "Hist. of Eng.," p. 400.   [2] "Affaires Étrangères."

they would they could not move the jury. The good men and true retired for a short space, only to return with an acquittal, a verdict of "ignoramus" against the bill.

A scene of excitement then took place such as our grave English courts of law have seldom seen. No rebukes could still the frantic shouts of joy which were taken up outside, and all through the night, while the city blazed with bonfires, the streets rang with shouts of "A Shaftesbury! a Buckingham!"

In London, surrounded by his "brisk boys," Shaftesbury for a time remained the popular hero. But in the country the publication of his papers by the Government made him an object of general execration, and deep as the cleavage had grown between himself and Buckingham as regards Monmouth, their influence sprang too much from the same causes not to suffer the same decline.

In the spring of 1682 James of York returned to England, and by dint of violence and intrigue the Court finally secured the return of sheriffs devoted to their interests. This was the death-knell of the Opposition. Already the staunch Whig jurymen were their only bulwark against destruction, and it was evident to the meanest intelligence that Tory sheriffs would now strike a Tory panel.

Shaftesbury we know would have risked an appeal to arms, but Buckingham seems to have withdrawn from these dangerous plots. When the conspiracy miscarried and Ashley fled to Holland, George Villiers was therefore able to remain in England. Had Shaftesbury lived, his old comrade-in-arms might have been drawn again into the vortex of politics. But a few weeks later, after agonising suffering, the mighty schemer breathed his last in the house of a friend at Amsterdam.

Separated as they had been by recent controversies, the passing of Shaftesbury nevertheless marked an epoch in the restless activities of the Duke. Their differences probably sprang rather from envy on Buckingham's part of Ashley's commanding genius than disapproval of his aims and methods. With no other statesman had the Duke been so long and intimately associated, and when death called the one, oblivion claimed the other.

To be forgotten was, indeed, the ambition of the Opposition leaders at this juncture. "As soon as Lord Shaftesbury was gone,"[1] Bishop Burnet tells us, "the lords and all the chief men of the party saw their danger from forward sheriffs, willing judges and bold witnesses; so they resolved to go home and be silent; to speak or to meddle as little as might be in public business; and to let the present ill-temper the nation was fallen into wear out."

No actual prudence and silence could, however, entirely blot out the recollection of Buckingham's glaring indiscretions in the past, and it is almost unaccountable that during this era of retribution none of his political sins came home to roost. It cannot have been for lack of enemies or want of proof. But probably Brian Fairfax is right; and threadbare as the friendship between George Villiers and Charles Stuart had worn, the memories of many an hour of youth spent in study or revelry together still pleaded the cause of his frolic Grace with the easy-going master.

[1] Burnet, vol. ii. p. 351.

Buckingham did not presume on the Royal indulgence. No longer did Alderman George hatch plots with friend Jinks in sailors' taverns. No longer did he creep like Nicodemus in the gloaming to hold counsel with the French Ambassador. He, too, "went home and was silent." When he came to Court at all, it was because, as he told Barillon, Lord Shaftesbury and the Duke of Monmouth had brought matters to such a pass that he dared not dispense with paying his respects to the King and the Duke of York.[1] Absence would be interpreted as adhesion to the party of the conspirators.

But though he had renounced all participation in matters political, in 1685 he broke silence in a novel and unexpected manner. He published a little pamphlet entitled, "A short Discourse upon the Reasonableness of Men's having a Religion or Worship of God."[2]

The saintly Baxter once said that if "George Villiers was of no religion, but notoriously and professedly lustful, yet he was of greater wits and parts and sounder principles as to the interest of humanity and common good than most lords in the Court."[3]

Buckingham had undoubtedly given serious offence to all decent-minded people by his loose talk and ribald sermons, and it was the more inexcusable, since he frequented meeting-houses, and prayed as lustily as any Anabaptist, or Leveller. His contemporaries had no hesitation in ascribing

---

[1] "Affaires Étrangères," 9th August 1683, No. 150, f. 212.
[2] Duke of Buckingham's Works, "Phœnix," XXVIII., vol. ii. p. 519.
[3] Baxter, p. 21.

these spiritual vagaries to hypocrisy pure and simple. And it is impossible to deny that these devotional exercises strengthened his position with the Nonconformists. That

> "He cast himself into the saint-like mould,
> Groaned, sighed and prayed while godliness was gain,
> The loudest bagpipe of the squeaking train,"[1]

was a charge far more applicable to him than to Shaftesbury, the friend of Locke. Yet our more psychological generation may be excused if it also sees in his conduct an unedifying instance of the unbridled emotional temperament, and ventures to suggest that a man so cursed with a dual nature is not always consciously insincere. Nothing is more communicable than religious fervour. And Buckingham was the last person to resist the infection of such an atmosphere.

Liberty of conscience, the object of the Duke's pamphlet, has for many a long year seemed an unanswerable proposition to most creeds and most races in the civilised world. Then, it was far otherwise, and in advocating universal tolerance Buckingham deserves to rank with the noble army of martyrs, who, at great personal loss and hazard, fought the battle of Progress.

The methods by which the Duke demonstrates the "existence of God as the source of all human excellence" do not appear strikingly original to the modern reader. But having to his own satisfaction established this starting-point, he proceeds to ask " which is the virtue which men most value in their

[1] Dryden, "The Medal."

fellow men?" and he answers "justice." "For justice is that good quality or virtue which causes all other good qualities and virtues to be esteemed; nay, it is that virtue without which all other virtues become as vices; that is, they all become abhorred, because the more wit, judgment and valour he has the more certainly he will become a wicked man." Those, therefore, who hold the doctrine of Predestination, represent the Deity as Injustice, since He is bestowing eternal punishment for that which He Himself has compelled. Nor can God reprove a man for conceiving religion as it represents itself to his own mind. Hence "nothing more unmanly, more barbarous and more ridiculous than to go about to convince a man's judgment by anything but reason." Even at school "if boys are loggerheads enough to go to cuffs instead of arguing, they are whipt. Moreover religious persecution has ever been fatal to the Commonwealth who practise it. Let those who persecute be called 'anti-Christians,' since it is most contrary to the doctrine of Jesus Christ, and finally let men lead such lives as may save their souls . . . rather than cutting each other's throats about these things which they all agree are not absolutely necessary to salvation."

Such dangerous heresy was not allowed to go long unchallenged. A champion was soon raised up to the Church from the horde of anonymous scribblers, who swarmed and starved in London. In a leaflet, which bore the name of "A Short Answer to His Grace the Duke of Buckingham's Paper concerning Religious Toleration and Liberty of Conscience," the Duke's arguments were boldly traversed. Naturally, the "Short Answer"[1] provoked a retort from Buckingham, who, charmed to break a lance with "his nameless, angry, harmless, humble servant," in a few witty and spirited pages finally silenced that gentleman.

When James II. came to the throne, Buckingham withdrew still further from the world. He had ceased to be a force in politics, and was not troubled by those in power. Indeed James might claim some merit not only for leaving his ancient enemy unmolested, but for returning good for evil by attempting to snatch the Duke's battered soul from damnation. The pious mission of Father Fitzgerald, whom the King and Queen despatched to Buckingham on this errand, is the subject of one of the Duke's liveliest publications. Never surely was theological conference conducted—on one side at least—in so sprightly a fashion. But it is possible that the worthy father found the Duke's Rabelaisian apologue less humorous than does the dainty Horace Walpole. It is included amongst Buckingham's collected works, but would probably obtain little favour with a generation which, as a rule finds many even of the classics of that age too coarse for enjoyment.

With a Plantagenet pedigree the Duke had also inherited from his mother a fine estate in the North Riding of Yorkshire, and here, in 1686, he went to live. Like his splendid palace of Burley-on-the-Hill, now sold to Lord Nottingham, Castle Helmsley had suffered grievously in the civil wars. The huge breach in its walls spoke eloquently of its obstinate resistance to Fairfax, and only a

[1] "Phœnix" XXIX.

portion of the old keep remained intact after the siege. A few rooms, however, which even now bear on chimney-piece and frieze the scutcheons of Manners and Villiers, were habitable, and here the Duke installed himself. Occasionally also he wandered to Fairfax House at York, which, being part of his wife's fortune, he had not been able to alienate, and sometimes he stayed for sporting purposes in a tenant's house at Kirkby Moorside.

Had it not been for the chase it is indeed difficult to see what the Duke would have devised to cheat the melancholy of solitude. But with the wonderful elasticity of his versatile character he flung himself into this pursuit, as if the hunting field had always bounded his ambition. He kept the Bilsdale hounds, and a remembrance of his riding feats is yet retained in the songs and traditions of the countryside. To this day there is a hunting song in Yorkshire which keeps his memory green.

> "Oh! with the Duke of Buckingham
> And other noble gentlemen,
> Oh! but we had some fine hunting!"[1]

The old friends who did not share his pastimes could not however bring themselves to believe that the man they had known as the Alcibiades of the Restoration was now content to live a fox hunter's life in a Yorkshire farm. Etherege,[2] writing from Ratisbon, voiced their impression when he declared that he received the news of Buckingham's retire-

---

[1] "Quarterly Review," 109.
[2] Sir G. Etherege to Duke of Buckingham, Ratisbon, 12th November 1686.

ment "with no less astonishment than I should hear of his Christian Majesty turning Benedictine monk, or the Pope's wearing a long periwigg, and setting up for a flaming beau in the seventy-fourth year of his age. . . . Who could have prophesy'd (though he had a double gift of Nostradamus's spirit) that the Duke of Buckingham, who never vouchsafed his embraces to any ordinary beauty, would ever condescend to sigh and languish for the heiress-apparent of a thatch'd cottage in a straw hat, flannen petticoat, stockings of as gross a thrum as the Blew Coat boy's caps at the Hospital, and a smock (the Lord defend me from the wicked idea of it) as coarse a canvas as ever served an apprenticeship to a mackeral boat? Who would have believed that Your Grace . . . the most polished, refined epicure of his age, that had regaled himself with the most exquisite wines of Italy, Greece and Spain, would in the last scene of Life debauch his constitution in execrable Yorkshire ale? and that he who all his lifetime had either seen princes his playfellows or companions would submit to the nonsensical chat and barbarous language of farmers and higglers."

If the following undated and unaddressed letter was Buckingham's reply to Etherege, it shows that "the most polished and refined epicure" had not grown indifferent to the opinion of his quondam associates, and indeed was anxious to explain and justify his enforced retirement.

I am not ashamed[1] (he writes), to owne that I neither am nor desire to bee out of the world, but

[1] Add. MSS. 27872 f. 40, Duke of Buckingham. No clue to whom addressed, nor date.

I confesse I am growne olde enough to be unwilling to loose my time, and therefore having lately observed the playing of two games of which neither were tending towards the publick good, and both (as I humbly conceive) managed by bunglers that did not understand what they were about, I thought it better to doe nothing by my selfe than to play the foole in company, which I take to bee so farre from being out of the world that I am apt to believe there are a world of people in England of the same opinion. When the present warre of witnesses is over, all men then will begin to thinke how to settle the nation, and that can never bee done but by coming up to publick measures which may quiet the minds of the people in order to the matter of Government as well as of religion. When this honest game comes to be played, you will find a world of people who will be very industrious, and who (though perhaps they will not often outrun the constable, as the late politician with a witnesse has done) yet I am confident they will be able to do theyr King and country much more service. Till then I shall be very intent about looking after my farme, and though wee farmers neither have nor will have to doe with courtiers, but in order to the securing to every man in England his religion and liberty and estate (things which wee conceive to bee of some importance, though they have not of late been much talked of), yet those courtiers, that can see anything, doe soe well foresee that these points must bee thought of, that I am apt to believe they will not refuse an honest farmer any honest request; it is not out of theyr thoughts to reconcile themselves to the farmers against that time comes.

That I beleeve anything they can be persuaded to doe, they would bee as willing to doe at this time to oblidge the farmers as any other sort of people now in England of the same opinion

But however much Buckingham might affect to be engrossed with affairs bucolic, even the stillness of that lonely country could not charm his wayward spirit into quietude.

If we are to believe Oldmixon, the character of his diminished household at Castle Helmsley was much the same as in the stormy days of affluence at Wallingford House. Buckingham[1] therefore had no difficulty in enlisting the assistance of his retainers when in obedience to an order of Chancery the tenants refused to hand over the rents to him; and thanks to his "company of ruffians" the Duke was able to seize on the moneys. But the sturdy Yorkshiremen did not give way without resistance, and the business culminated in a serious riot at an inn.

In the seventeenth century a Duke — even broken and banished—was a great personage, but had he lived a few weeks longer Buckingham must have stood his trial for contempt of court. His Grace's adventures were however numbered. He was now close on sixty, a ruined, disappointed man. During the whole course of his feverish existence he had spared his health as little as his fortune, and under the increasing strain even his vitality was fast becoming bankrupt.

In April 1687 he contracted a chill from sitting on the damp ground when heated after a run out foxhunting. Like most of his generation he had been a sufferer from ague, and, at first, does not seem to have paid much heed to his ailment, though he took to his bed in the farmhouse at Kirkby Moorside, of which mention has already been made.

[1] Oldmixon, p. 128.

The chill rapidly developed into fever, and though he longed to be moved from the bleak moorlands either to his own mansion at York or to the faithful Brian Fairfax's house, it soon became apparent that his journeyings were done. It was fortunate for the Duke that his last illness was not long drawn out in a place where, even had he not been well-nigh penniless, the simplest comforts were unattainable. Save that it was not at an inn, but in a substantial yeoman's house that he breathed his last, Pope's description is accurate enough, and well-known as are the lines no study of the Duke of Buckingham would be complete without them.

> "In the worst inn's worst room, with mat half hung,
> The floors of plaster and the walls of dung,
> On once a flock-bed, but repaired with straw,
> With tape-tied curtains, never meant to draw,
> The George and Garter dangling from that bed,
> Where tawdry yellow strove with dirty red,
> Great Villiers lies."

At this juncture, Buckingham's cousin, Lord Arran, the future Duke of Hamilton, chanced to be passing through York and posted to his relative's assistance. His narrative and that of a neighbour, a certain Mr Gibson who does not appear to have been scared by "the Duke's company of ruffians," give us a detailed account of the last moments of George Villiers. The picture they draw is indeed so vivid it would be a pity not to give it in their own words.

My Lord,[1]—Mere chance having thrown me into these parts by accident as I was at York in my

[1] Ellis, "Correspondence," vol. i. p. 276, Letter of Duke of Hamilton to Dr Sprat, Kirkby Moore Syde, 17th April 1687.

journey towards Scotland, I heard of the Duke of Buckingham's illness here, which made me take a resolution of waiting upon His Grace to see what condition he was in. I arrived here on Friday in the afternoon, when I found him in a very low condition; he had long been ill of an ague which had made him weak, but his understanding was as good as ever, and his noble parts were so entire, that though I saw death in his looks at first sight, he would by no means think of it. He told me he was on horseback but two days before, and that he found himself so well at heart that he was sure he could be in no danger of his life. He described his symptoms, but believed by applying warm medicines the swelling would fall and he would then be at ease, but it proved otherwise, for a mortification came on those low parts and rapidly ascended so that it soon occasioned his death. As soon as I had arrived I sent for one Dr Waler, for I found him here in a most miserable condition: he desired me to stay with him, which I very willingly obeyed. I confess it made my heart bleed to see the Duke of Buckingham in so pitiful a place and in so bad a condition: and what made it worse he was not at all sensible of it, for he thought in a day or two he should be well: and when we minded him of his condition, he said it was not as we apprehended. The doctors told me his case was desperate, and though he enjoyed the free exercise of his senses, a day would kill him; but they durst not tell him of it, so they put a hard part upon me to pronounce death to him; which I saw approaching so fast, that I thought it was high time for him to be thinking of another world, for I saw he could not long continue in this. So I sent for a very worthy gentleman, Mr Gibson, a neighbour of His Grace's, who lives but a mile from this place, to be an assistant to me in this work; so we jointly represented his condition to him, who I saw was at first very uneasy; but I think we should not have discharged the duty of honest men or of a faithful kinsman if we had suffered him to go out of this world without desiring him to prepare for death and to look into his conscience.

After having plainly told him his condition, I asked him who I should send for to be assistant during the short time he had to live; he would make me no answer, which made me conjecture, and having formerly heard that he had been inclining to be a Roman Catholic I asked him if I should send for a priest; for I thought that any act that would be like a Christian was what his condition now wanted most, but he positively told me he was not of that persuasion, and so would not hear any more of that subject, for he was of the Church of England: but hitherto he would not hear of a parson, though he had declared his aversion to my offering to send for a priest. But after some time, beginning to feel his distemper mount, he desired me to send for the parson of this parish, who said prayers for him, which he joined in very freely but still did not think he would die; though this was yesterday at seven in the morning and he died at eleven at night. Mr Gibson asked him if he had made a will, or if he would declare who was to be his heir; but to the first he answered that he had made none, and to the last, whoever was named, his answer was always "No," and to see whether he would change in any way the answer or manner of it they asked him if my Lord Purbeck was to be sent for, but to that he answered, "By no means." I did fully represent my lady Duchess' condition to him, and told him it was absolutely fit during the time he had the exercise of his reason, to do something to settle his affairs; I desired he might die as a Christian; and since he called himself of the Church of England the parson was ready here to administer the Sacrament to him; which he said he would take: so accordingly I gave orders for it, and two other honest gentlemen received with him, Mr Gibson and Colonel Liston, an old servant of His Grace's. At first he called out three or four times, for he thought the ceremony looked as if death was near, which for the strength of his noble parts (they not yet being affected) he could not easily believe, for all this time he was not ready to take death to him, but in a few minutes he became calm and received the Sacrament with all the decency imaginable, and in an hour afterwards he lost his speech, and so continued till eleven that night, when he died.

Mr Gibson's account, written many years later, confirms Lord Arran's letter.

WELLBURNE, 27th February 1705.

SIR,[1]—As it fell to my share to know as much of the last moments of the late Duke of Buckingham as any then about him, so, at your instance, I shall readily give answer to satisfy any that he died in the best house in Kirkby Moorside (which neither is nor ever was an alehouse), and that when he was moved to receive the Sacrament he consented to it, and received it from the hands of the minister of the parish, with great decency and seeming devotion; while we, who received with him, were doubtful of his swallowing the bread because of his weakness and pain. Hence we had reason to conclude he had died in the Communion of the Church of England, and none about it questioned it that I heard of. Indeed, my Lord of Arran (who was then there) could not be prevailed with to communicate with His Grace and us. What my lord's

---

[1] Fairfax, "Correspondence," J. Gibson—Brian Fairfax, vol. iv. p. 268.

reasons were for that unwillingness I know not, but my lord (now Duke of Hamilton) is a witness of the truth of His Grace's thus receiving, his lordship being (if I am not mistaken) in the room then.

I omit, at present, many particulars which I could give some account of, as to making his will, his naming his heir, etc., which His Grace would not be persuaded to. If you please to command any farther account of the very last passages of his life, the respect and honour I had from him, and for him, engage me to answer you in favour of his memory. I had not the honour to converse with him any long time before his dying days; but so far as I had any discourse with His Grace, he was always pleased to express a love for good men and good things, how little able soever he was to live up to what he knew.

The efficacy or futility of death-bed repentance will always provide a fruitful subject for the dogmas of the theologian and the theories of the philosopher.

> "The moving finger writes; and, having writ,
> Moves on; nor all your piety nor wit
> Shall lure it back to cancel half a line;
> Nor all your tears wash out a word of it."

Nevertheless, the piteous cry of a soul in such extremity of anguish as the following letter reveals must surely touch a chord of pity in the heart of every man born of woman.

DEAR DOCTOR,[1]—I always looked upon you to be a person of true virtue and know you have a sound understanding; for however I may have acted in opposition to the principles of religion or the

---

[1] Duke of Buckingham to Dr. Barrow, "Quarterly Review," pp. 109, 110.

dictates of reason I can honestly assure you I have always had the highest veneration for both. The world and I shake hands, and I dare affirm we are heartily weary of each other. Oh! what a prodigal have I been of that most valuable of all possessions —Time.

To what a situation am I now reduced! Is this odious little hut a suitable lodging for a prince? Is this anxiety of mind becoming the character of a Christian? From my rank I might have expected affluence to wait upon my life: from religion and understanding peace to smile upon my end; instead of which I am afflicted with poverty and haunted by remorse; despised by my country, and I fear forsaken by my God.

I am forsaken by all my acquaintances, neglected by the friends of my bosom and dependants on my bounty; but no matter! I am not fit to converse with the former and have no abilities to serve the latter. Let me not however be forsaken by the good. Favour me with a visit as soon as possible. I am of opinion this is the last visit I shall ever solicit from you.

My distemper is powerful; come and pray for the departing spirit of the poor unhappy

BUCKINGHAM.

The poignant bitterness of the man who in his last hour realised "how little he had been able to live up to what he had known" breathes in another dying saying of Buckingham's. The first question of the well-meaning clergyman, whom Arran had summoned to the bedside, was to ascertain "what His Grace's religion was." And a truer sense of the essence of religion than that of the worthy precisian lives in the Duke's answer. "It is an insignificant question," he said, "for I have been a shame and disgrace to all religion; if you can do me any good, do."¹

Thus, on 16th April 1687, died George Villiers, Duke of Buckingham, and it was characteristic of his whole career that though, as Arran says, "there was not so much as one farthing to defray the least expense," or to mitigate the squalor of his end, the funeral was on a scale of princely magnificence. Indeed it far exceeded that of Charles II., for whom no mourning was given, and whose body, when it lay in state at Westminster, was placed in a room "furnished only with coarse cloth,"² and surrounded by tallow instead of wax candles.

But appalled as was Lord Arran "at the state of confusion not to be expressed" that he found in his relative's affairs, and though evidently nervous of being involved in them, it never seems to have occurred to him to depart from the pompous routine then observed.

He "took upon himself" to order the body to be embalmed and carried to Helmesley, where it lay in state. And in the presence of Brian Fairfax and Mr Gibson, for he was too prudent to do anything without witnesses, Lord Arran searched the Duke's strong box for a will. But will there was none, only "some loose letters of no concern," which he sealed up and sent to the Duchess with the little plate and linen that was still left to her spendthrift lord.

June had come before the last arrangements were complete and the slow train of mourners reached the capital. Young Robert Fairfax, good

---

¹ Echard, p. 842.   ² Supplement to Burnet's "History," p. 143.

Brian Fairfax's son, was one of the bearers who carried the coffin through the House of Lords into the Prince's Chamber.

The ingenuous youth cannot contain his satisfaction at the "very good mourning" allotted him. "Cloth at eighteen shillings a yard, with sword, belt, stockings, gloves and cravat, with two white dimity waistcoats," so absorb his thoughts that he has no leisure to enlarge on the closing scene.

And yet the least imaginative should have been impressed when at the dead of night the mortal remains of George Villiers were lowered into the family vault, whither forty years ago his young brother had preceded him.

Apparently the duties of the executors ceased with the pomp of the final pageant. The love of wife and Royal friend gave the first Duke a magnificent memorial in the Abbey. The resting-place of the second is unmarked by tomb or effigy; while James II. contemptuously declared that, but for his charity, the widow of his old enemy must have starved.

Such was the end of George Villiers, Duke of Buckingham, and it must be admitted that never did career afford a finer theme for the warnings of the moralist.

Seldom indeed did man start more happily endowed in the race of life. It would seem that at his birth the presiding genius sought to show how futile are all the gifts of intellect and person if that great quality which Englishmen worship as "Character" be lacking. If justice is only another word for the balance of mind that springs from self-control, undoubtedly he traced his own epitaph when he wrote of justice "as that without which all other qualities and virtues become as vices." This was particularly the case as regards his wonderful adaptability and imagination. He found it so easy to substitute one scheme for another that the process inevitably led to juggling with ideals.

Considering how susceptible Buckingham was to feminine influence, it is remarkable that he should never have met the woman capable of supplementing his defects. It may be said that it was his fault, but other sinners have been less unfortunate. At an early age circumstances estranged him from his good but foolish mother. It is only necessary to glance at Mary Fairfax's portrait to understand why that excellent lady could never hope to retain George Villiers' errant fancy, and Madame Henriette, with all her charm, was too much a Stuart to show the way to higher things.

Then came Lady Shrewsbury. Till the fatal siren beckoned him across the Rubicon that divides the libertine from the criminal he might plead that his iniquities had not worn a darker hue than those of others whom the King delighted to honour. But from the hour he left the "close" at Barn Elms his nature and career experienced a rapid deterioration. In Lady Shrewsbury's train came the seven devils that vex mankind, and henceforward disappointment, misfortune and ruin marked him for their own. The blight, that settled upon all he owned or touched, did not even spare the remarkable personal beauty to which, rather than to his wit, he loved to impute his successes.

With the exception of the *Rehearsal*, Buckingham's literary efforts were ephemeral. Nor can a different fate be claimed for his ventures in statecraft. Contrary to the usual order of things, the evil he did was interred with his bones. His happy inspirations, the belief in freedom of thought, and the naval supremacy of England, have wrought for good in the hands of his successors. The ambition to lead and represent the democracy, which inspired the Whig aristocrats in the coming century, may also be claimed as part of his political heritage.

Such was George Villiers. As he sinned so he suffered. Nor can it be counted the least retribution that he died in the blackest hour of England's history. The one selfless aspiration, to which through a thousand changes he remained true, was universal Liberty of Conscience. But even the sight of the Promised Land was denied him, and the vault had long since closed over his remains when William of Orange landed at Torbay.

INDEX

A

AGLIONBY, DR, 20
Airlie Castle, 45
Aix-la-Chapelle, court at, 68; peace of, 201
Albemarle, Duke of, 144, 145, 193
Amsterdam, Capt. Wendy Oxford at, 63; Prince of Orange at, 264; death of Shaftesbury at, 385
Anglesea, Lady, 8
—— Lord, 294, 318
Anglo-French Convention, 262
Anne of Austria, 2, 121
Antrim, Randal M'Donnell, Earl of, 15
Argyll, Marquis of, leader of Presbyterian party, 35; treatment of King Charles, 43
Arlington, Lord, letters to Buckingham, 127, 128; on commission to examine Buckingham, 180; summary of character, 189, 190; reconciliation with Buckingham, 217; subscribes Treaty of Dover, 218; Buckingham's colleague, 230; subscribes Treaty of D. second time, 237; relations with Buckingham, 251-253; in Holland, 255; Embassy to King of France, 272; advance in peerage, 273; becomes Lord Chamberlain, 306
Arran, Richard Butler, Earl of, betrothal, 140; Hamilton at Buckingham's death-bed, 394; funeral arrangements, 400
Arras, 69
Arundel House, 195
Arundel, Lord, subscribes Treaty of Dover, 218; in the Tower, 351
Ascham, 74
Ashley Cooper. *See* Shaftesbury
Atkins, Samuel, 356, 357
Aylesbury, Mr William, 30

B

BAMPFYLDE, COLONEL, 73, 81
Barbon's Bridge, 51
Barillon, intrigue to separate Charles and William of Orange, 335; relations with Buckingham, 342, 367; with Montagu, 362
Barkstead, Colonel, 97
Barlowe, George, 53
—— Mrs, 53
Barn Elms, 194
Bearcroft, Serjeant, 172, 173
Beaumont, Sir John, 1
Beauvais, 36
Bedloe, 351
Beerwaert, Isabella von, 190
Belasyse, Lord, 349, 351
Bellasis, Sir H., 151, 174
Bellefonds, de, Maréchal, 280
Bellings, 218
Belvoir, 3
Benedictines, Abbess of the, 78
Bennet, Harry. *See* Arlington, 188
Berkeley, Charles, 70
Berkshire, Lord, tutor to Charles II., 18; in Parliament, 294
Beverling, 269
Birmingham, 31
Blackheath, 276
Blague, Colonel, 52
Blanquefort, M., 158
Blood, Colonel, 239, 240-41
Blorepipe House, 53
Booth, Sir George, 106, 107
Borough Bridge, 110
Braganza, Catherine of, friendship with Duchess of Buckingham, 86; illness, 127; proposed divorce escapade, 213; proposed kidnapping, 214-15; ballet at Whitehall, 243; plot against, 360
Breda, Charles at, 39; return of Court, 113

405

INDEX

Brian Duppa. *See* Duppa
Bridgeman, Sir Orlando, demands Great Seal from Clarendon, 185; resigns office, 273
Bridges, Mr George Rodney, 296, 333
Bristol, Earl of, 115, 294
Brudenell, Anna Maria. *See* Shrewsbury
—— Lord, 153
Bruges, 77, 78
Brunkhard, 199
Buckhurst, Lord, friendship with Buckingham, 135, 136; suspicions against Buckingham, 176; journey to the Tower, 180
Buckingham, old Countess of, 4, 6
—— Katherine Manners, first Duchess of, marriage, 5; a widow, 8; birth of Lord Francis, 9; return to Church of Rome, 10; second marriage, 15
—— Mary Fairfax, second Duchess of, marriage, 91; saves her husband's life, 166; assists him to escape from Owthorp, 172; goes to London, 174; leaves her husband, 198; ballet at Whitehall, 243; supports her husband, 295
—— George Villiers, first Duke of, birth of son, 1; marriage, 5; expedition to La Rochelle, 7; assassination, 8
—— George Villiers, second Duke of—
1628 birth and christening, 1, 2
life at court, 12
life at Cambridge, 19
1642-1643 escape from college to join the king at Oxford, 20
travels in France and Italy, 20, 21
1645 in Paris, 21
influence on Prince Charles, 22
1648 with Lord Holland at Reigate, 23
escape to St Neots, 25
joins Prince Charles, 25
confiscation of property, 26
appearances in disguise in London, 28
retreat to Holland, 30
1649 letter to Earl of Denbigh, 32
Order of the Garter bestowed by Charles, 34
advises King to accept Covenanters' terms, 35
1650 sails with Charles for Scotland, 41
becomes Secretary of State, 43
appointed General of the Eastern Division, 46
1651 marches south with Charles, 48
flight from Worcester, 51, 52
takes refuge at Nottingham, 53
lands in Rotterdam, 54
pretensions for Mary Stuart's hand, 59
dismissal from her court, 60
1653 return to England, 65
suitor for Cromwell's daughter, 66
in Paris, 68
Siege of Mouzon, 69
Siege of Arras, 70
return to Paris, 71
1656 in Turenne's army, 75
at Valenciennes, 75
friendship with Fairfax, 81
attentions to Mistress Fairfax, 85-89
1657 marriage, 91
escape from Nun Appleton, 91-92
York House, 93
visit to Cobham, 94
arrest by Colonel Gibbon, 94
sent to the Tower, 95
relations with Sir A. Ashley Cooper, 98
1658 release from the Tower, 103
life at York House, 104
1659 plot to join General Monk, 108
meets Charles at Dover, 114
1660 pardon under the Great Seal, 117
accompanies Princess Henrietta to France, 119
recalled, 121
1661 becomes Lord-Lieutenant of Yorkshire, 122
1663 rising of Rymer and Oates, 124-130
at Court, 133-136
1665 at Council of War, 142
failure to gain naval command, 142-144
1666 joins Duke of Albemarle, 144
return to York, 146
scientific researches, 28, 147
friendship with Sir G. Savile, 149, 150
entertains Shrewsburys, 153
supports Agricultural Bill, 156
quarrel with Ossory, 158-160
in the Tower, 161
1667 attempt on life, 165, 166
betrayal by Braithwaite, 167
escape from Owthorp, 172, 173
appeal to the King, 179

INDEX

Buckingham, George Villiers, second Duke of (*contd.*):—
1667 in the Tower, 180
set at liberty, 182
meets the King, 183
restoration to favour, 185
reads Clarendon's letter to the Lower House, 187
return of power, 188
1668 duel with Lord Shrewsbury, 194
at the opening of Parliament, 198
Foreign Affairs, 201-206
a zealous Protestant, 211
reconciliation to Arlington, 217
1669 appointment at St Germains, 220
reception in France, 221
return to England, 229
letters to Louis XIV., 232, 233
Treaty of Dover, 237
kidnapping of the Duke of Ormond, 238
birth of Lady Shrewsbury's son, 244
extravagances, 246
becomes Chancellor of Cambridge University, 248-250
1671 goes to Dunkirk, 251
appearance of *The Rehearsal* at Drury Lane, 257
1672 in Holland, 265-268
interview with Prince of Orange, 269, 270
Lord High Steward of Oxford, 365
1673 in York, 276
withdrawal of promised command, 277
1674 appeal to the Commons, 282
cross-examination at Westminster, 285
result, 288
defence before the Lords, 292-294
separation from Lady Shrewsbury, and forfeiture, 295
recantation in Parliament, 296
letter of remonstrance to the King, 298
compensation allowed, 302
retirement to private life, 302
1675 return to Parliament, 306
confession of faith, 310
1676 speech in Parliament, 315-317
disappearance, 319
imprisonment in the Tower, 321, 322
set at liberty, 329
affairs with France, 338
1678 goes to Paris, 342
Popish Plot, 351
letter to Louis, 352
warrant issued, 370
in hiding, 371
return from Paris, 376
1680 plot against Louise de Kérouaille, 378
at Wapping, 380
Lord Shaftesbury's case, 383
1682 retirement, 386
1685 publication of pamphlet, 386
1686 life in Yorkshire, 390
1687-88 illness, 393, 394
letter to Dr Barrow, 398
1688 death, 400
summary of character, 402, 403
Buquinham, M. de, 354
Burnet, Dr, 349, 350
Butter, 258

C

CABAL MINISTRY, 99; members of, 237; origin of name, 274
Calais, 188
Canterbury, Archbishop of, 185
Carbisdale, 41
Cardigan, Lord and Lady, 152
—— Earl, 295
Carlisle, Earl of, 140
Carnarvon, Robert Dormer, Earl of, 363
Caryll, Francis, 357, 358
Castlemaine, Lady, in favour with Charles, 116; relations with Buckingham, 133; assists interview between the King and Buckingham, 183; loss of power, 228
Cellier, Mrs, 372, 375
Chaise, Pere la, 346
Channel Islands, 35
Charing Cross, 29
Charles, Prince of Wales, schoolfellow of Buckingham's, 18, 21; in the Downs, 25
Charles II., King, Scottish Covenanters, 35-39; in Scotland, 41; attempt to join Royalists, 44; coronation at Scone, 46; march south, 48; defeat at Worcester, and flight, 51; in Paris, 57; at Aix and Cologne, 68; landing at Dover, 114; public entry into London, 115; coronation in

Charles II. (*continued*)—
London, 122 ; immorality of Court, 77, 139 ; passing of Cattle Bill, 156 ; interview with Braythwaite, 167 ; Buckingham's trial, 182 ; dismissal of Clarendon from office, 185 ; reconciliation to Buckingham, 186 ; attitude to Roman Church, 211, 218 ; relations with his brother and sister, 213 ; rejection of the plot against the Queen, 215 ; visit from William of Orange, 238 ; proclamation for Blood's arrest, 240 ; grant of free pardon, 241 ; godfather to "Earl of Coventry," 244 ; cancels Declaration of Indulgence to Nonconformists, 279 ; letter of remonstrance from Buckingham, 298 ; secret agreement with Louis, 312 ; adjourns Parliament, 323 ; influence of Louise de Kéroualle, 332 ; reconciliation to Louis, 312 ; dissolves Parliament, 323 ; creation of new Privy Council, 368 ; illness, 369 ; summoning of Parliament at Oxford, 380 ; dissolves Parliament, 382 ; diminution of friendship with Buckingham, 385
Choisy, de, Colbert. *See* De Choisy
Churchill, Jack, 229
Clarendon, Lord, sympathy with Ascham's murderers, 74 ; supreme at Court, 133 ; opposed by Buckingham, 155 ; refusal to see Buckingham, 178 ; forced to give up office, 185 ; impeachment, 186 ; in exile, 187 ; death, 188
—— Countess of, 184
Clark, Colonel, 101
Claypole, Mrs, 83
Clergis, Dr, 107
Cleveland, Barbara Villiers, Duchess of, joins alliance against York succession, 216 ; loses support of Buckingham, 228 ; ballet at Whitehall, 244 ; relations with Montagu, 361
Clifford, Lord, member of commission, 180 ; subscribes to Treaty of Dover, 218 ; member of the Cabal, 237, 287 ; receives a barony, 273 ; resignation, 274
—— Martin, 258
Cobham, 94
Coke, Sir Edward, 7
Colchester, 23
Coldstream, 108
Coleman, secretary to the Duchess of York, 345 ; examination of, 352 ; death, 360

Colepepper, 74
Colinaar, Mr Justus, 30
College, 382
Cologne, 68
Condé, Prince de, 38
—— Princesse de, 69
Conway, Lord, 199
Courtin, 313
Covenanters, Scottish, 35
Coventry, Earl of, 1, 7 ; false title, 244
—— Mr Henry, 323
—— Sir William, commission to examine Buckingham, 180 ; ally of Duke of York, 206 ; committal to Tower, 208
Cowley, Abraham, at Trinity College, Cambridge, 19 ; poem on Buckingham's marriage, 91 ; at Windsor, 98
Cozens, Dr, 11
Cromwell, Henry, Lord Deputy of Ireland, 83
—— Mrs, 83
—— Oliver, campaign in Ireland, 30 ; battle of Dunbar, 43 ; battle of Worcester, 51 ; refusal to receive Buckingham, 63 ; trial of Lilburn, 64 ; alliance with Mazarin, 76 ; treatment of Buckingham, 82 ; effect of Buckingham's marriage, 91 ; arrest of Buckingham, 94 ; death, 96
—— Richard, character, 83 ; Protector of England, 96 ; government, 105

D

DAMPORT, MRS, 175
Danby, Lord, becomes Lord Treasurer, 275 ; increasing power, 396 ; negotiates marriage between Princess Mary and William of Orange, 334 ; letter to Montagu, 362 ; defence by Lord Carnarvon, 364 ; in the Tower, 368
Dangerfield, 372, 375
De Bellefonds, Maréchal, 280
De Buquinham, M., 354
De Choisy, Colbert, assists Louise de Kéroualle, 230 ; interview with Buckingham, 254
De Guiche, Count, 121
De Kéroualle, Louise, Charles' admiration for, 227 ; journey to England, 229 ; at Dieppe, 230 ; ballet at Whitehall, 243 ; mock-marriage, 252 ; increase of power, 274 ; entertained by Buckingham, 343
De Lionne, M., 221

INDEX

De Lorraine, Chevalier, 219
De Louvois, M., 271
De Montmorency, Charlotte, 38
De Penancöet, Seigneur Guillaume, 227
De Pomponne, M., member of Council, 271; letter from M. de Buquinham, 354
De Ruvigny, Marquis, Buckingham's friend, 280, 297; sent to London, 335; effort to bribe Charles, 340
De Ruyter, at North Foreland, 145; puts to sea, 262; escape after Southwold Bay, 264
De Saulx, Comte, 226
De Witt, 145
Declaration of War, with Spain, 76; with Holland, 262
Denbigh, Basil Fielding, Earl of, 31
—— Lady Susan, 11, 31
Derby, Earl of, letter from Buckingham, 48; joins King at Warrington, 49
Dieppe, 230
Don Alonso, 78
Don John, 75
Doncaster, 122
Dorchester, Marquis of, 161
Dorislaus, 74
D'Orleans, Philippe, Duc, betrothal, 118-120; character, 216
Dormer. *See* Carnarvon
Dorset, Duke of. *See* Buckhurst
Dover, Treaty of, 218, 237
Dryden, 258-261
Dudley, Duke, 15
Dugdale, 382
Dunbar, battle of, 43
Dunkirk, 296
Duppa, Brian, Bishop of Salisbury, 18

E

"Ecce Homo," Titian's, 27
Edinburgh, 41
Essex, Lord, supporter of Exclusion Bill, 377; present at Shaftesbury's case, 383
Etherege, Sir G., 390
Evelyn, Mr, 147
Everard, 381
Exclusion Bill, 377, 379

F

Fairfax, Brian, biographer, 85; carries message to Coldstream, 107, 108; on Buckingham's death, 400

Fairfax, Lady, 87
—— General, Lord, blockades Colchester, 23; character, 79-81; intercedes with Cromwell for Buckingham, 92; petitions Parliament for Buckingham, 98; supports Monk against Lambert, 108-110; enters York, 111; letter from, 130-33
—— Mary, meets Buckingham, 81; obstacles to marriage, 85; personal appearance, 86; Buckingham's proposal, 87; Buckingham's letter, 88; marriage, 91
—— Robert, 400
Farnley Wood, 124
Fauconberg, Lord, 150
Felton, 7
Feilding, Basil. *See* Denbigh
Finch, 317
Fire of London, 153, 154
Fisher, 11
Fitzgerald, Father, 389
Fitzharris, 381
Flanders, 338
Fleetwood, Lord, messenger from Council to Fairfax, 93; Commander-in-Chief, 106
Floyd, 11
Fowler, 357
Frazer, Dr, 43
Fryr, 176

G

Gerard, Lord, instructs Buckingham, 20; siege of Arras, 70
Ghent, surrenders to Louis, 336; King Charles at, 39
Gibbons, Colonel, at Colchester, 23; letter to Thurloe, 94
Gibson, Mr, 394, 400
Giffard, Mr, 52
Gloucester, Duke of, with Turenne, 69; death, 118
Goadby, 3
Godfrey, Sir Edmundbury, 346-348
Goodman, Abraham, 166
Goring, 23
Gower, Mr, 110
—— Sir Thomas, 124
Grafton, Henry, Duke of, 190
Grammont, Count, 134, 136, 219
Greathead, Colonel, 124
Grey, Lord, supporter of Monmouth, 373; present at Lord Shaftesbury's case, 383
Grice, 176
Guiche, Count de, 121
Gwyn, Mrs, 324

INDEX

H

Hacker, 110
Hague, the, King Charles at, 112; Prince of Orange at, 264; Buckingham at, 268
Halifax, Marquis of, meets Buckingham, 149; character, 150; sent to France, 265; Dutch sympathies, 272; Popish Plot, 351; member of Privy Council, 368; combats Exclusion Bill, 379
Hamilton, Duke of, member of Privy Council, 34; in Scotland, 43
Hampden, Mr, 369
Harcourt, Mr Vere, 91
Harley, Sir Edward, 330
Harlowe, Mr Robert, 87
Hastings, Sir Henry, 14
Hatton, Lord, 71
Havre de Grace, 119
Haynes, 383
Hazlerig, 105
Helmsley, death of Buckingham, 24; property of Katherine Manners, 79; in the Civil Wars, 389; lying-in-state, 400
Henrietta Maria, approval of Duchess of Buckingham's marriage, 15; grudge against Montrose, 35; secret marriage with Jermyn, 59; supports Buckingham, 68; takes daughter to France, 119
Henrietta, Princess, marriage, 118, 119; re-visits England, 216; death, 218
Herbert, Charles, Lord, betrothal, 10; marriage and death, 15
—— Philip, 15
—— Lady, return to Court, 16; second marriage, 17
Hertford, Lord, 18
Hewet, Dr, 83
Heydon, Dr, false title, 169; letter to Duchess of Buckingham, 174, 175
Hobbs, tutor to Prince Charles, 22; dismissal, 61
Holland, Buckingham's retreat, 30; war declared, 262; peace declared, 306
—— Lord, at Reigate, 23; escape to St Neots, 25; death, 25, 26
Hollis, 338
Holmes, Sir Robert, Buckingham's second, 193; attempt to capture Dutch fleet, 262, 286
Horsted Keynes, 56
Howard, Mr Bernard, 193
—— Sir Robert, 179

Howard, Thomas, marriage with Duchess of Richmond, 140; relations with Lady Shrewsbury, 152; given Colonel's commission, 350
Hyde, Sir Edward, goes to Spain, 34; in Paris, 57; at Aix, 68; return to England, 113; becomes Earl of Clarendon, 116

I

Ireland, 30
Ireton, Mistress, 67
Irwin, Lord, 153

J

James I., King, 1, 6
Jenkins, Mr, 193
Jermyn, Harry, marriage, 60; relations with Lady Shrewsbury, 152
—— Lord, policy with Henrietta Maria, 36; secret marriage, 59; supports Buckingham, 68
Jersey, 91
Jinks, 371

K

Kéroualle, Louise de. See De Kéroualle
Killigrew, Harry, despatched to Court, 144; relations with Lady Shrewsbury, 152; brawl with Buckingham, 191; attack on highway, 209
King, Dr, 40
Kingston, 23
Kirkby, 344
—— Moorside, 390, 397
Kirke, Mrs, 24
Knaresborough, 109, 110
Knyvett, Frances, 3

L

La Ferté, 75
La Rochelle, 7
Lambert, 48
Lambeth, 17
Laud, Dr, Bishop of Bath and Wells, 2
Lauderdale, Lord, opposes scheme to join Royalists, 44; prisoner at Windsor, 98; ally of Buckingham, 156, 220; Anglo-French agreement, 230; Treaty of Dover, 237; attack on, 281; vote of censure, 339

INDEX

Lawson, 107
—— Miss, 378
Leighton, Ellis, friend of Buckingham, 54, 55; pleads with Cromwell for Buckingham, 63; sent to Paris, 202; in prison, 352
Lennox. *See* Richmond
Leopold of Prague, Archduke, 26
Lionne, M. de, 221
Lesley, David, 47, 49, 236
Lichfield, 20
Lilburn, John, 62
Lilburne, 109
Liston, Colonel, 397
Lloyd, Dr, 348
Lockhart, 70
Long, 43
Lorraine, Chevalier de, 219
Lothian, Lord, 44
Louis XIV., King, ally of the Dutch, 145; invasion of Franche Comte, 200; influence over Buckingham, 203; negotiations with England, 211; Treaty of Dover, 218; reception of Buckingham, 221; presents to Buckingham, 225; letters from Buckingham and reply, 232-235; victories over Holland, 264; reception of Embassy at Utrecht, 271; appeal from Buckingham, 280; secret agreement with Charles II., 312; surrender of Ghent, 336; affairs with England, 337-339; reconciliation with Charles, 340; financial arrangements with Charles, 381
Louvois, M. de, 271
Lowestoft, 144

M

MADRID, 74
"Mall." *See* Villiers
Mallet, Mrs, 136
Malton, 110
Man, Captain, 74
Mancini, Olympe, 59
Manners, Lady Katherine, 3, 79
Mansell, Colonel Roderick, 374
Marvell, Andrew, 330
Mary, Princess, 334
Massey, 47
May, Mr Bab, 213
Mazarin, alliance with Cromwell, 76; Ambassador's despatch, 114
M'Donnell, Randal. *See* Antrim
Mealtub Plot, 377
Middlesex, Lord, 323
Middleton, Lord, with Royalists in Scotland, 43; death, 175, 176

Mildmay, Colonel, 101
Modena, Mary of, 280-281
Mohun, Lord, 311
Monk, General, in Scotland, 106, 107; goes to London, 112; reception by Charles, 114; at Lowestoft, 144
Monmouth, Duchess of, 243
—— James, Duke of, in command, 271; election as Chancellor at Cambridge, 302; plot in his favour, 314; plot against the King, 366
Montagu, English Ambassador in France, 278; quarrel with Buckingham, 279; estrangement from Danby, 361
Montague, Abbé, 9
Montgomery, Colonel, 45
Montmorency, Charlotte de, 38 .
Montrose, raises troops, 35; defeat at Carbisdale, 41; death in Edinburgh, 41
Morrice, Sir William, commission to examine Buckingham, 180; secretary, 206
Mouzon, siege of, 69
Mulgrave, Earl of, 261

N

NEIVERBRUGGE, 269
Newburgh, Lord, 52
Newcastle, Duke of, tutor to Prince of Wales, 18; admitted to Privy Council, 34
Nicholas, Sir Edward, 38, 54, 57
Nimeguen, 340
Nonesuch, 23
North Foreland, 145
Northumberland, Earl of, tutor to Buckingham, 9; goes abroad, 20
Nottingham, 20
Nun Appleton, marriage of Buckingham, 91; escape, 92; Brian Fairfax at, 108

O

OATES' RISING, 124
Oates, Titus, denounces Popish Plot, 343, 345
Olivolo, 15
O'Neale, Mr, 116
Onslow, Mr, 98, 101
Orange, Princess Mary Stuart of, forbids Buckingham her court, 55; a widow, 58; her brother's guest, 77; death, 118

INDEX

Orange, William of, birth, 58; visit to England, 238; Captain-General of Forces, 264; Stadtholder, 265; interview with Buckingham, 269, 270; forces French to retreat, 306; marriage, 334
Orleans, Philippe, Duc D'. *See* D'Orleans
Ormond, Duke of, supreme at Court, 133; opposed by Buckingham, 155; supports Buckingham, 294; letter to Clarendon, 177; kidnapped, 238, 239
Osborne, Sir Thomas. *See* Danby
Ossory, Lord, challenges Buckingham, 158-160; speech in defence of his father, 242
Owthorp, 172
Oxford, 20
—— Captain and Mrs Wendy, 63
—— Lord, 323

P

PAGE, MR, 247
Palmer, Sir Guy, 14
Paris, King Charles in, 57; Leighton sent to, 203; Buckingham in, 342
Pembroke, Lord, 10, 17
Penancöet, Seigneur Guillaume de, 227
Penderel, 52
Penn, William, 128
Pepys, Mr, 356
Peterborough, Lord, 143
Petition of Right, 7
Petre, Lord, 351
Pett, Commissioner, 198
Philippe, Duc D'Orleans. *See* D'Orleans
Pomponne, M. de. *See* De Pomponne
Pontefract, 124
Popish Plot, 343
Porter, George, 141
Portsmouth, Duchess of. *See* Kérouaille
Powis, Countess of, 373
Pritchard, 350
Pudsey, Mr George, 366

Q

QUESNOY, 75

R

REHEARSAL, THE, 257
Reresby, Sir John, 6, 151

Richmond, Charles Lennox, Duke of 302
—— Duchess of, marriage, 17; transferred from Whitehall to Windsor, 29; hides Buckingham, 53; joins Henrietta Maria, 71; daughter's betrothal, 139; third marriage, 140; ballet at Whitehall, 243; plot against Louise de Kéroualle, 378
—— Duke of Lennox and, 17
—— Ludovisa, Duchess of, 261
Robinson, Sir John, 329
Rochelle, La, 7
Rochester, Earl of, a wit, 135; assault on Dryden, 261; friendship with Buckingham, 303-305; letter to, 331; poem, 378
Roos, Lord and Lady, 212
Rosherville, Lord, 317
Rotterdam, 54
Rouen, 188
Rufford, 149
Rupert, Prince, instructs Buckingham, 20; supports Buckingham, 68; at Lowestoft, 145, 146
Russell, Lord, leader in Lower House, 335; Protestant Opposition, 338, 352; supporter of Exclusion Bill, 377; present at Lord Shaftesbury's case, 383
Rutland, Countess of, 5
—— Francis, sixth Earl of, marriage of daughter, 3-5; sponsor to Lord Francis, 9; death, 12, 13
Ruvigny, Marquis de. *See* De Ruvigny
Ruyter, De. *See* De Ruyter
Rymer, 124

S

SACKVILLE, CHARLES. *See* Buckhurst
St Albans, 173
St Albans, Lord, 120
St Evrémond, 137
St Germains, 220
St Johnstone's, 42, 45
St Martin's Church, marriage of Buckingham, 5; recantation of Duchess of Buckingham, 11
St Neots, 25
St Sebastien, 221
Salisbury, Lord, defends Buckingham, 317; in the Tower, 318, 323; set at liberty, 329; present at Lord Shaftesbury's case, 383
Sandwich, Lord, 120
Saulx, Comte de, 226
Savile, Sir George. *See* Halifax

INDEX

Savile, Henry, 207
Schomberg, Marshal, in command for Holland, 276; Commander-in-Chief, 286
Scilly Isles, 35
Scone, 46
Scotland, 41
Scott, Mr, 353
Scroope, Colonel, 25
Shaftesbury, Lord, friendship with Buckingham, 98; character of, 99-101, 156; affairs with France, 220; Anglo-French agreement, 230; Treaty of Dover, 237; advancement in peerage, 273; advocate for Countess of Shrewsbury, 295; plot in favour of James Monmouth, 314; defends Buckingham, 317; a prisoner in the Tower, 318, 321, 323, 329; case at the Old Bailey, 383, 384
Sheldon, 74
Shrewsbury, Lady, Buckingham's passion for, 89; character, 151; scandal with Harry Killigrew, 190-192; lives with Buckingham, 198; pension from Louis XIV., 226; in convent at Dunkirk, 296; marriage with G. R. Bridges, 333
—— Lord, forbearance, 152; challenges Buckingham, 192; duel, 194; death, 195
Sidney, Colonel Robert, 30
Smithson, Colonel, 124
Southampton, Earl of, 176
Southwold Bay, 263
Spain, King of, alliance with William of Orange, 277; Protestant Cause, 306
Spain, War with, 76
Sprat, Dr, marries Buckingham and Lady Shrewsbury, 245; *The Rehearsal*, 258
Stafford, Lord, chosen for military command, 349; in the Tower, 351; attack and death, 377, 380
Stamford, 173
Strangways, Captain, 110
Strickland, Lord, 93
Stuart, Miss, 133-35
Suffolk, Earl of, 2
Sunderland, Lord, 342, 372
Sweden, Queen of, 71

T

TALBOT, SIR JOHN, 193
—— Lord, 51

Temple, Sir William, Triple Alliance, 201; advice to Charles, 368
Test Act, 274
Thurloe's spies, 73, 76
Titus, Colonel Silas, 56, 117
Tonge, Dr, 350
Tournai, 336
Trayleman, Mr John, 26
Trevor, Sir James, 206
Triple Alliance, 200-201
Tuke, Colonel, 74
Turberville, 382
Turenne, instructor to Dukes of York and Gloucester, 69; at Valenciennes, 75
Turnour, Dr, 247

U

UTRECHT, 265, 271

V

VALENCIENNES, 75, 337
Valois, Charles, 30
Van Beuning, 269
Vane, Sir Harry, 102, 105
Vaughan, Lord, 180
Vavasour, Mr Thomas, 110
Vendome, Duke of, 273
Versailles, 222
Villiers, Barbara. *See* Castlemaine
—— Francis, birth, 9; life at Court, 12; life at Cambridge, 19; travels, 20-21; at Reigate, 23; death, 23
—— George. *See* Buckingham
—— Jacobina, 1
—— Lady, 3
—— Lady Mary or "Mall," 2; betrothal, 10; goes to the Earl of Pembroke, 12; marriage, 15

W

WAKEMAN, 350
Waler, Dr, 395
Wales, Prince of, 16, 18, 21
Walker, Sir Edward, 43
Wallingford House, 1, 2, 118
Walpole, 11
Walters, Lucy, 58, 366
—— Mr, 129
Wapping, 380
Warrington, 49
Wentworth, Lord Strafford, 15

Westmoreland, Earl of, 290
Wharton, Lord, defends Buckingham, 317; sent to the Tower, 318; set at liberty, 329
Whitehall, Duchess of Richmond, imprisoned at, 29; Buckingham at, 82, 85; ballet, 135
Whiteladies, 52
Whorwood, Mr Broome, 366
Williams, Dr, Dean of Westminster, 5
Williamson, Sir J., in Paris, 203; secretary, 306
Wilmot, John. *See* Rochester
Windsor, Duchess of Richmond at, 29; under Richard Cromwell, 97
Witt, De, 226
Wood, Sir Henry, 37
Woodstock, 365
Worcester, battle of, 51
—— Marquis of, 102
Wright, Alderman William, 366

Y

YORK, Lilburne's garrison, 109; reception of Buckingham, 123; return of Buckingham, 146; raising of recruits, 276
York, Duke of, Buckingham's schoolfellow, 18; in France, 69; at siege of Arras, 70; smallpox, 187; refuses command to Buckingham, 142; conversion to Rome, 211; Anglo-French Agreement, 230; naval preparations for War with Holland, 262; retirement from office, 274; marriage, 280; opposes Buckingham's promotion, 330; banishment, 366, 377; return to England, 384
—— Duchess of, supports Clarendon, 185; conversion to Rome, 216
—— House, valuables, 9, 27; marriage of Lady Mary Villiers, 15; marriage of Lady Herbert, 17; given to General Fairfax, 79; Buckingham takes up residence, 93; installation of Buckingham, 249
Ypres, 337

Z

ZIMRI, 260, 261